THE DEATH OF MAO
The Tangshan Earthquake
and the Birth of the New China

JAMES PALMER

ff

faber and faber

First published in 2012
by Faber and Faber Limited
Bloomsbury House
74–77 Great Russell Street
London WC1B 3DA
This paperback edition first published in 2013

Typeset by Donald Sommerville
Printed in the UK by CPI Group (UK) Ltd, Croydon CRO 4YY

A CIP record for this book
is available from the British Library

ISBN 978–0–571–24400–3

FSC
www.fsc.org
MIX
Paper from
responsible sources
FSC® C101712

2 4 6 8 10 9 7 5 3 1

James Palmer was born in 1978. In 2003 he won the Spectator's Shiva Naipaul Prize for travel writing. He has worked with Daoist and Buddhist groups in China and Mongolia on environmental issues, and now lives in Beijing. His first book, *The Bloody White Baron*, was shortlisted for the 2008 John Llewellyn Rhys Prize.

Further praise for *The Death of Mao*:

'James Palmer's book weaves together these two narratives of natural disaster and elite political intrigue to provide a lucid account of one of the eeriest moments in modern Chinese history . . . Palmer's account is written in enviably elegant prose. The narrative never flags and its judgements are humane and nuanced . . . This account of the links between natural disaster and elite politics in China is a fine work of history. But its real relevance may be that it shows how much has changed in China, and yet how little, since 1976.' Rana Mitta, *Guardian*

'The terrifically detailed description of this road trip from hell to the inner precincts of power in Beijing is emblematic of the tricky balancing act Palmer mostly pulls off in *The Death of Mao*. His book is both a masterly recreation of the horrors of the earthquake and of the power struggles going on in Beijing as Mao Zedong lay close to death in a hospital visited frequently by anxious doctors and senior leaders . . . Palmer excels at creating a three-dimensional docudrama of the earthquake . . . *The Death of Mao* renders beautifully these moments of tragedy.' Rahul Jacob, *Financial Times*

'Mr. Palmer takes us through these events with skillful ease, weaving history, politics and geophysics into a complete narrative.' *Wall Street Journal*

'This is an eye-opener for many to a side of the world we hardly look back

---

by the same author

THE BLOODY WHITE BARON

For Claudia He,
who is incomparable

Contents

Plates

Students at the Tangshan Public Library, 1962. *Tangshan City
Museum*

Tangshan's railway station, among the first in China, in the
1930s. *Tangshan City Museum*

A clock at the Tangshan Coal Power Station shows the exact
time the earthquake hit. *Chang Qing*

Ruined factories in Tangshan, July 1976. *Chang Qing*

Aerial view of the ruined city. *Chang Qing*

Local Party committee members hand out food. *Chang Qing*

A political message atop the damaged sailor's club in
Qinhuangdao. *Tangshan Earthquake Museum*

Tangshan's rail track, ruined by the quake. *Chang Qing*

Two images of PLA soldiers hurrying to aid the stricken
city. *Tangshan Earthquake Museum*

PLA soldiers haul rubble in Tangshan. *Tangshan Earthquake
Museum*

Tangshan residents and rescuers in the Xiaoshan
district. *Chang Qing*

The People's Liberation Army struggles to recover
survivors. *Chang Qing*

Survivors walk through a cleared path in early August
1976. *Tangshan Earthquake Museum*

Clothing hangs among reconstructed houses. *Chang Qing*

Children study in an open-air classroom among the ruins of
Tangshan. *Chang Qing*

Tangshan students learn 'Father is good, mother is good, but
Chairman Mao is best.' *Tangshan Earthquake Museum*

Hua Guofeng is applauded by city officials on a visit to
Tangshan, 1978. *Chang Qing*

Introduction

Tangshan is an ordinary Chinese provincial city, a two-McDonald's town of heavy industry, factories and cheap hotels. Building work is everywhere, the pavements are cracked and broken, and the ubiquitous dust of the Hebei plains ruins clothes and electronics. Thirty-five years ago, its population of one million people made it one of China's larger cities. Today it is double the size it was in 1976, but there are dozens of bigger conurbations.

Migrant workers, brought in busloads from the countryside, huddle around small fires in the night to cook their noodles. They live in tents near the construction sites, where they labour for a few dollars a day. Anyone with ambition or education, however, tends to make their way to Beijing or Tianjin; nobody studying at the local universities plans to remain, unless they have a promise of a very well-paid, or well-connected, job. The city is run by the normal coalition of businessmen, gangsters and officials, a network of relationships smoothed by cash, drink and girls.

The only remarkable thing about Tangshan is that it exists at all. On 28 July 1976, the city was flattened in the space of a few minutes, all but obliterated in one of the world's worst earthquakes.

For many Chinese, though, the Tangshan disaster was only one small part of the 'cursed year' of 1976. It was the last of the 'ten years of chaos' spurred by the Cultural Revolution. As Mao Zedong lay dying in the capital, his potential successors squabbled around him. The Cultural Revolution had frequently exploded into outright battles between different factions, bloody street fights that left hundreds dead at a time. Tens of thousands more had been killed in political persecutions. Beijing was split between potential reformers and the fanatics who had ridden the chaos to power.

The Chinese have many sayings about the relationship between Heaven and Earth, and between high politics and everyday life. One of them is 'The heavens crack, and the earth shakes'. As Maoist rule in China cracked that year, the second part of the saying came true in all too literal – and lethal – a fashion.

Maoism claimed to be a people's movement: the very name of the new China, the People's Republic of China (PRC), proclaimed it. The Cultural Revolution could never have happened without Mao's ability to tap into popular discontent and turn it to his own ends. By the end of his life, however, the public was sick of violence, disorder and fanaticism. While the leadership in Beijing was locked in battles over the succession, the people spoke, launching mass protests that played a critical part in determining the future of the country.

A terrible year, it was also a turning point; it was the year that China began to recover, and that the relative normalcy, peace and prosperity of modern Tangshan, and the rest of China, was achieved. This is the story of 1976 in China, of the fights to determine the fate of a country of 800 million people, and of how over half a million of them lost their lives in the middle of that struggle.

A NOTE ON STATISTICS AND NAMES

Chinese statistics, even today, are inherently unreliable. This is partly due to the size of the country, and partly due to the systematic misrepresentation of statistics by local governments for political purposes. I have an acquaintance whose job is to provide economic growth figures for the county where he's employed as a low-level (but fast-tracked) government official; when I asked him how he gets them, he told me, quite simply, that he makes them up. With performance evaluation linked to GDP growth and little independent or external oversight, the motivation for local officials to deceive is enormous.

Take something seemingly as simple as population. How many Chinese are there? The official estimate of China's population is 1.3 billion, but the real figure is likely somewhere between 1.4 and 1.5 billion, perhaps even higher. Apart from size and inefficiency, the root cause of this is the One Child Policy, which has produced tens, perhaps hundreds, of millions of unregistered births.

It has also induced local family planning officials systematically to under-report population growth in order to make it seem as if they're doing a better job. (The One Child Policy has had a striking effect on reducing family size, but anyone with rural acquaintances will find that they usually have two or three siblings; it's just not the seven or eight it would have been in the past.) Grassroots officials report fake numbers to their superiors, who massage the statistics when giving them to their bosses, who in turn tweak them further to meet the regional or provincial goals they've been set, and by the time the figures reach the top their relationship with reality is tenuous at best.

The situation in 1976, with the country barely recovering from one of its most chaotic decades and much of the countryside deeply isolated, was even worse. In 1976, the National Bureau of Statistics in Beijing had *forty-eight* people to cope with the whole of China, and the political motive for lying about figures was even stronger than today. All statistics in this book, save for those gathered directly from the lowest levels, therefore have to be taken with a grain of salt. I've noted likely biases and made estimates of what the actual numbers might be at various points, but these are extremely loose guesses for the most part.

All names are given in the Chinese style of family name first, and in Pinyin, the standard romanisation system developed in the PRC in the 1950s. Unfortunately, this system was largely based around Russian sounds, which can make it a tad unintuitive for English-speakers.

Unfootnoted direct quotations are taken from interviews conducted in Tangshan or Beijing during 2009–11. It was rare for interviewees to consent to being recorded, and so I wrote up the accounts from my notes as soon as I could afterwards, checking details by follow-up phone calls where possible. Speaking to strangers is still not easy in China, though the situation has improved immeasurably from the past. Many of my Tangshan interviewees preferred to remain anonymous, or wanted to give only a last name; I have occasionally given people invented personal names for the sake of readability, since the Chinese journalistic habit of 'a witness surnamed Zhang' sounds distinctly odd in English.

The technical terms in 1976 for rural communities were 'communes', for those containing roughly 15,000–25,000 people, and 'brigades', which had around 600–1,200, but I've chosen instead to talk of 'towns' and 'villages', and ignored the technicalities of administrative divisions in many cases for the sake of ease of reading. Equally, many senior figures held numerous titles and official positions; I've given only the most important or immediately relevant.

It seems redundant to point this out, but China is a very large place, and the Chinese an extraordinarily diverse people. When I say 'the Chinese' or 'Chinese culture', please take it as read that there are numerous exceptions, counter-examples and regional idiosyncrasies in whatever statement follows.

1 Who will protect us now?

On 9 January 1976, He Jianguo left Tangshan and took the train to buy a goldfish. She had been the only girl in her dormitory able to get time off that day, and her dorm-mates had picked her to go and get a pet – not for pleasure, but as an alarm system.

There had been at least two moderate earthquakes in the region every year for the previous six years; some of the older people said quietly it was a sign that things were bad in China. So Jianguo and the others had, like thousands of people in Tangshan, decided to get a goldfish, based on media reports that animals could predict earthquakes.

Cats or dogs were difficult to keep, especially in the city, and to find food for, but fish were easy enough. If it got agitated, Jianguo reasoned, she would know a quake was coming and at least she could get outside. But goldfish were too much of a luxury item to be bought in Tangshan. You had to go up to Tianjin on the train.

It was a long trip, but a nice break for Jianguo. Most people on the train were wrapped in long grey-green overcoats, made in army-imitation cut; there was no heating and the carriages were freezing. She didn't talk with her fellow passengers much, but stared out of the window at the beautiful white fields, munching sesame seeds.

She had tramped through half a foot of snow, grey with pollution from the Tangshan factories, to get to the railway station in the first place. It still beat her job as a secretary for a ceramics factory, spending the whole day copying documents by hand or bringing people tea. Nor was there much to do in her spare time, and she was bored with political rallies, books and opera.

Sometimes it was fun to get together and chant slogans and bang drums, but most of the time it was just another work obligation. You couldn't even play cards or mah-jongg, considered signs of degenerate gambling. Only two of the girls in the dorm had proper boyfriends, and they rarely found time or space to be with them.

There was no make-up, and hairdressers barely went beyond chopping for length, and so the girls wore their hair in the same long, thick plaits, and tried to make themselves pretty with ribbons or artificial flowers. In the winter you could have snowball fights at least, but it was too cold to spend a lot of time outside, so gossip was the main pastime, though this could be nasty, even lethal, when it turned to certain topics. Quite apart from politics, illicit sex, especially adultery, could get you years in prison if people found out.

Like many of her generation, born in the patriotic fervour of the fifties, she had a name that aspired to great things. *Jianguo* – 'Build the country!' She had wanted to go to a university, but they had been closed down in 1970. Now only technical and political colleges were still open. Missing her chance to go to university was only one way the years of chaos had affected her life. Although the Cultural Revolution had started when she was only eleven, in 1966, she never lost the sense of it being something unnatural, an overturning of the right order.

She remembered seeing a box of gold in her home town, crafted into gold bricks and delicate leaves, pulled out of a waste pipe by a sewer worker. Someone had flushed it down there, knowing that if they were caught with it in their house, it would be taken as a sign of hoarding, of counter-revolutionary feeling or even be imagined to be a foreign bribe to a spy. A small crowd was gathered round, mouths open at the gold shining through the shit, but nobody wanted to pick it up. It could have bought half the town in ordinary times; now it offered only the chance of shame or death.

When she was a girl, she had shouted slogans – 'Destroy the Four Olds!', 'Victory to Chairman Mao!' – along with the other 'little Red Guards' in her school. Her older brothers and sisters[1] had been Red Guards proper, rampaging about China in the late sixties before Mao decided to curb them in turn, after which they had found themselves sent off to the countryside to 'learn from the peasants'.

At least she had an idea where her older siblings were. One girl in her work unit was from a big village in the north-eastern province of Liaoning. From there, all the students over fourteen had gone to Beijing in 1967, travelling for free on the train, as Mao had promised. Nobody in the village had ever heard from them again.

Jianguo's uncle, who worked in Tangshan, had managed to secure her a job there. Now she lived with seven other girls in a cold room in a twenty-year-old block-built building. In the winter, when their coal ration ran out, they would sleep together under the blankets like rabbits in a burrow.

All of them were thin and small; when they were children, the famine caused by collectivisation was at its worst, and they were malnourished and stunted. These days there was barely enough, and they ate in the communal canteen, a steady, dull diet of rice and vegetables. China had been on rationing for over twenty years. People traded ration tickets for favours, sweets, or sex sometimes, but Jianguo and the other girls were able to get by on theirs.

When she arrived in Tianjin, she saw the faces of some people were red with crying, and white banners hung everywhere. For a few minutes she wondered who they were for. So many of the Party's leaders were sick and old. Then she saw Zhou Enlai's face embroidered on one of the banners, and felt sad for a moment. She had liked the Prime Minister; he seemed kind, like an uncle. There wasn't time to mourn, though. She bought the goldfish from an old peasant woman, paying two mao[2] for it, and gingerly carried it in a bag back to the train station. She decided to call it *Xiao Hong*, 'Little Red', a good revolutionary name. It would be nice to feel safe.

The radio announcement was made that morning, but Zhou Enlai had died the day before. It was not unexpected; he had had bowel cancer for years. Foreign governments hurried to pay their regards. A dapper, handsome man, he had studied in Paris when young, like so many Asian communists, and spoke French fluently, and a couple of other languages too. Well-read and cosmopolitan, he was always the acceptable face of the regime, delighting diplomats with his gnomic wisdom, an Oriental sage ever-ready with a comment on Lenin or Dickens or the French Revolution. Over the last years he had entertained over a thousand foreign delegations, from the Young Pioneers of Hungary to US Republican Congressmen.

In private, he had lived in fear, pain and regret. In some ways, death must have been a relief. He had seen his oldest allies in the government systematically disposed of by Mao and his clique during the course of the last ten years. Among the first and most significant was Liu Shaoqi, one-time president of China and an old comrade of Mao and Zhou; he had been publicly castigated for a year before being placed under arrest as a 'traitor, spy and renegade'. After two years of humiliation, he was, according to some accounts, stripped of his clothes and locked in a bank vault, where he died of exposure; it was several weeks before his naked, vomit-smeared body was brought out.

Many of those killed had stood up to Mao over his disastrous agricultural and industrial policies and subsequent war on peasant 'hoarders' in the 1950s. This was the so-called 'Great Leap Forward', intended to transform Chinese agriculture and industry, but which had instead resulted in at least thirty-two million deaths by famine, and perhaps over fifty million. Peng Dehuai, the fiery, brilliant peasant general who in 1959 had confronted Mao directly over the famine, losing his army positions as a result, was arrested in 1966. He was beaten so badly that half the bones in his body were broken and his liver permanently damaged.

Zhou had done nothing to stop the Great Leap Forward himself. But he had done what he could to protect Peng and others, sending soldiers to escort and protect Peng after his arrest. Even in his lowest moment, Peng had reacted strongly to news that Zhou had described him as a 'comrade', putting his head into his hands and shaking with emotion. But in the long run Zhou had been able to do nothing to protect him from numerous public humiliations and torture. At one public 'struggle session', the crowd had broken Peng's ribs, leaving him to be carried in agony back to his cell. He'd been under house arrest, denied doctors, till he died in 1974.

Zhou's other attempts to save old comrades were no more successful. After the old general He Long personally pleaded with him, he let him into his house for protection, but ended up putting his own stamp on a document approving the case against He. The best he could do for Zhang Linzhi, the minister for coal and mining, was to order an autopsy on his body after he was either beaten to death or driven to suicide.

And Zhou had betrayed people, slavishly proclaiming his own devotion to Mao. He wrote statements he knew to be lies, proclaiming that Liu was 'a big traitor, big scab, big spy, big foreign agent and collaborator who sold out the country. He is full of the five poisons and a counter-revolutionary guilty on more than ten accounts!'[3] Towards the end, he was haunted by his memories of failure and collaboration. He dreamt of Chen Yi, an old friend purged in 1969. 'Chen and I were half way up a hill . . . Chen slipped and fell, and I couldn't grab him in time. Then both of us tumbled together over a cliff.'[4]

For ten years before his death, Zhou had feared his own end was near. Mao sadistically subjected him to a series of petty ordeals, such as swapping out his chair at diplomatic meetings and forcing him to sit, racked with pain, on a hard backless seat. Denying his rivals medical treatment was one of Mao's favourite tricks, and after Zhou was diagnosed with cancer he suddenly found it hard to get pain medication and reliable doctors. There was an unstated rule that any major operation among the elite of the Party had to be approved by the Central Committee, due to the time it would remove them from work, meaning that Zhou, like others, was also medically hostage to the Chairman's whims.

Then there was the political harassment. The 'Criticise Lin Biao, Criticise Confucius' campaign, launched in 1974 and seemingly eschewing the values of the Chinese past, was in fact aimed at Zhou and made constant reference to the 'slave state of Zhou', ostensibly referring to an early Chinese kingdom praised by Confucius. This kind of historical–cultural code was common in Chinese politics, especially during the Cultural Revolution, one of the first salvos of which was an attack on a play about honest Ming officials, which was taken to refer to Peng Dehuai's criticism of Mao during the Great Leap Forward.[5]

The Chinese language itself, with characters that could be altered with one stroke into a new meaning, contributed to this kind of coded reading, which infected everyday life. Even among half-literate villagers, accidentally miswriting a character could be read as evidence of counter-revolutionary feeling, leading to humiliation, exile or death.

But Zhou remained too respected, and too popular with the public, for Mao to dispose of him completely. He and the rest of the Party elite targeted by Mao were hardly innocents. Zhou had done his share of political purging and execution in the twenties, thirties and forties, during the bitter internecine struggles in the revolutionary movement, and he and the others had had no objections to the mass murders of 'rich peasants', 'bandits' and 'traitors to the Chinese people' carried out after 1949. They had also been complicit in supporting Mao to begin with, and in creating a system which allowed his personality cult and murderous ideology to take root. From the start of the Cultural Revolution Zhou had reluctantly been pressed into backing Mao in persecuting others, and his own writings, when not tuned to please a Western audience, expressed the usual vicious banalities against 'counter-revolutionaries' and 'class enemies'.

Mao's motivations in launching the Cultural Revolution had been manifold. It was an opportunity to cleanse the Party leadership of those who had turned against him in the Great Leap Forward, mostly military men who were getting above themselves. It was a chance, too, for him to solidify an already developing personality cult. But there was also an ideological, or at least psychological, element. Mao delighted in being the one constant amidst the chaos, seeing it as a cleansing and purifying force. He took joy in turning the world upside down. It helped that he had an utter disregard for ordinary people's lives – although, like all dictators, he occasionally practised sentimentalities on those around him, asking after their families and arranging small favours – and firmly believed that you couldn't make an omelette without killing a few hundred thousand people.

Compared to millions, Zhou had it lucky. Outside the central leadership, any number of his habits, from his love of art to his contacts with the hated Nationalists (Guomindang) in Taiwan and his fluency and delight in foreign languages, not to mention his general air of cosmopolitanism, would have been enough to get him tarred 'black', in contrast to revolutionary 'red'.

Mobs harassed, tortured and murdered people for wearing too much hair pomade, for having studied in Europe, for having a globe of the world (for who needed to know about anything outside China?), for having had a Nationalist husband, wife or brother, for once owning land and so on. Anyone with any pretensions to intellectualism suffered.

If Zhou had been a schoolteacher or a writer, or even a regular Party cadre, he might well have ended up kicked to death on the street, or hanging himself to escape months of relentless persecution, insults and forced self-criticism. At the least he would have been shamed, forced on the streets wearing a dunce's hat and with a mocking billboard around his neck, made to clean the toilets in a commune or to break rocks in a quarry. His statues would have been smashed, his books burnt, his writings ripped to shreds – mostly by childish mobs barely out of their teens, egged on by the words of Chairman Mao.

Yet, for many ordinary Chinese, Zhou was seen as a great protector, almost a protective deity. His wife, Deng Yingchao, couldn't have children. She had had an abortion as a young revolutionary worker, without telling Zhou, fearing that pregnancy would detract from her ability to carry out the work of the Party, and then suffered a miscarriage when fleeing from a Nationalist purge. She was childless and not particularly attractive, but unusually for the Communist elite, and Chinese men generally, he had not divorced her. This added considerably to his reputation as a wise moderate, a man of Confucian virtue and strength. So did his patrician ways; he had the manner of a benevolent court official of some earlier dynasty. He claimed to see the people of China as his children, and this paternal benevolence seemed very real to many, who called him 'Father of the Country' – a term never applied to Mao. He occupied the same pedestal in people's minds as Ataturk in Turkey or that Nelson Mandela would in post-apartheid South Africa.

During the worst times of the Cultural Revolution, Zhou did what he could to protect the temples, old city walls and palaces of Beijing and elsewhere, deploying People's Liberation Army (PLA) units loyal to him to guard sites such as the Forbidden City and the Temple of Heaven from mobs of Red Guards. Over most issues, though, he kow-towed to Mao, and he saved more monuments than people. Nevertheless, his reputation as a moderate, as a sane, wise man in these times of chaos, endured.

Zhou enjoyed much popular affection, but it paled compared to Mao's own personality cult. From the very start of the PRC, Mao's portrait had been placed in the centre of even small and remote villages. 'Mao Zedong thought' was a compulsory topic of discussion for everyone from scientists to schoolchildren.

After the Cultural Revolution began, devotion to Mao reached new heights. His 'Little Red Book' of quotations was compulsory reading – five billion were printed, enough for every citizen to own six copies. Terms previously reserved for emperors, like *wansui* ('Live ten thousand years!') were now appropriated for Mao, and his statues went up in every square.

Mao was turned from leader into god. Wherever his image appeared, it had to be 'red, bright, and shining'. In posters, he transformed from a saintly but still human figure, blessing troops or workers, to a disembodied head floating above the people, the 'sun which makes all things grow'. His portraits spread from public areas to private homes, where they often occupied the spot previously kept for household deities. Like Muslims offering daily prayers, people 'asked for instructions in the morning, thanked Mao at noon, and reported back at night', each time bowing three times before Mao's portrait or bust, reading from his works, and stretching their arms in praise.

Three portraits had decorated most homes in the sixties: Zhou, Mao and Lin Biao, the then vice-chairman of the Party. Lin had been one of the most spectacularly successful Communist generals, a close ally and slavish sycophant of Mao's, and a prominent supporter of the leftists when the Cultural Revolution began. But his portrait had come down overnight in September 1971. His own efforts to consolidate his power base in the military, while systematically undercutting and persecuting other leading generals, had made others, including Mao, nervous. They set out to undermine him in turn.

Yet nobody had expected the swiftness of Lin's fall. Once Mao's chosen successor, he had disappeared after an attempted coup and supposedly crashed in Soviet-controlled Mongolia when escaping by plane to the Soviet Union. Lin seems to have seen that Mao was turning against him, and decided to risk it all rather than endure the slow ostracism and humiliating fall that he had helped inflict on so many others.

The details of the coup are still unclear, and it's faintly possible that the whole affair was fabricated to dispose of Lin. But if so, it would have been politically premature: the campaigns against him were only just beginning. There were persistent rumours that he, and his family, had simply been rounded up and shot, but the coup, escape and crash (possibly shot down by either a Chinese or Soviet missile) seem to have been real. Within a few days he was transformed from hero of the nation to despised traitor. It was a grim reminder of how precarious life at the top was.

But, despite the campaigns to undermine him, Zhou had died with his portrait up. Throughout China work shut down for days, as each work unit offered its individual tribute to Zhou. They waved white silk banners in the air, with Zhou's face embroidered on them, sang revolutionary songs, read his speeches and books and vowed to carry on his work. This was certainly not state-mandated mourning, though, but a genuine outpouring of public sorrow: old women tore their hair, young men sobbed together in unashamed grief. Among the mourners there was a certain element of self-promotion, as different work units competed to appear the most elaborately devoted to Zhou's memory.

Beijing was like a ghost town throughout that January. People wondered whether this year was cursed. January was a month of liminal uncertainty in the new China; traditionally the New Year didn't start until the lunar Spring Festival in January or February, but officially the country now used the Western calendar. Grief was mixed with anger; Beijing, along with Shanghai, had been an epicentre of political violence during the Cultural Revolution, and people were sick of it.

Ten years before, in the summer of 1966, Mao had summoned the Red Guards, as the radical student groups that had sprung up across the nation were known, to Beijing. The Red Guard movement had been started by a dozen young teenagers at a middle school attached to Tsinghua University, seized upon and promoted by Mao, and spread across the country like a raging fever. Their formation had been encouraged by rhetoric from the centre, and local authorities had been forbidden from shutting the groups down, but many of them had arisen semi-spontaneously. Their motivations were initially mixed, from determined hardline class struggle to a desire for social experimentation and travel, but Mao would turn them, as he had intended from the start, into a political weapon for his own use, even if one he could never fully control.

Millions of young people came, moved by ideological fervour, free travel and the chance to run riot. They milled in Tiananmen Square, in the centre of Beijing, like teenagers at a Beatles concert, screaming for Mao. On 19 August, Mao had appeared to a million Red Guards, praising their spirit and repeating a favourite phrase of his, 'To rebel is justified!'

And they rebelled all right. They saw themselves as 'soldiers going out to war against an old world',[6] and there were no civilians in this war. The impetus for the Cultural Revolution had come from the top, but it was seized upon by China's youth with a fervour that went above and beyond even Mao's call for rebellion. A central policy document approved by Mao forbade the police from interfering with the students in any way, giving the Guards carte blanche to go wild. At that Beijing meeting, a young girl, Song Binbin, had been given the honour of pinning an armband on Mao. When he heard her second name, Binbin, Mao laughed at its meaning ('refined and courteous'), and advised her instead '*Yao wu ma*!' ('Be violent!'). She changed her name accordingly.

Teachers and other figures of authority were the favourite targets, and Tsinghua and Beida, the capital's two great universities, among the first battlegrounds. The Guards wore quasi-military yellow uniforms, with a red armband and a heavy leather belt, which was often used to whip victims. Its heavy copper buckle could inflict serious damage. Among themselves, the Guards discussed the most effective beating techniques. Which angle could cause the most pain to the enemies of the revolution?

There was a child-like sense of experimentation in many of the cruelties, like torturing frogs or insects. One Red Guard:

. . . dragged [his teacher] Peng into the classroom where he had once been master. [He] found a broken chair. Discarding the wooden seat, he took the intact iron frame and shoved the makeshift stocks over

Teacher Peng's head, arms, and chest. Then he forced Teacher Peng to walk on his hands and knees all around the room. [His] peers were fascinated by this invention, and proceeded to break the other chairs [to use on other teachers].[7]

Lecturers were denounced as monsters, freaks, dogs and demons. The lucky ones were forced to clean toilets, others were beaten to death. Teachers were forced to sing 'the howling song' to show their degradation. Originally composed at a Beijing middle school, it spread around the country.

I am an ox-ghost and snake demon
I am guilty, I am guilty.
I committed crimes against the people.
So the people take me as the object of dictatorship.
I have to lower my head and admit to my guilt.
I must be obedient.
I am not allowed to speak or act without permission.
If I speak or act without permission
May you beat me and smash me
Beat me and smash me.[8]

Some among the Red Guards called for peaceful revolution, but they were soon swamped by those hungry for violence. Children as young as eight imprisoned and tortured adults. Elementary school teachers were forced by their pupils to swallow balls of shit and nails. In Beijing No. 6 Middle School, across the road from Zhongnanhai, the palaces that housed the Party leadership, the music classroom was turned into a prison, with 'Long Live Red Terror' written on the wall in blood. Three people were beaten to death there.

Hundreds of thousands of these improvised prisons were set up across the country. They were called 'cow-sheds', originally from a popular term of abuse for the targets, 'cow-demons'. In many cases in the countryside, however, they literally were cow-sheds, or disused barns or the back rooms of local village halls.

Teachers were not the only victims. Virtually anybody could become a target, for as little as giving wrong directions to a group of Red Guards or failing to hang a picture of Mao in their home. Fellow students became frequent victims, especially if they dissented from the violence or had politically suspect parents. At Beijing First Middle School, 200 students from 'problem families' were labelled 'children of dogs' by their fellows, and forced to work for them. At another middle school, a schoolboy from a 'bad family' was tied inside a sack and beaten to death by his classmates.

Returned scholars were among the most frequently persecuted. They found the violence particularly incomprehensible. (I ran, quite by chance, into Eric Gu, a Princeton-educated mathematician, at breakfast one morning in Beijing, and we talked about his imprisonment forty years earlier. 'They *beat* me,' he said, with the uncomprehending horror of a wounded child.) They had given up the chance of a prosperous life in the West to come back and help build a new country, only to find themselves denounced as spies, counter-revolutionaries and traitors.

One doctor was imprisoned in his town morgue for five years. He was a Canadian-trained obstetrician, who had come back to teach country midwives modern birthing techniques in an attempt to lower China's appalling rates of death in childbirth. At night in the winter, he wrapped himself in winding sheets to avoid freezing to death. To stay sane he would stand on a chair, so that he could see out of the room's one small, high window, and recite the Gettysburg Address as he looked at the sunlight.

Torture went well beyond locked jails. The Red Guards held public 'struggle sessions', where the victims were mocked, humiliated and beaten. Howling children forced people into the 'aeroplane position', their head pressed down and their arms raised high behind their back, where they would be kept for hours as the crowd jeered and abused them. People were paraded through the streets wearing dunces' caps, with placards listing their crimes hung around their necks.

Struggle sessions could be repeated for weeks or months, with prominent victims being brought out for ritualised daily abuse.

Luo Ruiqing, a former army chief of staff, broke his leg in a suicide attempt in 1966 after having being denounced as a fellow plotter of Peng Dehuai's the year before. The Red Guards would pile him in a wheelbarrow or drag him in a basket to take him to his struggle sessions; without proper medical care, his leg had to be amputated.

There was an unconscious religious aspect to the public humiliations. Public confession could be a means of redemption and cleansing, an idea with as strong roots in China – in Daoist 'hygiene cults' members confessed to their sins before the whole congregation – as in Europe. More often, though, struggle sessions were an exercise in sadistic humiliation. Chinese culture placed a high value on public reputation as part of a sense of self-identity.

The way others saw you was a critical part of how you saw yourself, and it was extremely common for those subjected to repeated humiliations by the mob to kill themselves, such as the Beijing revolutionary dramatist Lao She, who walked into a lake with his pockets full of stones after being tormented for two months.

The idea of suicide as an act of defiance or romanticism was also a standard trope of Chinese literature and history; one of the country's main traditional festivals, Dragon Boat Day, celebrated the suicide of the scholar Quan Yu, driven to the deed by an unjust king. Suicide was sometimes a way of sending a message: 'I am not the person you say I am.' Notes left behind highlighted the deceased's loyalty to the Communist Party, or defiantly declared that he or she was not a spy, a counter-revolutionary or a traitor to the country. More often, suicide was a product of sheer despair.

Lao She was sixty-seven, his tormentors around sixteen or seventeen, an additional indignity in a society that traditionally valued the seniority of age. Literary suicides were the most famous, such as those of Lao She and the poet Wen Jie, who gassed himself in 1971 after falling in love with one of his former tormentors (and she with him) and being denied permission to marry her. But tens, perhaps hundreds, of thousands of ordinary Chinese were driven to suicide in those years. Others came close to it. The mother of the historian Xing Lu, for instance, came home crying that she wanted to kill herself after her best friend at her workplace put up a poster accusing her of being a counter-revolutionary and a rich peasant.

It was often ambiguous, however, whether individual cases were suicide or murder, such as Zheng Meipian, the daughter of the memoirist Zheng Nian (Nien Cheng), who died in typically dubious circumstances during a struggle session by Red Guards in Shanghai. The ones who most commonly killed themselves were the very young, like the teenager who threw herself in front of a train after weeks of mockery for her 'bad family', and those who had once enjoyed positions of dignity and status.

Drinking pesticide was a common method; truckloads of it had been produced as part of the 'Campaign Against the Four Pests' of 1958–62, when the state had declared war on sparrows, rats, flies and mosquitoes. (Millions of sparrows had been killed in an attempt to stop them eating grain seeds, which then resulted in huge locust swarms, since the sparrows were no longer around to control them. It was perhaps the emblematic campaign of the era: encourage people to kill to solve a problem, unleashing forces much worse than the original problem.)

The Red Guards targeted far more than just people, however. With the thoroughness of the present-day Taliban, they looked to purge the country of any sign of 'old ideas, old culture, old customs and old habits'. The most harmless side of this was imposing revolutionary nomenclature on parts of the cities, so that you could stroll down Revolution Avenue, turn into Anti-Imperialist Boulevard, and end up in Mao Zedong Square.

They attacked any sign of bourgeois culture, foreign influence or traditional thinking – women were dragged off the street by young patrols of purity police, their high heels broken and their long hair forcibly cut. Pleasant pastimes like kite-flying, chess, tai chi and poetry became politically suspect, and art that wasn't tuned to political ends was deemed a sign of dangerous indulgence.

Despite wars, revolution, pillaging imperialists and opportunistic archaeologists, China's cultural heritage had remained among the richest in the world. That didn't last. There were 6,843 historic or cultural sites in Beijing in 1966; by 1976 fewer than 2,000 were left, and most of those were either so small as to be overlooked or so large and important that Zhou Enlai and others had to send the army to protect them from the vandalism of the Guards.

It was a pattern repeated across the country, from attacks on the Bund in Shanghai to the destruction of medieval temples in Tibet. Art and literature hardly fared any better, as the Red Guards made bonfires of books, sculptures and paintings. Numerous suicides wiped out a generation of artists and writers.

In a rare moment of political honesty, the information board at the Yonghegong, a magnificent Tibetan Buddhist temple in Beijing, today records the battle between a mob of students intent on burning the temple complex to the ground and the soldiers sent to defend it. Religious institutions were singled out, since they represented a doubly hated legacy of tradition and superstition. The Communists had sought to stamp out religion even when they only controlled limited areas of China, by smashing village shrines and forcibly laicising monks, but the Cultural Revolution took these practices to new heights.

Even ordinary household rituals, like smearing honey on the Kitchen God's lips during the Spring Festival, or burning incense before exams, could invite violent denunciation. There was no space for ceremony any more, only for rituals dedicated to the new gods of Maoism. Being caught reciting the Buddhist sutras or the Christian gospels could be cause for a beating. Temples, churches, shrines and mosques were all destroyed as signs of outdated superstition, while passages from Mao's works were recited each morning and his Little Red Book was proclaimed to have the power to heal the sick.

The madness wasn't limited to the young. Across the country 'mass organisations' and 'rebel groups' rallied. In Shanghai, in January 1967, the 'Workers' Command Post' group, made up of a loose alliance of factory workers, students and opportunistic Party intellectuals, seized control of the city in the 'January Storm'. Other groups seized power in cities and counties nationwide, as China shuddered under a thousand small coups, accompanied by the denunciation and persecution of the previous leaders.

In the countryside, the movement became a pogrom against 'rich peasants' and 'landlords'. There had already been one wave of violence against these groups, just after the founding of the PRC, back at a time when the terms actually meant something, although a huge number of the killings then had been arbitrary. According to Maoist theory, however, class status carried through the generations, and so now the children and grandchildren of those who had once been better off were targeted too. So were the descendants of 'counter-revolutionaries' and 'rightists', lumped together with the other two as the 'Four Black Groups' – a number which swelled to five, and then to seven, as 'bad elements', 'capitalists' and 'black gangs' were included among the persecuted.

In some places, this meant social ostracism, heavy workloads and reduced rations. In others, it led to mass murder. Quanzhou County, Guangxi, was one example. There, according to the records, on 3 October 1967,

... the militia commander Huang Tianhui led [the brigade militia] to engage in a massacre. They pushed off a cliff and killed seventy-six individuals of the brigade – former landlords, rich peasants, and their children – in snake-shaped Huanggua'an canyon ... From July to October [another] 850 individuals [in the county] – the four-type elements and their children – were executed with firearms.[9]

It didn't take long before the various groups started to turn against each other. The Red Guard movement soon became as ideologically divided as any group of activists, while Party leaders, knowing that they could be next on the chopping block, allied with some mass groups against others. Meanwhile, the army involved itself, looking to restrain the violence in some places and solidify military power in others.

The country was plunged into a civil war with no two clear sides, only a multitude of local factions. Broadly speaking, any given area would have a 'rebel' group whose members saw themselves as ideological purifiers and overturners of the corrupt old order, and a 'loyalist' group made up of an old guard equally convinced that they were the true Communists, and determined to protect their positions. But 'rebel' groups as frequently fought each other as the loyalists, and local politics, ethnic rivalries and old squabbles created a tangled mess of political violence.

In most places the battles were fought with spears, knives and improvised explosives. Home-made hand grenades were still being unearthed forty years later. In the industrial city of Chongqing, the centre of China's armaments industry, the battles escalated to tanks and artillery. A single clash there left a thousand dead.

In Wuhan, where the Party leadership rallied its own 'Million Heroes' against the Red Guards, young teenagers were hired as mercenaries. One recalled, after attacking a group of young Red Guards:

I killed five kids with my star-knife . . . one got it in the waist, the second, third, and fifth ones in the back, and number four in the neck. They were all maybe eight, nine years old. Killing a young boy would get you 20 yuan.[10]

Near Beijing, hungry farmers were paid in grain to attack soldiers. The vast city factories, built in the fifties in a frenzy of heavy industrialisation, were major battlefields in fights as bloodily intimate as Stalingrad. The economy collapsed as work came to a standstill, while precious machinery was smashed beyond repair. Defeat in battle produced further slaughter, as in the Dao County massacre of 1967, where the losing side in a factional battle decided to prove their superior political consciousness by massacring upwards of 4,000 people in a month.

By October 1968 the chaos had grown too much even for Mao, and he ordered the PLA to disperse the Red Guards. They were sent 'up to the mountains and down to the villages', rusticated to stop them causing further trouble. The army fought pitched battles against the more tenacious groups.

The end of the student movements, however, did not mean an end to the violence. The killings in the countryside worsened in 1968–70. The 'Cleansing of the Class Ranks' campaign, launched in 1968, prompted whole new waves of brutality, including bizarre cases of politically inspired cannibalism. In Inner Mongolia, for instance, 790,000 people were persecuted, 22,900 killed, and 120,000 crippled, out of a population of around 14 million people. In total, perhaps somewhere between one and two million people were killed in those years, and tens of millions persecuted.

It was only by 1971 that the violence abated, as the new revolutionary organisations found themselves in charge, and the number of targets had decreased. Mass killings had mostly ended, but political persecution, often to the point of suicide, continued.

Even in 1975 there were still horrific incidents. An extreme case was the Muslim village of Shadian, in the borderlands of southern Yunnan. Ethnic and religious conflicts, sparked by Red Guards burning mosques and shredding Korans, created civil war between Shadian's 'Muslim Militia Regiment' and the local Han Chinese. A peace treaty had been brokered by Beijing, only to fall apart in an argument over the handing-in of weapons, and eventually the PLA itself was called in. On 29 July, the army was unleashed against Shadian and six other Muslim villages; a month later, when the fighting had finished, the town was razed, and 1,600 people were dead.

In present-day China, the Red Guards tend to be treated as an aberration, a perverse generation of murderers. But the violence they used didn't come from nowhere. They'd grown up in an atmosphere where brutality was normal, especially if they were from the countryside. During the Great Leap Forward, in 1959–61, violence was normalised. Those who couldn't work, usually because of physical exhaustion, or who were found to be hoarding or stealing food, were subject to the same public criticism sessions the Red Guards later used, already a standard Maoist technique.

One villager recalled:

The victim was forced to stand on a table, [kneel down] and confess to everyone in the crowd . . . If the explanation was acceptable, then the person being criticised would be spared, but if the explanation was unacceptable, then the village leaders would beat the person. On some occasions, the village leaders would suddenly knock down the table on which the victim was standing, and the victim would fall to the ground and suffer injury.[11]

Many of the Guards had therefore seen their parents or older siblings beating or being beaten, as well as witnessing other tortures. In one commune of 40,000 people, among 4,605 deaths in 1959–60, most of them by starvation, '398 were beaten to death, 148 driven to suicide, and 105 were frozen to death after being stripped of their clothing'.[12] Out of the over 30 million deaths of those years, perhaps as many as 2 million were due to political violence linked to the famine – around the same as the high estimates of deaths during the Cultural Revolution itself.

At the top, thousands of leaders were targeted in Beijing alone at the end of 1959. 'The struggle should be profound, and should be carried out according to our principles, whether it is against old comrades-in-arms, colleagues or even husbands and wives!' one of Mao's allies proclaimed in language 'auguring the Cultural Revolution'.[13]

Before that, of course, there had been the long violence of the civil wars and the Japanese invasion. Even in the Anti-Japanese War, most of the violence was Chinese fighting Chinese. The Chinese 'puppet army' fighting for the Japanese always outnumbered the Japanese in the country, and they were much easier targets than Japanese soldiers.

Back then live burial (also a staple of Russian peasant killings) had been a common means of execution, used both by the puppet armies and by the resistance fighters. This was followed by the mass killings of landlords, rich peasants and supposed collaborators and Nationalist supporters in 1949–51, when any wild accusation could result in a lynching. 'Superstitious and feudal' practices, from Daoist exorcisms to the transport of corpses thousands of miles for burial in their home towns, were punished with anything from lectures to beating to hanging.

Sporadic political violence continued throughout the fifties, whether used against 'rightist' intellectuals or in local village disputes. In 1956 Mao promised intellectual freedom and called for dissenting voices to be heard with his slogan 'Let a Hundred Flowers Bloom', and then crushed those who had spoken out in the vicious 'Anti-Rightist' movement that followed. Most of the dissenters were about as right-wing as Trotsky, but 'rightist' had long since become a generic term of abuse, like 'bourgeois' and 'counter-revolutionary'.

It was in 1957 that a professor wrote, in a public letter to Mao:

We have applied to intellectuals methods of punishment which peasants would not apply to landlords and workers would not apply to capitalists. During the social reform campaigns, unable to endure the spiritual torture and humiliation imposed by the struggle . . . the intellectuals who chose to die by jumping from tall buildings, drowning in rivers, swallowing poison, cutting their throats, or by other methods, were immeasurable. The aged had no escape, and pregnant women were given no quarter.[14]

None of the cruelties of the Cultural Revolution were new to the People's Republic; they were just enacted on a horrendously larger scale than ever before.

Even regular countryside life was (and is) rough. Most villages had their local thugs or hooligans, and even normally peaceful farmers could get violent with relatively little provocation.

Political and ideological violence never ceased altogether, and, at a local level, one round of it was often revenge for the last. Villages were close-knit places, often dominated by one or two local clans, and each slight, humiliation, theft, murder or other abuse of power stuck in people's memories and could be used against the former leaders when the next cycle of political upheaval began.

Yet many of the Red Guards came from urban middle-class backgrounds, where their experience of violence was relatively limited. The youth of the perpetrators, however, was something new. At one level, they weren't that different from their student counterparts in the West, young, idealistic, and fed up with an old order that seemed to have become stagnant and complacent. They had grown up on stories of revolutionary martyrs and liberation from a feudal past, but around them they saw the same old corruption, superstition and backwardness.

After 1949, Party officials had rapidly become as drunk and petty with power as the landlords, collaborators or Nationalists they had replaced. Periodic anti-corruption purges from the centre did little to change the lack of judicial or public oversight that gave Party cadres, in many cases, free rein to plunder, beat, rape and rob those beneath them. Life was still cripplingly poor for the vast majority of the population.

From the point of view of the young, the system had promised so much and delivered so little – but, suffused with Maoist ideology, the conclusion they drew was that the system had failed because it had not been red enough, that the black stains of old ways of thinking were still smeared across the nation. Or it had been betrayed by saboteurs and counter-revolutionaries. What other explanation could there be?

Student revolution had a long history in China, starting with the angry protestors of the 'May 4th' movement in 1919, who had denounced the post-WWI handover of Germany's colonial territories in China to Japan by burning the homes of government officials. During the Anti-Japanese War, 'the bravest of the terrorists were the young students in the middle-schools', who would make the sudden decision to murder a collaborator because, 'It is intolerable that we should breathe the same air as him.'[15] Their terrible sincerity was not far removed from that of their juvenile descendants, if arguably directed to better ends.

And their schoolbooks taught them to kill. The necessity of violence was drummed into Chinese children from a young age. So was an acute and resentful class consciousness: 'Family origin was important: those of us from good backgrounds had to be certain not to stray from the path, and those from bad backgrounds had to struggle against their inferior inheritance,' one writer remembered.[16]

Second-grade[17] textbooks in the sixties told a story of a wolf who disguised himself in sheep's clothing and ate many sheep without the shepherd realising it. When the shepherd found that out, no leniency was possible: 'The shepherd raised the wooden stick in his hand and struck fiercely at the wolf, saying as he struck: "Death to you, you wolf in sheep's clothing! Death to you, you wolf in sheep's clothing!"' By fourth grade, students had learnt about the Farmer and the Snake: 'The snake was freezing on a very cold day. When the farmer saw it, he held it against his chest to give him warmth. When the snake awakened it bit the farmer, who died.'[18] Teachers made sure the message came across clearly: the wolf and the snake were class enemies. They could never be trusted, and they deserved only death.

Money was another motivation. Especially at the village level, being a Red Guard was often an opportunity to steal from others with impunity. And beneath all the ideological fervour, sometimes there was just the appeal of running free and wild, shouting and killing, and revelling in the joy of mayhem. One participant remembered:

I was in my third year of junior high school when the Cultural Revolution got going. It was No. 27 High School, a real dump. I don't care what other people say about why they got involved; I know I became a Red Guard just for the hell of it, to have a chance to lash out and rebel. Up till then alley-kids like me were always treated like dirt.

But, fuck, when the Cultural Revolution came along, I was suddenly one of the five red categories, a child of the workers and peasants who had been oppressed by the revisionist line in education . . . I took part in pretty much all the big events: being reviewed by Grandad Mao in Tiananmen, destroying the Four Olds, the great link-ups, armed struggle: anything that involved beating people up and smashing things and taking stuff.

Man, it was fantastic! Me and my buddies got baseball bats and worked our way up the street from south to north. We must have busted every damn shop sign along Xidan. Just try doing that today! The cops'd be all over you after the first hit. But back then, they didn't dare. We were fuckin' Red Guards; we were destroying the Four Olds! . . . You could get away with beating up anyone, like it was for free, as long as they were class enemies. You could beat them to death and no one would care.[19]

Beyond the violence, it was the sheer all-pervasiveness of the Cultural Revolution that had left people so exhausted. Yan Xuetong, a Tsinghua professor, summed it up well in an offhand remark. 'Even during the Japanese invasion,' he said, 'there were people selling sunflower seeds [a popular Chinese snack] on the street. In the Cultural Revolution, there was nobody selling sunflower seeds on the street.' In 1975, as the government backed off from past excesses under pressure from Zhou and his allies, it seemed as though the worst times were over, but with Zhou dead, everything suddenly seemed uncertain again. As they wept for Zhou, Beijingers were also voicing their own fears.

From his palace bed, himself close to death, Mao could hear the cries of mourning for Zhou. It probably disturbed him, as did any sign of too much popular support for other leaders, even the dead, but now, confined to his bed, he could hardly do anything about it. Mao had once been a man of formidable endurance, a long-distance swimmer who had reasserted his personal authority at the beginning of the Cultural Revolution in mid-July 1966 by swimming the Yangtze unassisted – at the age of seventy-three. In 1976 he could barely walk by himself, and his speech was slurred and barely intelligible.

He was now eighty-two, and it was astonishing he had lived so long. Although he grew up a pampered child in a rich farmer's house, he had lived as a guerrilla and a renegade under the harshest conditions since his twenties, travelling thousands of miles across China. Since taking power he had kept himself fit, exercising every day, but he had indulgent tastes, gorging himself at banquets and coercing young dancers from his home province of Hunan to his bed, dismissing his doctors' warnings about personal hygiene and his recurrent venereal diseases with the blunt exclamation, 'I wash my dick inside them!'

He had made his name as a guerrilla leader and theorist, writing brilliant essays on how successful revolutionaries 'swam among the people', and leading a battered Communist insurgency through Nationalist betrayal, civil war and Japanese invasion to ultimate triumph. He had also come up through a Party hierarchy in the twenties and thirties where infighting, backstabbing, undermining, accusations of treachery or political deviance, and the ruthless disposal of political enemies were common practices. It was a climate that inevitably spawned someone like Mao, a genius at internecine political warfare. He'd been using internal purges to dispose of potential rivals since 1926, when he'd manipulated rumours of an 'Anti-Bolshevik League' of Nationalist spies within the Communist Party to bolster his own position, a technique he'd repeated in similar purges in the Communists' mountain redoubts in Yanan in 1944–5. He used the same methods he had developed as a guerrilla leader against his political enemies, never striking directly when he could first insinuate, undercut and harass. He was a master at playing factions against each other, picking out a favourite here and a protégé there.

Lin Liguo, Lin Biao's son, had accurately summed up Mao's tactics in a speech given to fellow plotters during the coup attempt in 1971, and later distributed in internal Party documents:

Today he uses this force to attack that force; tomorrow he uses that force to attack this force. Today he uses sweet words and honeyed talk to those whom he entices, and tomorrow he puts them to death for some fabricated crimes. Those who are his guests today will be his prisoners tomorrow. Looking back at the history of the past few decades [do you see] any one whom he had supported initially who has not finally been handed a political death sentence? . . . He will hurt you all the way, and he puts the blame for all bad things on others.[20]

Mao was a huge man, especially by rural Chinese standards. Nearly six feet tall and broad-shouldered, often unkempt, when younger he had the air of a shambling bear. His height added to his authority; he towered over most of his political opponents. He was a moody man, given to sudden sulks followed by outbursts of raucous humour; these had only worsened in old age. He had extraordinary personal charisma. Women were drawn to him – he was a notorious flirt and tease – and men followed him, both in battle and in politics. He liked to drop into peasant demotic – 'Fuck your mother!' – to make his points, but was equally adept at classical poetry or high-flown rhetoric. What really kept the whole of the leadership circling around him, even at eighty-two, was that he had crushed almost everyone inside the Party who had ever opposed him.

Like the rest of the Party elite, Mao lived in Zhongnanhai. Literally meaning 'Central [and] South Sea', it was part of a series of palace complexes built by the Chinese emperors over the past seven centuries, attached to the Forbidden City in the centre of Beijing. Under the Nationalist government of the thirties it had been a park, but the Communists had taken it for the headquarters of the government in 1949. The vanguard of the workers' revolution now lived in the old houses of the imperial elite, attended by servants and guards.

The Zhongnanhai buildings ran along the lakes that gave the site its name. The traditional wooden structures of the Qing emperors had been supplemented with concrete office buildings, albeit topped by faux pavilion-style roofs. It still retained the air of a park, very different from the overcrowded compounds most Chinese lived in, with plenty of green space and the delicate design touches of master architects. The most venerable buildings tended to be used for meetings, China's elite gathering around heavy antique tables to discuss the fate of hundreds of millions. A few dozen members of the leadership lived there in courtyard homes, as did their families, staff and doctors. Often this meant being crammed into shared apartments, with relatively little space; however, they also had far larger seaside villas a few hours away on the coast.

Being near the centre of power was worth a little overcrowding for Zhongnanhai's residents. Zhongnanhai was marked by Mao's presence – literally, since boards emblazoned with his calligraphy hung over both major entrances. The standard of living was far higher than that of the ordinary Chinese, complete with luxuries like refrigerators, colour televisions and record players that were almost unknown elsewhere in China. The heating bill for one Zhongnanhai family of five was higher than that of a nearby high school with 2,000 students.

Mao needed such creature comforts more than most. He had been diagnosed with Lou Gehrig's disease in 1975, a form of motor neurone disease. The doctors gave him two years at the very best. Unable to eat by himself, he had to be fed a liquid diet by his young female attendants, lying on his side on a couch like a Roman emperor. If he swallowed water too fast he choked and spluttered, and his hands shook so badly his writing was almost unintelligible.

When he met foreign leaders, he put his head back in the chair and drooled. Paralysis was not his only health issue; he had three bullets in his left lung, was half-blind from cataracts, even after an operation, had pulmonary and coronary heart disease, and numerous infections. He was still mentally alert, but drowsy most of the time.

A medical team led by Western-educated doctors was kept on twenty-four-hour alert. Prominent among them was Dr Li

Zhisui, who had been treating Mao for several years. An idealistic Communist at first, he was growing ever more sceptical as he witnessed Mao's callousness and debauchery. Mao, however, distrusted Western medicine, and came to rely more and more upon a female assistant and quack doctor, Zhang Yufeng, whom he had picked from obscurity in 1962 to be his 'secretary'. They were no longer lovers, but she increasingly controlled access to him; foreign diplomats were kept waiting for hours because Zhang Yufeng was sleeping. She could understand his grunts and scribbled characters better than anyone – or so she claimed – and the wisdom of the Great Helmsman, as Mao was known, was increasingly filtered through this half-literate former railway worker.

Surrounded by women, Mao barely saw his own wife, Jiang Qing. She preferred the more spacious quarters at Diaoyutai, another former imperial residence, where she assembled her personal court. There she could indulge her love of fashion and costumes, sometimes having whole boxes of them brought to her so that she could play at dressing-up. In 1972 she befriended the American anthropologist Roxane Witke, who spent hours watching her play billiards, discuss imported movies and run her fingers through fine silks and cottons with ecstatic exclamations of appreciation that would have landed any of her less powerful countrywomen in very deep trouble. She occasionally recognised the hypocrisy of her revolutionary posturings and her own love of beautiful things. 'We are the real capitalist roaders,' she once said of her clique.

A short, pop-eyed figure, just into her sixties, she had once been an actress in Shanghai, and something of a looker. Her love life had been complex, and marked by frequent betrayals on all sides. 'Sex is engaging in the first rounds, but what really sustains attention in the long run is power,' she once remarked, and she had a remarkable nose for where power in China was shifting.

In 1937, at twenty-three, she had thrown her previous life aside and travelled to join the Communists in their mountain fastness around Yanan, where she contracted a clandestine marriage to Mao, and had a daughter. In her youth, she certainly possessed a fiery charm; and it had been one of the things that drew Mao to her. They had never been deeply in love – she was his fourth wife, and he her third husband – and they had used each other with great political ruthlessness, but he had been surprisingly dependent on her at one stage, unhappy and fretful unless she was at hand, looking after his needs. After 1949 they drifted apart personally, becoming more political partners than husband and wife, and since 1966 she had increasingly associated herself with three other radicals, Zhang Chunqiao, Yao Wenyuan and Wang Hongwen.

They all had roots in Shanghai, with a strong support base there. Shanghai embodied some of the same contradictions as Jiang herself; it had once been China's most cosmopolitan city, and Shanghai women, even in 1976, were desperate for a semblance of fashion. They hitched their skirts short or wore daring hairstyles, and risked being pulled aside and harassed by the people's militias that were self-appointed guardians of revolutionary purity. Yet Shanghai was also a fiercely left-wing city that produced the most hardline ideologues of the Cultural Revolution. They constantly called for more purges, more violence, more strikes against the enemies of the revolution. Jiang used her new political power to take petty vengeance against critics and directors who had once snubbed her, or actresses with more talent or looks than she.

After her fall, Jiang would come in for far worse criticism than any other figure of the day, criticism that was charged with naked sexist hatred of Jiang as a woman. She would be called a 'female devil' and a 'white-boned demon'. One of the few undoubted achievements of the Communist take-over of China had been the liberation of women, who enjoyed far greater status than they had in the past. But China still had almost no prominent female political leaders, and Jiang was seen as being somewhat unnatural in her eagerness for power.

Jiang was, without doubt, an egocentric, unscrupulous and ambitious woman, who delighted in comparing herself to the great empress of the seventh century, Wu Zetian. A *Beijing University Journal* article of 20 August 1974 praised Wu as 'experienced in using violent dictatorship, which enabled her and her innovative political group to rule for as long as fifty years' – an inspiring model for Jiang. Others were drawn to Jiang by her fiery rhetoric and by the scent of power.

One story told about Wu Zetian, however, applies rather better to Mao than Jiang. He liked to tell it about himself, in fact. During Wu's rule, she often had her ministers executed. A particularly brave official challenged her. How, he asked, could she expect people to keep serving her if she kept killing them off? She told him to come and visit her at one of the imperial halls that night and, trembling, he did so, nervous that a terrible fate was in store. Rather than the executioner, though, he found the empress herself, holding up a torch. Moths flocked to the open flame, burning up as they approached. Mao understood the point as well as Wu did: he could use up as many people as he wanted, since more would always be drawn by the bright allure of power.

In Jiang's case, two of her closest allies were Yao Wenyuan and Zhang Chunqiao, both power-hungry pseudo-intellectuals with little round glasses and blank sociopathic stares. You could imagine them holding forth on the need for bloody revolution against the fascist state in a West German café in 1967, or publishing articles on the Reich's need for racial hygiene thirty years earlier.

As old Shanghai allies of Jiang, both of them had been critical in laying the groundwork for the Cultural Revolution nationwide, but they'd also taken part in local power games. They'd provided the intellectual weight, such as it was, for the seizure of power in Shanghai in January 1967. Alongside Wang Hongwen, they'd ruthlessly disposed of not only the previous leadership of the city but also any other rebel faction they disliked.

Zhang, born in 1917, was fourteen years older than Yao. They hated most of the old revolutionaries and army leaders, partly, one feels, out of jealousy at their greater achievements. Their careers had been mostly spent in propaganda, journalism and the universities, not the brutal guerrilla wars against the Nationalists and the Japanese. Their vision was narrowly fanatic, but they had climbed all the way to the top.

Zhang was the country's premier political theorist, responsible for finding the ideological excuses to get rid of factional opponents or old rivals. Yao Wenyuan was a propagandist, a skilful and poisonous writer. They had managed to close down newspapers, such as *China Youth Daily*, which opposed them, and ran the two most influential papers in the country, *People's Daily* and *Red Flag*, as their own fiefdoms. Yao had written the attack on the play *Hai Rui Dismissed From Office*, which had marked the start of the Cultural Revolution – and, not incidentally, led to the death of its author, the historian and Beijing politician Wu Han.

Jiang and Zhang had only joined the Party in the late thirties, and, caught between one generation and the next, they sought to identify themselves with the 'struggle' of the Cultural Revolution, portraying themselves as newer, more enthusiastic, more earnest revolutionaries than an older generation tainted by bourgeois and capitalist ideals.

Another close ally of Jiang's was Wang Hongwen. Wang's journey to power had been the longest and highest 'helicopter ride' of any Cultural Revolution leader. He was, quite literally, a political bruiser. When the violence began in 1966, Wang was on the security staff of a Shanghai textile factory, a Korean War veteran and Party member of no particular importance. When angry workers from several factories joined together to declare themselves the 'Shanghai Workers' Revolutionary Rebels General Headquarters' – one of the qualities shared by Marxist groups worldwide in the sixties and seventies was fabulously redundant and grandiose names – the tall, charismatic Wang had ended up as their leader and spokesman.

Amid the violence and chaos, Wang stood out, soon rallying more than 100,000 workers behind him. What made his name was an attack not on the old guard, but on another 'rebel' faction in Shanghai on 4 August 1966, when his men had stormed the headquarters of their enemies, the Workers United, killing eighteen people and wounding a thousand.

Wang was handy with his fists, and anything else that came to hand, but his real talent was for incendiary speeches. By January 1967, he'd helped seize power in the city, and brought his men to bear against yet other potential claimants to the revolutionary mantle, helping spark the war of a thousand factions that tore China apart.

After he moved on to Beijing, Wang built up a little personality cult of his own in Shanghai, where his old office and apartment were preserved as pilgrimage sites, and dozens of sycophants turned out admiring works and commentaries on his speeches. Visitors were treated to a potted history of the Cultural Revolution, emphasising Wang's key role; in the short book he had published on the events, his own name appeared 200 times. He ran Shanghai's political affairs from the Jinjiang Hotel, once a colonial apartment block. Even amidst the austerity of the 1960s, it was infamous for girls, drink and extravagant banquets.

At the beginning of the Cultural Revolution in 1966, Mao had made great use of Jiang, Yao and Zhang as willing cat's paws against his enemies, using them to steer the country into the chaos that he dreamed would create a glorious new order. Jiang had come to prominence addressing the Red Guards in Tiananmen Square, calling on them to strike hard against the enemies of the revolution. 'I was the Chairman's dog,' she famously remarked later, 'and I bit who he wanted me to bite.'

Despite their zeal, in 1975 Mao had grumpily labelled Jiang and her allies the 'Gang of Four', and told them not to 'gather together like a little clique' and for a few brief months had seemed to be turning against them. They had been forced to undergo the humiliating process of self-criticism, reading out lists of their own faults to Party meetings, and had avoided each other to reduce suspicions of their factionalism.

Mao had also promoted Deng Xiaoping, a hated rival of the Gang, back into positions of power, beginning with his restoration to the Central Committee in 1973. Meetings of the Chinese Politburo had been convened to reassess developments of the last nine years, working on Mao's stated formula that the Cultural Revolution was to be judged as '70 per cent positive, 30 per cent negative'.

Deng had launched an 'overall rectification campaign' in early 1975 that targeted regional factionalism and incompetent new officials, restored some of the old classics, and attempted, with some success, to kick-start a stagnant economy. But now the pendulum seemed to be swinging back towards the left, and the Gang of Four were once again in the ascendant. Zhou's death was a happy moment for Jiang and her allies. Jiang had been a major instigator of the 'Criticise Lin Biao, Criticise Confucius' campaign. She saw Zhou as an enemy, the epitome of the old guard who had to be torn down, gloating after one meeting in January 1974, 'We pushed Premier Zhou to his wits' end! . . . In the campaign of criticising Lin Biao and Confucius, I stand at the front line of attack.'[21]

She had used Zhou's patronage of traditional art to attack him, displaying hundreds of paintings in an 'Exhibition of Vicious Art' at the Ministry of Culture, with the introduction, 'The emergence of these black paintings was the result of a certain person's encouragement and support.'[22] In articles about Confucius, the writers were again instructed to model him on 'a certain person'. It was a fine example of the insinuating style of politics at the court of Mao, a long, vicious campaign to wear out Zhou physically and mentally and send the signal that his power was fading.

It would take more than that to wear out Deng, however. The Gang recognised his power and endurance. In 1975, Wang Hongwen had warned visitors to Shanghai that, if Deng didn't fall, they would need to start another civil war to stop the counter-revolutionaries seizing the nation. Deng was the ultimate survivor.

He belonged to the first generation of revolutionary leaders, which in itself was a source of massive prestige, although it hadn't saved the lives of many of his former colleagues. Revolutionary and wartime credentials were important, especially in a political culture that was constantly harking back to the past, whether to praise or condemn.

From a well-off gentry family, Deng had joined the Communist Party while a twenty-year-old guest worker in France, and then proceeded to Moscow. There he had studied at the 'University of the Toilers of the East', an institution mainly designed to churn out anti-colonial troublemakers in Asia and elsewhere. He had held his first Party position at twenty-three, gone on the Long March, commanded battalions against the Japanese, and been a member of the national leadership since 1949. He had, in short, a splendid revolutionary pedigree.

Barely five foot tall and portly, he looked like a mischievous but wise gnome. He had survived successive exiles from the start of the Cultural Revolution, when he had been condemned as a rightist and repeatedly forced into the countryside. For three years he lived in an abandoned military school, raising chickens, playing bridge and reading in the evening. Several of his political allies, such as Liu Shaoqi, had been killed, as had his youngest brother, Deng Shuping, a local politician in Guizhou province, who had been driven to suicide by the Red Guards in 1967.

In a way his exile provided some relief from the attacks he and his family had experienced in Beijing, of which the worst had been the fate of his son, Deng Pufang. After months of humiliations, a torture session at Beida University ended with him being thrown from a fourth-storey window, leaving him a paraplegic. Anti-Deng posters contrasted the 'great red banner' of Mao Zedong thought with the 'rotting black counter-revolutionaries' Deng and Liu Shaoqi.

Deng himself was protected by his contacts in the military where he had a strong enough power base to make attacking him directly politically risky even for Mao. Mao had never been able to dominate the military completely. There was no equivalent in China of the NKVD, which had thoroughly penetrated the Soviet Red Army.

Organised secret police forces were very small in China, where the machinery of repression operated through mob rule and local police and militia, though for many years outside observers, confused by the system's surface resemblance to the Soviet Union, vastly exaggerated the role of intelligence agencies and policemen. The closest equivalent was the Central Committee Examination Group, established in 1966 and used to direct persecutions against the top leadership by Mao's intelligence chief Kang Sheng, who had died in 1975.

And after a quarter century of continuous warfare, from 1927 to 1953, first against the Nationalists, then the Japanese, and then the Americans in Korea, the army had a very well developed sense of its own identity and rights. The military was armed and ready to defend itself. Its leaders looked down on the fanaticism of the Red Guards, sneered at the Gang of Four as parvenus, and protected their own.

Deng had also been protected by Mao himself. Unlike most of the other top leaders eliminated in the first years of the Cultural Revolution, Deng had never opposed Mao over the Great Leap Forward, which, for Mao, had been the ultimate test of loyalty. In a rambling attack on the rest of the leadership given in 1959, Mao had named every single politician present, with the sole exception of Deng, as having opposed him and been proven wrong.

Deng's own speeches in the aftermath of the Great Leap Forward show a mixture of guilty conscience and dogged loyalty. Speaking in 1961, after millions of his fellow Sichuanese had died in the famine, he said, 'In the past, procurements were too heavy in some regions, for instance in Sichuan, where they have been heavy for quite a few years, including this year, but there was no alternative. I approve of the Sichuan style, they never moan about hardship, we could all learn from Sichuan.'[23]

Deng had other allies. Many believed that he must be a member of the Hakka, the 'guest people' of south-west China,[24] since he was so closely supported by a number of prominent Hakka, particularly the army marshal Ye Jianying. In fact, he was a Han Chinese from Sichuan province, where feelings ran strong in defence of the local boy made good.

No amount of propaganda could wear away Sichuanese loyalties to Deng. When Deng had fallen in 1966, farmers and townspeople across the province had rallied against the attacks on him, even burning local Party buildings in protest. The protests were put down by militia units led by newly promoted Party members who weren't part of the networks Deng had built up over the years, but the old attachments still lingered.

For Deng, revolution had always been a means to an end. Like many of the 1920s generation, he saw communism as a way of achieving both national strength and personal prosperity: a chicken in every pot and a tractor in every shed. In a country acutely conscious of its own humiliations over the past century, and where much of the population was cripplingly poor, it was tempting to follow the path the Soviets claimed to have forged to material prosperity. To Deng, as to many others, the value of communism didn't lie in abstract principles of justice or moral values, but in tangible success – and when policies didn't work, they could be changed. The famous line, 'It doesn't matter if the cat is black or white, so long as it catches mice,'[25] wasn't original to Deng – if, indeed, he ever said those exact words at all – but it precisely summed up his pragmatic approach to government problems.

Deng's flexible communism contrasted sharply with the ideology of his chief enemies, the Gang of Four. They practised the usual hypocrisies, especially Jiang Qing, who denounced pets, foreign music and foreign luxuries, while keeping songbirds, dancing to jazz and stocking her Zhongnanhai apartment with movie projectors and refrigerators, but they were still revolutionary purists. For Jiang Qing and the others, communism was a process of continual revolution and self-purging, both nationally and personally. A true communist state would constantly cleanse itself, lest counter-revolutionaries and right-wing deviators destroy it. For them, the Chinese people were a means to an end; for Deng, the good of the people was an end in itself.

They believed that the soul of the revolutionary state was far more important than its material success. The obsession with revolutionary purity had a long pedigree in both the European left-wing tradition and Chinese culture. Young Chinese, meanwhile, had been fixated on the elusive quality of *chengyi*, 'sincerity', since at least the 1890s. The older generations lacked sincerity, and thus only the pure hearts of the young could carry through revolution.

That revolution had been frustrated by Deng's re-emergence and the general cooling down of the Cultural Revolution in the mid-seventies. Now, however, they saw themselves as being on the brink of seizing power. It was obvious that Mao had months left at best, and Jiang Qing followed his medical reports closely. Yet Deng still stood in the way. The day after Zhou's death, Wang Hongwen telephoned colleagues in Shanghai, advising them, 'You should turn grief into strength. Criticising Deng is the first priority.'[26]

Before 1975, Deng and Zhou had never actually been that close. Indeed, Deng had signalled his loyalty to Mao, during his own return to power, through a few carefully acid remarks aimed at Zhou. But over the course of the year, Zhou had come to see Deng as his only possible successor, and a reliable bulwark against the Gang of Four. Mao, in turn, had come to see Deng as a potential threat once more, launching in December a propaganda campaign, 'Counterattack the Right-Deviationist Reversal-of-Verdicts Trend',[27] aimed at taking him down again.

Now, Deng was asked to give Zhou Enlai's funeral oration. This was an honour, but also a risk. Although the terms he planned to use were boilerplate honorifics, with no hint of internal politics,

2 Living in coal country

Yu Xuebing was one of the seven black elements, and she wasn't happy about it. Her family had been branded as class enemies a long time ago, during the Anti-Rightist campaign of the 1950s, and the label had stuck. Being 'black' made it hard for her to find boys willing to go out with her – and although she was only fourteen in 1976, she liked boys. And if they weren't too scared of her family's reputation, they tended to like her.

Unusually, she was an only child, with elderly parents; her mother was already sixty. She had four cousins, though, who in the Chinese fashion she called sisters and brothers. Space was cramped in their house, so quite often they slept over at hers.

Her family had been harassed in the last ten years, because they had once been rich. In the 1950s they had even owned a private car, which at the time was about equivalent to owning your own yacht. Her uncle, however, had got drunk and driven it into a ditch in the early sixties. Nobody in the county had been able to fix it, and it was left to rust by the side of their house.

In the early years of the Cultural Revolution, her uncle had been driven mad after being dragged out of his home for daily public criticism and beatings. Some of her relatives were in Taiwan now, having fled in 1949; her father sometimes wished aloud that he had gone with them.

During the first few years of the Cultural Revolution, Yu had lived in constant fear. She was only a small child at the time, but she picked up on the terror of the adults around her. She was disturbed by pictures of Liu Shaoqi's wife being humiliated in public, since the same was happening to her family. The local Red Guards broke into their house several times, looking for signs of bourgeois wealth that they could steal. They stripped the floorboards and the roof for hiding places, and came away with a gold bracelet, a gold ring and 90 yuan. They also took the family's precious sewing machine. After Deng's rectifications of 1974, power in the village shifted, and her family was compensated for the lost cash, but they never saw the jewellery again.

Yu lived in a small village about a dozen miles outside Tangshan, with thirty-three other families. The road was still lined with crude effigies of Lin Biao, put up there in mockery after his 'flight' to Mongolia, along with more recent political slogans like 'Earnestly study the theory of the dictatorship of the proletariat'. For her, Tangshan was the city – it had a cinema, a library, a theatre, even a university. Going there was a rare treat. To outsiders, though, Tangshan was a backwater, overshadowed not only by Beijing but by the neighbouring city of Tianjin, an hour's train ride away.

Tangshan was indeed a backwater, but it was also a power-house of heavy industry, nicknamed the 'Coal Capital' of China. Tangshanese coal drove Chinese industry, which was recovering strongly after years of decline. The first railway in China, only 7 km long, had been built in Tangshan to haul coal. Tangshan was still a major producer of rolling stock for China's ever-expanding rail system.

It was a mining town, founded with British and Belgian money in 1877 to exploit the massive coal deposits nearby. They, like other foreign powers, had even won the right to station troops there after the Boxer Rebellion, though only the Japanese ended up sending soldiers there. After the foundation of the PRC, nationalisation had transformed the mines from an outpost of colonial power into a symbol of the new China's industrial might.

The Kailuan mining complex, China's first coal company, produced 5 per cent of the whole country's coal. It had been designed by Herbert Hoover, later to be US president, during his stint as a mining engineer in China. Tangshanese liked to boast that, with about a million people, they were only a thousandth of the population of China, but produced a hundredth of the output. Economically, a single Tangshanese factory worker or miner was worth ten farmers. Pictures of new Tangshan industrial plants were among the first propaganda images produced by the PRC.

The city centre was on a low-lying plateau. Like most of Hebei, it was dry land, and in the spring winds choked the air with sand and dust. A few miles from the centre the hills started, scored with quarries and vast slag heaps that formed an eerie grey desert. Heavy trucks trundled across worn roads, bearing Tangshan's coal to fuel the cities and steel factories of northern China.

Tangshanese prided themselves on being direct, blunt-spoken and strong. The workers of 1976 had been children during the grinding famine of the Great Leap Forward, and their growth had been stunted by malnutrition and starvation. Medical records from the Kailuan mines show an average height of only 1.57 metres, or just under 5 ft 2 in.

A stocky build was ideal for mining, and there was a strong Stakhanovite cult among the miners, with exceptionally productive workers receiving special bonuses, and a powerful sense of comradeship among the work gangs. Chinese miners had a long history of fierce leftist politics. In the first stages of the Cultural Revolution, the miners had formed their own revolutionary committees. The last five years had seen many 'model workers' drafted into politics or sent to universities to 'instruct the educated youth'.

About a quarter of the city was given over to heavy industry, mostly in the eastern mining district. The whole city covered about fifty square kilometres, and most people lived in one-storey houses, with thick load-bearing walls made of brick or stone. They often had heavy concrete roofs made of cast-offs from the mines. It was a style of building pioneered by the British as workers' housing. They had carried out seismological surveys of the planned mining area and found fault lines, but none serious enough, in their evaluation, to warrant putting up structures built to survive earthquakes. Only the houses and offices of the foreign staff were solid enough to withstand a severe quake.

Even after the foreigners left, newcomers to the mines had copied the buildings around them, throwing up weakly built, insecure houses, the roofs held up by heavy metal rods. In the fifties, new buildings, including multi-storey dormitories to house factory workers and university students, were thrown up with equal carelessness and speed.

Although regulations on earthquake-resistant building had been issued nationally in 1955, they weren't enforced. In the early years of the PRC, construction was modelled on the 'fraternal advice' given by the Soviet Union. The taller new buildings, like the official hotels and university dormitories, were built using plans provided by the Soviets, as were some of the factories. As in other Chinese cities, a couple of hundred Russians had been stationed in Tangshan in the fifties as technical advisors and overseers of the aid the USSR was supplying at the time. There would prove to be a marked difference in survivability between the buildings the Soviets directly supervised and those put together on Soviet blueprints, but with inexperienced Chinese architects.

Despite Tangshan's industrial might, unemployment and underemployment were high. Many young people couldn't find jobs, and spent their days doing occasional shifts at their parents' workplaces or helping the local militias. Full employment was supposed to be one of the defining characteristics of the socialist state, but the combination of population pressures and economic stagnation made this impossible even in a country of farmers and make-work schemes.

In the previous twenty-five years, the country's population – or, at least, that portion of it which the census-takers could find – had nearly doubled, from 583 million in 1953, a figure already 100 million more than the government expected, to over 900 million. Family planning policies had been contradictory and confusing, depending on the whims of the leadership: contraceptive drives one year, encouragement of fertility to ensure a stronger country the next.

Mao had commented in the fifties that, 'We need planned births. I think humanity is inept at managing itself. It has plans for industrial production . . . but not the production of humans,'[1] but efforts at population control had been denounced repeatedly in the sixties. The government was now providing free condoms in many areas, and the city birthrate was dropping, but in the countryside people still married young and had plenty of kids.

Economic growth had not kept pace with population growth. The Cultural Revolution included three years of outright recession, and many more of minimal growth. It was hard to make anything when supervisors kept being purged, technicians exiled, and more time was spent on political meetings and rallies than on the factory floor.

This fed into the Revolution itself. The denunciations of middle management, factory overseers and village heads were at least as motivated by the desire to take over their positions as any ideological fervour. With new agricultural techniques developed during the worldwide green revolution reverberating even in China, farmers were producing more than ever before. But the job situation in the cities was poor, even in an industrial powerhouse like Tangshan. In theory, every citizen was supposed to have a *danwei* (work unit) and a job; in practice, tens of millions of young adults survived on their parents' incomes and worked at whatever was available.

Even relatively comfortable families couldn't afford much. The average worker's income was about 300 yuan a year – roughly $115 at 1976 exchange rates. One yuan would buy five kilos of potatoes, or a treat like a honey melon, or two packs of cigarettes, or five packs of cherry gum, or ten packs of nuts.

Household phone lines were completely unknown; only major institutions and businesses had phones, and making a call involved going through operator after operator. The four great luxuries were a sewing machine, a watch, a bicycle (ideally a

'Flying Pigeon', a Tianjin brand that became synonymous with prosperity) and a radio, all of which required months of saving. Monochrome photographs were treasured mementos, and a village or a factory would consider itself lucky if it had a single black-and-white TV. Toilet paper was an urban luxury, and soft toilet paper unknown. Confectionery was limited to a few brands, such as the much-prized 'White Rabbit' vanilla sweets of Shanghai.

Factory workers described daily life back then as:

. . . just like living in North Korea now, I imagine.[2] It was very normal. You'd get up, go to the factory, have political meetings afterwards, come back home, sleep, just like that. We didn't have big dreams. Everything was paid for by the country. You just wanted to be warm and have enough to eat, though the really hungry times were over by the seventies.

Status didn't make life much better, except for government officials, who enjoyed entertainment budgets that allowed for luxurious banquets. Zhu Yinlai was a university student, which was a rare and privileged thing in 1976. He hadn't had things easily before, though. At seventeen, Zhu had been a 'sent-down youth', bundled from the city into the countryside in 1968. Millions of 'educated youth' were sent 'up to the mountains, and down to the valleys' to lose their soft city privileges and learn from the peasants. It was part of a wider response to the rampages of the Red Guards; dispersed and sent into the countryside, the young couldn't escape control as they had in the wild years of 1966–8.

For most, it was a hideous experience. They were thrown into communities that didn't want useless, unskilled extra mouths. Some found a second home with kind families, others were left entirely to their own resources, sometimes in the hardest landscapes in China. One student, exiled from Tangshan to a village only a couple of dozen miles away that he found grindingly dirty, backward and hostile, made a small crossbow to hunt birds for his supper. Many died through exhaustion, starvation or accident; they were often called upon to operate machinery with which they had no acquaintance, or to fight natural disasters like forest fires for which they were utterly unprepared. Others, especially young women, were sexually abused by local cadres. Suicide was common.

Zhu had had to do everything for himself: cook, clean, wash, dig and mend. He was constantly hungry; the villagers gave him meagre rations, and he learned to eat whatever he could find. He became adept at improvising and scrounging. Having survived his rural exile, he was now twenty-five, and relatively privileged. He had managed to get into the re-opened Mining and Technology University when it resumed classes in 1974.

Tangshan was an academic backwater, but even the small technical colleges there had seen ideological clashes in the late sixties; the 'College Union' and 'Red Guards', which were mostly made up of students, had brawled with the 'Big Red Flag', who were factory workers and miners. The conflict had never reached the levels of everyday murder seen in other cities, but there had been deaths, as each faction strove to prove itself more revolutionary than the other.

Of late the situation was more peaceful – and boring. Zhu's department, mining engineering, had sixty students, but only ten of them were women, and Zhu and his friends had no chance of dating any of them. The students lived in six-storey concrete blocks, five to a room, and ate corn mush twice a day, sometimes with scraps of meat. The only source of entertainment was a film every Saturday night. Occasionally they would try to sneak into the nearby militia headquarters to see more films, because there was nothing else to do other than study and exercise.

The choice of films was not extensive. Before the Cultural Revolution, the Chinese film industry had produced about a film a week, as well as importing Soviet movies. In a typical weekend in the 1950s, for instance, a cinemagoer could pick between Chinese films like *Pi Pa Lane*, *An Ideological Question*, *The Dove of Peace* and *Stand Up Sisters!* or Soviet perennials like *Lenin in October*, *The Fall of Berlin* and the children's film *Big Turnip*. Even some of the movies from the great pre-war era of Shanghai film-making were still shown.

Now anything made prior to 1966 was banned. Occasional exceptions slipped past the guards of cinematic purity, like the 'old fighting trilogy' of war movies, *Tunnel Warfare*, *Mine Warfare* and *Fighting North and South*. Other banned movies could be screened as 'negative examples', either by political enthusiasts or film buffs. No new films had been made during the first seven years of the Cultural Revolution, except for the adaptation of model operas and ballets. In the last three years, however, there had been a miniature revival in the film industry, which was one reason Zhu and other students were so keen to get to the movies.

Compared to others in China, their diet of weekly movies was positively rich. For village youths, seeing a film required extensive organisation. Mo Yan, who grew up to be a great novelist of the 1980s, once described the elaborate procedure he had to go through to see a film as a rural kid in the sixties. He made friends with the operator of his county's only phone, and bribed a shoe repairer who owned a bicycle, and so could travel around the countryside and report on any movie screenings. Eventually, after months of waiting, word came through that *The Red Detachment of Women* was going to be screened that evening in the next county, prompting Mo and his friends to run cross-country for three hours to get there on time.

The lengths people would go to in order to see movies seems baffling, given how appallingly crude most of them were. Only thirty-four films had been made during the Cultural Revolution, most of which were clumsily didactic, like the recent *Song of the Mango*, about the struggle against enemies of the revolution by a workers' propaganda team in a technical institute; *The Fiery Years*, in which a steelworker uncovers foreign spies and domestic saboteurs in his factory; and *Breaking With Old Ideas,* where peasant students teach out-of-date professors the importance of learning from the people.

But in a culturally and visually starved country, movies were one of the few sources of fantasy. The most popular films were foreign – meaning Albanian, North Korean and North Vietnamese. They were just as propagandistic, but they were at least different. The 1972 North Korean weepie *The Flower Seller,* purportedly based on a novel by the country's dictator, Kim Il Sung, had audiences across the country sobbing into their handkerchiefs. Another kind of film-going pleasure could be glimpsed in the popular stills pinned up on dormitory walls, which showed the heroine of the most famous model opera, *The Red Detachment of Women*, doing split-legged shots in loose silk pyjamas.

Elsewhere, students were more adventurous. *Samizdat* literature circulated, surreptitiously copied on factory machines and discussed in clandestine literary salons. Sometimes these copies were made by hand, allowing the insertion of satirical references to local politics. With millions of restless and underemployed young people, *Catcher in the Rye* and *On the Road* were exceptionally popular among those who could get them.

In Tangshan there was little literary activity and the most common form of escape was into nineteenth-century novels, especially those of Stendhal, Dickens and Balzac. As in the Soviet Union, Western social realist novels enjoyed a limited tolerance as examples of the sufferings of the poor under capitalism, but many readers found in them a vision of a larger, freer world, far more compelling than the one they lived in.

The very young had their own games. Zhang Youlu was eight years old in 1976, a skinny whelp living in rural poverty. He lived in a small village on the outskirts of the city, the second of four children. His childhood was one of gnawing hunger, squabbling over food with his siblings and being taught to scavenge for edible plants from a young age. Much of their diet was made up of *bobo*, corn cakes stuffed with vegetable leaves. They had no toys, and instead amused themselves by playing with cast-off metal scraps from the factories, pushing them around with sticks. Alternatively, they played soldier; some of them had older brothers (or, in rare cases, sisters) in the People's Liberation Army. The PLA were always the good guys, but the villains shifted; sometimes they were Japanese, at other times Nationalists or vaguely defined counter-revolutionaries.

It was only a couple of kilometres from his village to the industrial area, but it was a different world. The villages were small, often with only thirty or forty households and a couple of hundred people, but clustered closely together. In a few places it was literally a stone's throw from one to the next, as sometimes demonstrated practically in fights between villages.

Being hungry was nothing new in the countryside, where over thirty million people had died in the Great Leap Forward. Agricultural reform and innovation were beginning to solve China's persistent food insecurity, but population pressures and the sheer inefficiency of collectivised agriculture meant that most people remained, at best, prisoners of a subsistence lifestyle.

Even in 1976, everything was rationed. People still starved, or were so malnourished that ordinarily survivable diseases carried them away. In the city, there was a system of coupons, which were often illicitly traded. In the countryside villagers earned a certain share of the commune's produce. The amount depended, in theory, on how hard they worked. But the most ardently Stakhanovite labourer couldn't compensate for a bad family background or a family squabble with the village head: 'black' families were routinely given half or a quarter of the food of those with more acceptable backgrounds. A man could starve to death because his grandfather had been a cloth merchant.

A 'black' family of six might be allocated only 500 kilos of rice and 50 kilos of cooking oil for the whole year. Farmers were allowed to keep small private gardens, typically a half *mu* (about a twentieth of a hectare) of land for a household. They often cultivated other scraps of land, growing sweet potatoes, and ate 'any green plant' they found growing wild. Village leaders deliberately under-reported the amount of land the village owned year after year to reduce government demands.

The foundation of the PRC had brought one great blessing to the countryside: peace. Armies of 'grey rats', as soldiers were called, no longer swept back and forth, pillaging crops, extorting 'taxes' and conscripting those who couldn't bribe their way out of military service. Older villagers remembered the yo-yoing of armies as they struggled for control of the region, one group of soldiers arriving to steal whatever the previous contingent had missed.

But peace came at the cost of forced collectivisation, a state as predatory and vicious as any mercenary army, and the destruction or neglect of traditional village rights and customs. The worst times had been in the Great Leap Forward, but even after the end of that first period of ideological madness, agricultural policies were dictated from the centre by know-nothing officials, sometimes based on the pseudo-scientific theories of Soviet 'peasant scientist' Trofim Lysenko. They ignored the complex and intensely localised nature of village economics and needs, forcing them into a crude one-size-fits-all model.

One of the cruellest aspects of the system was that it stripped away one of the most basic rights of small farmers everywhere: voting with their feet. The Chinese had always moved around, both in response to disaster and in search of opportunities. Until the 1950s, it was moderately unusual for someone to have both grandparents born in the same province. Calamities like famine or invasion pushed hundreds of thousands of people away from their homes, while growing cities like Shanghai drew millions looking for a future better than farming. It shaped reputations; the people of Henan, one of the larger provinces in China's heavily populated east, had a bad name as beggars and crooks because the region was exceptionally vulnerable to natural disaster, and Henanese refugees were a common sight.

Marxist-Leninist rhetoric demanded that the Chinese past be described as 'feudal', and the farmers as 'serfs', a clumsy imposition of European terms on a very different historical reality. But the imposition of the *hukou* (residence permit) system in 1958 brought the Chinese countryside closer to serfdom than any previous regime. Without the right *hukou*, farmers couldn't get food or housing, thus fixing them permanently in one region. It also made it easier for the regime to draft the rural population for corvée labour, putting millions of men to work on mega-projects – for which their families had to supply the food. Household registration and manpower control had been tried by previous governments in China, but never with this ruthless efficiency.

A rural *hukou* also made it exceptionally difficult for the holder to move to the city – another blow at one of the traditional escape routes. The villages had always depended on the cities, and people moved between them constantly. Now that was impossible. In the cities, those without the right permits were periodically rounded up and dumped back in the countryside by the truckload. In the Great Leap Forward, rural *hukou* holders, bound fast to the commune system, had starved while those with urban *hukou* continued to receive rations.

In the seventies the consequences were less fatal, though even in good times an urban *hukou* could bring three or four times the amount of food a country household received. Instead of starvation, the system produced a surplus of frustrated young men and women. In the past they would have sought work in the cities, becoming, at least at first, *dofu* vendors, umbrella sellers, professional beggars, builders, prostitutes, pedlars and cooks. Instead, most of them were condemned to eternal peasantry.

They still tried to get away – the 'floating population' of vaga-bonds and casual labourers was already reaching the low millions, and bus and train stations were so busy, even late at night, that militias worked overtime to track down 'wandering criminals' without the right permits, beat and lock them up, and deport them back to their home town. (In sharp contrast, the countryside around Tangshan nowadays is positively geriatric; the young have taken off to become part of the army of migrant workers.)

Ambitions weren't dead, even if they were limited. Plenty of young women, for instance, dreamt of being dancers in the same way as girls today fantasise about being movie stars or pop idols. In 1976, that meant working for a propaganda troupe, walking for dozens of miles between remote villages to perform set-pieces promoting the government and the revolution. But this was better than a future spent assembling pots or hoeing fields.

For young people, there was something off key about the constant rhetoric of 'Struggle! Oppose! Crush!' that still dominated political life. The militant era of the late sixties was dead, and the contrast between the dramatic language and the repetitive nature of compulsory political activity was obvious to the young. Their older siblings or younger aunts and uncles had dreamt of furthering or cleansing the revolution; this generation had more practical expectations. Like Yu Xuebing ('Learn from the army') or Yang Wuyi (*Wuyi* is literally 'Five-one', or May 1/Labour Day), they had been named after patriotic or revolutionary concepts, but they didn't have the grand goals to go with these names. That was partly because they could remember their earlier years and contrast them with the realities of their adolescence. In the economic mini-boom of the mid-sixties, life seemed to be getting visibly better, but they were then caught up in the stagnation and political confusion of the seventies.

They had enough education to feel discontented with their parents' lifestyle, and they found Maoist rhetoric increasingly bereft of relevance or meaning for their lives. 'Our parents only wanted to fill all our bellies,' one young farmer remarked; 'We young people want more out of life than that.'[3]

This was particularly the case in the countryside, where improvements in rural education, even as the university system was being destroyed, had created a semi-educated, ambitious generation. As one sent-down youth put it, 'It's the younger peasants who've been through several years of schooling. They simply don't want to work in the fields ... They dream of working in factories, shops or government offices.'[4]

For the Red Guards, the Cultural Revolution had held out politics as salvation. This generation didn't believe those promises, but that didn't mean political activity couldn't be exciting. A good rally was fun; it was exhilarating, particularly at a time when there was so little else to do, to shout and pump fists and wave banners.

Sometimes it had the reassuring familiarity and community of ritual. The most overtly religious elements of the personality cult, such as the morning praise and self-dedication performed in front of Mao's statue, and the self-examination of one's conduct against Mao's instructions before bedtime, had disappeared after the fall of Lin Biao five years earlier. Regular readings from Mao's works were still often a part of office, factory or village life, and political invocations, denunciations and performance formed the rituals of everyday life as prayers, Masses, and saints' days once did in a Catholic village.

By 1976, much of the glamour of revolution had rubbed off. What politics meant much of the time was a constant low-level stream of mind-numbing activities and the stifling boredom of routine meetings in which the expected ideological genuflections had to be made before work could be done. In 1974, for instance, protests had been organised across the country against the supposedly unfavourable portrayal of China in Michelangelo Antonioni's film *Chung Kuo, Cina*. Hundreds of thousands of people protested against a film they were not allowed to see, for an audience of other people who couldn't see it either.

One of the reasons why people sought comfort and ritual in political life was the eradication of everything else. The things that made life good for Chinese in the past had been relentlessly targeted as anti-revolutionary. Some of these habits, like gambling, drinking and 'loose' sexual conduct, were singled out for puritanical reasons. Legends accumulated around Li Chi, a semi-mythical trickster artist; he evaded politics, taught workers in 'proletarian art' classes to play secret gambling games with the pictures, and slept with the buxom daughters of Party leaders.

Other traditions, like village songs, dances, games and rituals to celebrate harvests or provide spiritual sustenance through a long winter, were debunked as 'superstitious' and 'backward'. In the city, the social clubs that had once been a vital part of Chinese civic society, gathering to discuss politics, literature and poetry, play music and chess, or study philosophy, had been broken up as potential hubs of bourgeois thought and counter-revolutionary activity.

Politics in Tangshan, then, was entertaining, ceremonial, routine, tedious – and murderous. Like almost everywhere else, Tangshan had suffered from the paranoia of the last decade. Factions fought in the streets, and a brutal wave of persecutions had been sparked off in 1967 by Chen Boda, at the time a major political figure.

Moscow-educated, Chen was one of the Party's leading theorists, and a frequent speechwriter for Mao. He had been instrumental in kicking off the Cultural Revolution, out of his own conviction of the need for ceaseless struggle and because he was acting as a proxy for Mao. A nervous, stuttering man, he'd nevertheless been a political fixer without any qualms, disposing of inconvenient figures like Peng Zhen, the mayor of Beijing, in order to lay the 'blasting fuse' of the Cultural Revolution.

He published a famous editorial in *People's Daily* on 1 June 1966. Titled 'Sweep Away All Cow-Demons and Snake-Spirits', it gave the Cultural Revolution one of its great metaphors, drawn from folktales about exorcists; enemies of the revolution were demons and monsters in disguise, but they could be revealed with the 'demon-repelling mirror' of Mao Zedong thought.

Chen brought the quest for demons to Tangshan the next year, when he came on an inspection visit in late December. At a meeting of the Party, the army, and various 'mass organisations', he told them:

East Hebei is a very complicated area, a strange situation. There are still British and Japanese agents here. And the local Party . . . maybe it's being operated by the Communist Party and the Nationalists at the same time, or maybe it's just being run by the Nationalists.

You miners are trying to get Fang Fei [a local Party figure] on your side, but he has admitted that he used to be part of the Nationalist county committee. Is he a Nationalist or a Communist? Is he Chinese or Japanese? Look into it carefully, don't be fooled! And the mayor in Tangshan, Bai Yun, I know her husband is a manor owner. He even built a garden with his own money after Liberation!

He moved on to more specific accusations:

Tangshan has always been the centre of the East Hebei Party. The former leaders were rebels! Actually, they were led by Liu Shaoqi and Peng Zhen. So what we suspect we have here is an organised group of rebels which has infiltrated our Party, government and army.

Interrogated about the speech later, Chen had little to say for himself. 'I didn't have any evidence. I made it all up.' Pushed on his claims of Japanese, British and Nationalist agents, he stammered, 'Maybe it was possible in some areas, in some parts of the Party, maybe,' and then admitted, 'Yes, you're quite right. Impossible.' Later, interviewed by the famous writer Ye Yonglie, he was blunt: 'I'm a criminal, and did a lot of stupid things in the Cultural Revolution. It was a crazy time, and I was a crazy man.'

His words set off a furious witch-hunt inside Tangshan. A special group to manage the 'East Hebei Spy Case' was established, made up of local ideologues and opportunists, mostly lower-ranking Party members or leaders from other organisations. Within a few weeks they had exposed their former bosses as members of the 'Yang and Bai Anti-Party Group', named after the Tangshan Party secretary, Yang Yuan, and the mayor, Bai Yun.

The group was secretly working for the 'traitor, spy and renegade' Liu Shaoqi to 'viciously attack Chairman Mao and the

Great Cultural Revolution, falsify the Party's policies, and seize opportunities to swing to the right'. Their houses were ransacked for evidence of their crimes, and big-character posters[5] plastered all over the city, while they were interrogated in 'struggle sessions' where accusations were screamed at them for hours, punctuated by blows and kicks.

Determined to be thorough, the special group was expanded from twenty to over 280 members by February 1968. They formed plans to 'dig deep' and uncover the full extent of the conspiracies and networks of saboteurs by sending teams to over a dozen other local towns. They coined the slogan 'One point, two lines', meaning that the central point of the conspiracy had been the East Hebei Party Committee, but that the lines of treachery ran through both the Tangshan social department and the industrial department.

The social department, they determined, was a 'nest of spies and rebels'. So, perhaps unsurprisingly, was the industrial department. They interrogated 1,604 Party cadres, determining that 737 of them were rebels, spies or Nationalists. They went deep into the past, examining the case files of 362 underground members of the Communist Party in the region between 1922 and 1949, men and women who had suffered vicious persecution at the hands of both the Nationalists and the Japanese. It turned out that 282 of them, no less, had been traitors, including over 80 per cent of the former heads of the East Hebei Party Committee.

Clearer minds might have wondered how the Communist Party ever got anywhere, given that so large a proportion of its membership had, apparently, been working to betray it all along. But espionage paranoia had permeated the People's Republic from its foundation. Spies were the villains of films, books and 'true story' magazines. At first, the main targets were Nationalist agents, supposedly left behind to sabotage the new regime. Later, the focus turned to 'wreckers and saboteurs', acting out of an ill-defined mixture of personal evil and nebulous backing from higher-level political deviants or foreign powers.

For the members of the Special Group, however, the exposure of the plot confirmed the reality of the media tale they'd been absorbing since they were young. It was evidence of both the constant need for alertness and the triumph of true Maoism. And the exposure of these spies and traitors left openings in the upper ranks that could be filled by the politically pure.

Having dealt with the leaders, the persecutors turned to civilians. They called it 'catching worms and bugs'. Torture was one way of exposing hidden spies, including driving nails under fingernails, water-boarding and forcing people to hold a painful fixed position for hours. Retired leaders were imprisoned or killed after being denounced as long-term agents and counter-revolutionaries. The dead were not free from suspicion: forty out of the 238 revolutionary martyrs buried in a local cemetery were found to have been 'rebels and spies' all along.

Not everyone accepted this madness blithely. In Tianjin, an hour or so from Tangshan, a local artist and teacher, Feng Jicai, had started recording stories of suffering after a friend, half-dead from torture, arrived at his house at the dead of night in 1967 and asked, 'Who will live to tell the real stories of our generation? Will we suffer for nothing?'[6] Feng wrote on small pieces of paper, changed names and dates and signed the stories with the names of foreign authors so that, if they were found, he could claim they were copied from nineteenth-century works. As an extra precaution, he hid the stories inside the cracks of his house, and covered them with revolutionary posters or pictures of Mao, a concealment technique inspired by stories of Confucian scholars hiding their works from the literary persecutions of the First Emperor.

Officially, the final total of suffering caused by Chen's remarks alone was 84,000 persecutions, 2,955 deaths, and 763 people left permanently disabled by torture. The Special Group exchanged information and conspiracy theories with similar groups elsewhere, tying the supposed spy networks back to higher-level leaders and eventually forming a picture of a counter-revolutionary 'conspiracy' that involved 24 government departments and 29 provinces. The ripples went through the country, but the sharp point of this particular persecution, one of hundreds nationwide, was concentrated around Tangshan. An almost-offhand speech had helped destroy tens of thousands of lives.

But the little persecutions could be as painful as the big campaigns. One of the defining features of Communist rule was chickenshit. Chickenshit, as originally informally defined within the US military in WWII, is 'petty harassment of the weak by the strong; open scrimmage for power and authority and prestige; sadism thinly disguised as necessary discipline; a constant "paying off of old scores"; and insistence on the letter rather than the spirit of ordinances. Chickenshit is so called – instead of horse- or bull- or elephant shit – because it is small-minded and ignoble and takes the trivial seriously.'[7]

When we think about authoritarian regimes and social catastrophes, we tend, understandably, to think about the big things: murder, torture, imprisonment, suicides, blindings, rapes. But the small things mattered too: the endless routine of political obeisance and cliché, the frustration at having free time filled up with tedious meetings, incompetent ways of doing things at work that couldn't be changed because they'd been put in place by someone with an acceptable political record or ties to higher-level leaders.

The amount of chickenshit depended on the village commune or work unit involved. There were villages where leaders pulled people together and did their best to mollify the insanities coming from above, and there were villages where the leadership was a brew of resentments, intrigues and petty sadism. Everything was worse for those labelled as 'black', of course, who became open targets for every piece of bullying and humiliation others wanted to heap upon them.

Politics affected every part of daily life, from farming to schooling to entertainment. But deep beneath the earth, massive elemental forces were building that cared nothing for red or black, reactionary or revolutionary.

Even a government as inept and self-tortured as China's in 1976 had to care about earthquakes. They had concerned successive Chinese authorities for over two and a half thousand years. One of the main tests for the survival of any Chinese imperial dynasty was how well it coped with natural disasters. The end of each regime was often marked by a succession of calamities that caused famine, flight, and eventually revolts that either overthrew the old order or weakened it to a point where foreign invaders could take easy advantage of this vulnerability.

Flooding was one of the most frequent disasters. Extensive waterways permeated large parts of eastern China, where a complicated system of levees and dams checked the great rivers and lakes that gave many provinces, like Hebei ('Northern River'), their names. The system required constant maintenance, usually carried out with forced labour, and when it failed, the results were calamitous.

Facing invasion from the north by Manchu horsemen in 1644, a desperate Ming dynasty had deliberately broken the levees on the Yellow River, causing mass flooding in an attempt to hold back the enemy, a tactic repeated 400 years later by the Nationalist government against the Japanese. Both times it killed hundreds of thousands of people, and barely slowed down the invaders.

In August 1975, the Communist government had discovered how fearsome China's waters could be when Typhoon Nina caused rivers in Henan to flood, leading to the destruction of one of China's largest hydropower projects, the Banqiao dam. There had been major dam or reservoir collapses in 1960, 1963 and 1971, each killing hundreds of people, but they were nothing compared to the Banqiao disaster. As much as 600 million cubic metres of water was released when the dam burst, and the whole of the local countryside disappeared under surging waves, like an inland tsunami.

Poor communications and disorganised local government meant that warnings to evacuate didn't reach most of the villages in time, leading to 26,000 deaths by drowning, and nearly 150,000 deaths in the subsequent famines and epidemics. The extent of the famine underscores how chaotic the country still was, and how close to starvation most people lived.

Maoist arrogance contributed to the Banqiao disaster. Mao was determined to prove that 'man could conquer nature', and gigantic hydrological projects such as at Banqiao were one way of demonstrating Communist mastery of the landscape. China's 80,000 dams and reservoirs were put up hastily, and without adequate safety measures – by 1981, 3,200 of them had collapsed. Western-educated hydrologist Chen Xing had repeatedly warned that the Banqiao dam was unsafe, but had been attacked for his lack of faith as a 'right deviationist' and purged, once in 1958 and again, after being brought back to work on the project, in 1961 for opposing the Great Leap Forward.

The disaster was swiftly hushed up, receiving almost no coverage in the news; even now, most Chinese have never heard of it. To get a sense of how strange this is, imagine that a natural disaster had killed, adjusting for population, 12,000 people in the UK in 1975 – and then imagine that almost nobody knew about it today.[8]

But earth could be worse than water, though the disasters fed into each other, as the shaking ground cracked dams and broke levees. In an earthquake, the government could do little to prevent the initial harm. It was how it coped with the chaotic aftermath that mattered, whether troops could be brought in to herd refugees to safety, or food moved from elsewhere in the nation to the afflicted areas and the power of the state reasserted. Without good government, disaster left power gaps that were rapidly filled by bandits. Chinese political thought was very clear on this; Ming officials wrote that 'hunger and cold make bandits' and 'civilians who refuse to die of starvation will inevitably become bandits'.[9]

The difference between bandits and rebels, as the rulers well knew, was thin; all it took was a charismatic leader, a national or ethnic cause, or a millennial impulse. In the famines of the Great

Leap Forward, some of the Communist Party's top officials had been worried that a mass revolt in the countryside could topple the government, and Chiang Kai-Shek, the exiled Nationalist leader in Taiwan, had been barely dissuaded from reinvading the country in the expectation that the peasants would welcome liberation from famine.

To rebel, after all, was glorious. One of the oldest concepts of government in China was the 'Mandate of Heaven' (*tianming*), the idea that an emperor's legitimacy depended on heaven sanctioning his just and fair rule. When a ruler became corrupt or unjust, this mandate was revoked by the gods, and rebellion was not only legitimate but presumed to be divinely sanctioned. In popular thought, among the chief consequences of this idea were natural calamities, which demonstrated that the ruling dynasty had lost the favour of the gods.

The legitimacy of the Mandate of Heaven was not judged by the mere occurrence of natural disasters, which were inevitably frequent in as huge a country as China. The disasters themselves didn't show that the rulers were doomed; the failure to manage or anticipate floods or earthquakes did. One of the most critical factors was tax relief; a government that kept trying to squeeze revenues or labour out of a devastated area showed not only a lack of justice but also a lack of sense and doomed itself to rebellion. Any large-scale disaster was, in effect, a challenge to the government to prove what it was there for.

Earthquakes offered some of the most critical of such challenges. China is one of the most seismically active countries. On average, an earthquake of magnitude 7 or higher, powerful enough to crack the ground and shake, or even raze buildings over hundreds of square miles, hits the country every year. Fortunately, the most frequently hit areas were in the sparsely populated west, but the country had still been racked by numerous disastrous quakes throughout history. The worst was the colossal Shaanxi earthquake of 1556, which may have killed as many as 800,000 people.

For Europeans, earthquakes were a theological and philosophical challenge. They were the ultimate example of nature's amorality, killing without regard to innocence or guilt, hard to accept for any believer in a just God. After the Lisbon earthquake of 1755, which struck on All Saints' Day and killed 40,000 people, many of them in church at the time, Voltaire was prompted to write, in a poem:

Will you say, 'It is the effect of everlasting laws
Which necessitates this choice by a free and good God'?
Will you say, seeing this heap of victims:
'God is avenged, their death is the payment of their crimes'?
What crimes, what bad things have been committed by these children,
Lying on the breasts of their mothers, flattened and bloody?
Lisbon, which is a city no longer, had it more vices
Than London, than Paris, given to doubtful delights?

The Chinese intelligentsia was not greatly concerned with such theodical conundrums. Explanations for earthquakes looked to practical matters. Earthquakes were not the will of an angry God, but the product of a cosmological imbalance, or of the movement of air underneath the earth. The court mathematician Zhang Heng devised the world's first seismograph in AD 132, a bronze bowl with dragons on each of the eight cardinal points. When a shock was felt, they spat balls into the mouths of toads underneath, reportedly detecting tremors up to 800 km away.

Like every other Chinese regime before it the PRC struggled with the problem of earthquakes. Fortunately, they were relatively few and far between in the post-war period. Two magnitude 8 quakes – thirty times as powerful as magnitude 7 – had smashed isolated parts of Tibet in 1950 and 1951, but the worst quake, a relatively low 6.8, had been in Xingtai, in southern Hebei, on 8 March 1966. It had killed 8,000 people and wrecked nearly five million homes.

Another significant quake had happened in the Bohai Sea, near Tangshan, on 18 July 1969; it had caused a small tsunami but done relatively little damage.

The Xingtai quake prompted Zhou Enlai to form a working group on seismology, which eventually became the State Seismological Bureau in 1971. The atmosphere of the times, when 'people's science' and 'cooperation with the masses' were ideological imperatives, meant that from the start the emphasis was on mass observation carried out by local enthusiasts. Over 100,000 amateurs were recruited to monitor possible signs of earthquakes, using methods based on both foreign experience and the reports from Xingtai.

Earthquake prediction is the most frustrating, bitter and unrewarding part of seismology. As one Chinese seismologist commented to me, 'People spend their whole lives trying to find a method for it. Then in their old age, they just give up and turn to the *I Ching* instead. In all honesty, fortune telling is about as good as any other method we have.'

The mass observation method was actually an eminently practical one, especially given the pseudoscience that pervaded academia elsewhere in China. Observers were trained to look for a variety of signs, most critically the sudden dropping of water levels and strange behaviour in animals.

The first is a well-attested forerunner of quakes, but the validity of the second remains in question. More often than not, animals behave weirdly for no reason – as I write this, my dog is running up and down the stairs of my apartment for, as far as I can tell, his own amusement – but usually we just ignore it. It may well be that supposed animal signs of earthquakes are only heeded in retrospect. Usually, howling dogs or chickens that refuse to go into the coop are simply ignored. Only when followed by disaster do they suddenly become remembered as dire warnings.

An important lesson learned from Xingtai was that a series of small quakes often foreshadowed a major one. It was this lesson that saved the small city of Haicheng in southern Liaoning province, a few hundred miles north-east of Tangshan. On 1 February 1975, reports of minor tremors started pouring in from all over the province. Three days later, on 4 February, the Seismological Bureau issued an official prediction that a major earthquake was likely, and the Liaoning Revolutionary Committee, the chief authority in the province, warned the whole area to take precautions. It was bitterly cold, but nevertheless work was shut down, over a million people evacuated from their houses, and medical teams and supplies kept ready. When a 7.3 magnitude earthquake hit the same evening, thousands of buildings were destroyed, but only 1,328 people were killed, and 16,980 injured.

Haicheng was a remarkable achievement, and one much trumpeted in the Chinese press as proof of the nation's heroic scientific progress, but it was no guarantee of future success. Sharp foreshocks had shaken the whole area, and people were already fleeing their homes prior to the evacuation warning. It was the clearest earthquake indicator possible, but it had little to do with the 'people's science' constantly touted in the press. The extent of success at Haicheng was also played up for propaganda. The toll of dead and injured was kept secret, and the public told that 'very few' had been killed. The propaganda convinced many among the public that the problem had essentially been solved, and that earthquake prediction was a simple business.

At an event congratulating those involved in Haicheng, Hua Guofeng had shaken the hand of every seismologist in the Bureau and asked them, 'After today, do you think you can predict earthquakes over magnitude 5 twenty-four hours in advance?'[10] They couldn't, and they knew it, though for months one group of seismologists within the Bureau was convinced that a serious earthquake was due to hit the Beijing–Tianjin area. The signs had been many, if hard to read: slow changes in water levels, frequent microquakes, and a long drought. The link to the last was a contentious theory mooted by one of the seismologists, Geng Qingquo, that high-magnitude quakes were connected to periods of drought.

Their report only predicted a magnitude 5 to 6 quake, but it also noted:

Based on the historical pattern of major earthquake activity, the study of regional seismicity, the influence of the Western Pacific seismic belt and those earthquakes with focal depths of 400–500 km on North China, some comrades believe that North China has accumulated enough seismic energy for an earthquake of magnitude 7 to 8.[11]

The scientists went on to hedge their bets, though, saying that others regarded it as unlikely, given the historically long gap between earthquakes in north China, that there would be a quake at all.

The language of the document, however, reminded the provincial leaders of their first priority, stating, 'We look to you to pursue the movement to "criticise Lin Biao and Confucius", and, at the same time, to carry out the central government policy of forecasting and precautionary work.' Politics still took precedence over scientific theory, although the rest of the document urged (along with some boilerplate language on the leadership of the Party and the role of the masses) 'careful attention to the work of seismic experts' and that 'every aspect of seismological work must be intensified'.

Document 69 undoubtedly helped save lives in Haicheng, but in many places it didn't mean that much. The provinces had a long history of ignoring central policy documents, especially at a time when local leadership was still fractured and divided by the legacy of purges and civil war. After all, this was the sixty-ninth policy document issued that year. Some rural counties didn't even receive the document until more than six months after it was issued. The first central policy documents of the year were traditionally important, but others could be neglected or ignored without serious consequences.

Earthquake education throughout Tangshan had been spotty. Later writers would exaggerate the extent of it for dramatic purposes. The usually excellent journalist Qian Gang, for instance, claims:

In almost every house a wine bottle was placed upside down on the table, the theory being that if it fell this was the sign of an upcoming earthquake. Families with babies placed milk powder and feeding bottles near the door, so that they could be swiftly snatched up as they made their escape. The parents of slightly older children sewed money into the lining of their clothes.[12]

Perhaps this was the case for a relatively well-informed urban elite. Milk powder and feeding bottles weren't even available in the countryside, where kids were often breast-fed until six or seven. Some survivors talk of buying goldfish in anticipation of the quake, like the young He Jianguo watching for signs of their agitation as a warning to leave the house. But most people, at least according to their accounts today, paid very little heed to earthquakes. Some remembered a short film on earthquake preparation being shown, but that was all. The Haicheng earthquake rattled a few, but only in the way that most people react when reading about natural disasters: a few moments of speculative fantasy on what they'd do if it happened to them, then pushing it to the back of their minds and getting on with more immediate concerns.

One county near Tangshan took far greater precautions. Qinglong was a rural county, high up in the mountains, about 185 km north-east from Tangshan as the crow flies, but a good five or six hours by car. It was a rugged place of winding roads and isolated villages. China's infrastructure was still terrible, and one in three villages in the country couldn't be reached by road; in Qinglong and similar mountainous areas it was more like half. Technically it was a minority region, though the practical differences between the Han and the northern Manchu peoples had been erased by intermarriage, the disappearance of the Manchu language, and Han settlement for decades.

Qinglong's Party head, Ran Guangqi, was a driven, self-educated leader, a veteran of dangerous propaganda work in Japanese-occupied territory in the 1930s. He'd only just been appointed to the position in 1974, and he took Document 69 seriously enough to start teaching himself about earthquakes. In November 1975, Ran made an enthusiastic 21-year-old administrator, Wang Chunqing, head of a disaster management team; he set up earthquake monitoring sites, ran slide-shows in schools and villages and distributed thousands of posters and leaflets on earthquakes.

But even in Qinglong many villages only a dozen miles or so away from the county centre remained completely unaware of the earthquake awareness programmes. With most people trudging through the mountains by foot, many village heads simply didn't bother turning up for meetings in the county centre, and educators frequently skipped smaller or harder-to-reach settlements.

By 1976, the Seismological Bureau was also finding it hard to concentrate on its work. The Bureau's head, Hu Keshi, was not a scientist, but a political ally of Deng Xiaoping. He'd been a deputy to Hu Yaobang, a prominent Party liberal, in the Communist Youth League and had been beaten and mocked alongside him in 1966.

The Red Guards had marched them on to the third-floor balcony of the Youth League building every quarter of an hour to be jeered at by the crowds. After years of exile, Deng's return had carried Hu Keshi back into government in late 1973, and, despite his lack of education, he had begun to establish himself as an authority on scientific matters.

But now that position was being challenged. In January the Chinese Academy of Sciences, the parent body of the Seismological Bureau, held a contentious meeting where the supposed swing to the right was fiercely criticised. Hu was publicly named as one of the rightists, a clear sign that he was being targeted. Understandably, he was fretful, and so was the rest of the Bureau. A new wave of purges was clearly about to be unleashed, and Deng Xiaoping and his friends were standing right in its way.

3 Tomb-Sweeping Day

It was a cold Beijing morning when the cavalcade of cars bearing Zhou Enlai's body set out from Tiananmen Square, but that didn't stop the crowds. Over a million people had turned out to see their premier on his last journey. They lined the 10 kilometres from Tiananmen Square to the Babaoshan Cemetery, at that time beyond Beijing's western outskirts.

The route and the timing were supposed to be kept a secret, but had soon leaked out. At Babaoshan, Zhou's body would be cremated, an idea the crowds objected to, at one point swarming the cortege and protesting that he should be buried, as was the tradition. It was only when Deng Yingchao, Zhou's widow, stepped out and told them that her husband had wanted his ashes scattered over the country that they calmed down and let the cars drive on. Incongruously, Zhou's body was carried in a large white coach of the kind used to ferry holidaymakers to the seaside. White was the traditional colour of mourning, though on the coach it was offset with revolutionary red flowers.

The crowd's faces were contorted with fearful grief. Clad in dull overcoats and furry hats, they wiped away cold tears. Everyone, young and old, was crying. Teenage girls clutched at each other, their faces snotty with tears, and howled their grief.[1] At Babaoshan, mourners lined up to buy pictures of Zhou, openly weeping as they handed over the money.

Before the cremation, the memorial ceremony had taken place in the Great Hall of the People, on the western edge of Tiananmen Square, the flag outside lowered to half-mast. His body had lain in state, with the hammer-and-sickle draped over it. One by one, liver-spotted old comrades came in to pay their respects, clutching at the hands of his widow and bowing their heads to his painfully thin corpse. Soong Qingling, the widow of Sun Yat-Sen, hailed as China's first president and a pre-Communist revolutionary hero, embraced Deng Yingchao, kissing her on both cheeks.

Inside the hall, Deng Xiaoping delivered a memorial address in his heavy Sichuan accent. Wearing a dark Mao jacket, he was dwarfed by the white floral tributes piled on each side. Every political figure of consequence in China, save Mao himself, was there, but Mao's wreath was the most prominent, with those of Zhu De and Ye Jianying, two old generals and military comrades of Zhou's, just behind. Deng's speech was not stirring stuff – 'He will be mourned by the military, the country, the people . . . he faithfully carried out Mao's doctrine' – but it still moved the audience to tears, old politicians and generals snuffling into hankies.

In Tangshan, He Jianguo watched the funeral on her factory's flickering colour TV along with her workmates. At first, all of them were crying, but as the camera panned over the lines of dignitaries, there were angrier words. 'Look at her,' one of the older men at the factory said, pointing at Jiang Qing, 'I don't know what she's doing there, the old sow.'

A chance to see the leaders in such intimate detail was rare, and audiences nationwide had harsh words for Jiang. She was accused of keeping her cap on, a clear sign, it was claimed, of disrespect – though several of the other dignitaries, including those close to Zhou, had done the same in the cold hall. Her ally Zhang Chunqiao was blamed for embracing Deng Yingchao too warmly, which was felt to be foreign and affected. It was acceptable for Soong Qingling to do it, but seen as inappropriate from a man, especially one of the Premier's enemies.

The funeral procession began in Tiananmen Square, the most politically resonant location in China. It was here, on 4 May 1919, that students had gathered to protest the handover of German colonial territories in China to Japan, rioting against a government they saw as complicit with the imperialist powers.

It was here that Mao had overseen the mass gathering of Red Guards in 1966, commanding them to go out and overturn the old order. And it was here that Mao had proclaimed the founding of the People's Republic of China on 1 October 1949. His portrait now hung there permanently, usurping the imperial gate.

Tiananmen was named after the entrance to the Forbidden City on its northern edge, the 'Gate of Heavenly Peace'. In 1976, though, the Forbidden City, the home of generations of emperors, was an overgrown park, closed to the public. The Red Guards had threatened more than once to burn it down; it had been Zhou sending army units there that had saved it, preserving one of the most beautiful parts of China's imperial heritage for generations to come.

Beijing was a fraction of its current size in 1976. Areas which are now one continuous urban sprawl were then fields and villages; the two universities of Tsinghua and Beida, now well inside the city boundaries, were isolated countryside campuses, surrounded by hemp fields. The modern city stretches beyond its Sixth Ring Road; the city then would comfortably fit within the Third.

Although there were many Soviet-style concrete blockhouse flats, many Beijingers still lived in *hutongs*, tangled alley complexes with numerous houses around cramped courtyards. They were a sign of the city's past, and the urban authorities disliked them, not least because, like backstreets and alleys everywhere, they were impenetrable to outsiders, and to the power of the state. The Party preferred vast avenues and squares, after the pattern of Haussmann's rebuilding of Paris. These were designed both to overawe the public and to provide routes through which soldiers could march and crowds could be channelled.

The square itself was unimpressive. Theoretically the world's largest, it didn't feel like it, because, unlike the Kremlin, on which it was partly modelled, it wasn't closed off on all sides, instead disintegrating into monumental buildings and alleyways.

It looked like a stony field, though when Richard Nixon flew into Beijing for his groundbreaking 1972 visit,[2] Tiananmen had been covered with potted flowers, a blaze of diplomatic colour in a grey city. Within days of his departure, Beijing citizens stole them all, sparking a rare fit of temper from Zhou Enlai.

The great flower theft represented a simple truth: the public was desperate for beauty. It was the same reason people plastered propaganda posters on their walls. No matter how banal the message, the pictures, with their bright colours and vivid action scenes, were the closest to art many people were going to get.

The conflict between the demands of politics and the hunger for art was acute in every field. Before the Red Guards denounced Western music, the radio regularly broadcast classical composers. In the early sixties, Chinese factories churned out (relatively) cheap violins in vast numbers for ambitious parents who knew that music, like sport, was one of the few specialisations that could potentially mean a way out of the farm or the factory for talented kids. But classical music came to mean far more than that.

As Red Guards burnt violins and smashed records, people, even those whose only experience of music had been as spectators, started to construct their own violins. One boy, exiled to a farm at thirteen, patiently plucked a single hair from a horse's tail every day, so as not to be noticed. It took him six months to build his own instrument.[3] Thousands like him spent hours practising every day, but had to do so in secret, for fear of being criticised, beaten or even murdered for their love of foreign decadence. Hidden caches of sheet music were passed on by defiant teachers, or copied by hand. By 1976, foreign instruments were just about politically acceptable, though they had to be used for revolutionary songs.

But domestic Chinese music, too, had fallen victim to political fervour. The most prominent example was the Chinese national anthem. Although never officially chosen, the de facto anthem before the Cultural Revolution was 'The March of the

Volunteers', a Marseillaise-inspired piece originally composed in 1934 for an anti-Japanese film from a Shanghai studio.

Rise up, you who would not be slaves
Build with your flesh and blood a new Great Wall
As China faces its greatest peril
Everybody is forced to give their last.
Rise up! Rise up! Rise up!
Our million hearts beat as one.
Brave the enemy's fire! March on!

With its stirring militarism, sense of imminent danger, and appeal to the masses, it seemed well suited to the Cultural Revolution. However, it had two flaws. The first was complete omission of mention of the Communist Party, and, in particular, of Mao Zedong.[4] The second was the political unreliability of the lyricist.

Tian Han, a young playwright when he wrote the original, eventually became the chairman of the Chinese Dramatists' Association and a critic, from an idealist communist perspective, of Maoist policies. He had almost been exiled in 1959 for speaking privately against the Great Leap Forward, but the Tibetan uprising that same year had saved him, after Zhou Enlai commissioned him to write a play emphasising national unity and the historical roots of 'China's Tibet'.

Mao's hunger for vengeance against those who had opposed him over the famine encompassed even a politically insignificant artist. In 1966, Tian Han was stripped of his official posts and attacked by Red Guards, eventually dying under a false name in a military hospital in 1968. His musical collaborator on the song, Nie Er, had been murdered by pro-Japanese thugs in 1935. Their two deaths neatly spanned China's national tragedies.

So at Zhou's funeral, instead of an epic of sacrifice and danger, they sang the approved alternative,

The East is red, the sun is rising
China has brought forth Mao Zedong

He works for the people's welfare.
Hurrah! He is the people's great saviour!
Chairman Mao loves the people.

Right at that moment, Chairman Mao did not love the people. Instead, hearing accounts of the crowds' attitude to the dead Zhou, he was bitter and resentful. '[Zhou] opposed me over launching the Cultural Revolution, [and] not a small bunch of veterans all listened to him [although] on the surface they supported me.'[5] He declared the mourning activities 'a cover for restoration', and told his nephew, Mao Yuanxin, to convey as much to the Politburo.

Deng recognised the attack on the mourning activities as another swipe at him. The culmination of the campaign against him was close at hand. Sure enough, a few days after the funeral, he was relieved of his duties. This was a soft landing as he remained in the Politburo; but it was also, he realised, a prelude to something worse. He stopped attending the Politburo meetings unless summoned directly. When forced to go, he would be 'criticised' non-stop by the Gang of Four, with others opportunistically joining the tirade.

It was the kind of humiliation that had driven some to despair or even suicide, but Deng bore the political blows easily enough. After all, he was used to it; this was his third time around on the political wheel, although he was nervous for his family. He even took the chance to wind up his opponents a little. Genuinely somewhat deaf, he would deliberately exaggerate it in order to ignore comments aimed at him at meetings.

'When Hua Guofeng, way at the other end of the table in a low voice announces "meeting adjourned", he hears it immediately and, pushing back his chair, gets up to leave!'[6] complained Zhang Chunqiao, one of Deng's fiercest critics. Deng pulled the same trick at a particularly heated meeting when some young students had been brought in to act as a claque for his critics. Amid catcalls and jeers, he got up and walked out, muttering

'I am a deaf old man and I cannot hear what you folks are yelling about.'[7]

Marshal Ye Jianying, one of Deng's close allies, also stopped going to the Politburo meetings. Ye was another of the old revolutionaries, a friend of Zhou Enlai, and one of China's greatest generals. His power base was in Guangdong, a massive southern province. He'd implemented relatively sane and mild policies there in the 1950s, trying to work with former landlords instead of condemning them wholesale, but had fallen victim to the hardline insistence on class struggle and had his policies rescinded by Mao and Lin Biao.

Like many of the founding Party veterans, he looked as though he should be playing with his grandson in a park, not running a country, but his wispy hair and thick-rimmed glasses concealed a still-sharp mind. Trained in Moscow, Ye had been chief of staff of the PLA in the war against the Japanese, and was a formidable tactician, organiser and analyst – skills he brought to politics as well.

In 1967 he tried to cut the Cultural Revolution off at the knees when, along with other prominent military men, he launched a fierce attack on the leftists at a meeting in Zhongnanhai, openly condemning the mess they were making of the country and the attacks on old cadres. It was a bold move, and if he had been dealing only with a rogue political faction, it might have worked. He hadn't realised that the leftists were acting for Mao, and how deeply Mao was committed to backing them. It had only been age and status that saved him and the other generals from being entirely destroyed, and he'd been forced out of high-level politics for four years until Mao brought him back to provide military backing for his moves against Lin Biao.

Now he was engaged in a tactical retreat. Nearly seventy-nine, he used his age as an excuse, pleading 'illness' to explain why he could no longer come to meetings, and instead staying with his family at his home in the western hills of Beijing. It was a subtle show of support for Deng, and a snub aimed at the members of the Gang of Four, whom he loathed. They'd gone after him again in 1973, after he'd worked with Zhou to build relations with the US, accusing him of 'right-wing capitulationism'. In private, he'd mock Jiang as 'the actress' (with much the same tone, one imagines, as a seventeenth-century Puritan would have used for the term) and Zhang as 'glasses'.

Deng's removal left Mao with a serious dilemma. Deng was obviously the most competent member of the Politburo, and he would have been the only natural choice to succeed Zhou. But now that was out of the question, and the decision couldn't be put off. Whoever Mao picked would be not only second-in-command, but would be seen as having his blessing as successor.

Mao knew the end was coming. As he grew weaker, questions of succession continued to trouble him. He could have followed the model of past Chinese revolutionary leaders, picking one of his own children and effectively creating a new imperial dynasty. That was Kim Il Sung's choice in Korea, although his personality cult had always been far more baroque than even Mao's. Mao's only surviving son, Mao Anqing, was tragically incapable of ruling. He suffered from severe mental illness, diagnosed by Chinese doctors as schizophrenia but possibly the result of trauma suffered during a vicious beating by the Shanghai police. Whatever the cause, he was depressive, occasionally delusional, and given to fits of anger to the point where he attacked people.

Anqing and his brother, Anying, had been left in Shanghai after their mother was executed by the Nationalists, and ended up on the streets, fending for themselves. It was only by luck that they had been found again: five of Mao's other children, two sons and three daughters, had been left behind in various villages and towns during the fight against the Nationalists and the Japanese, and were never heard of again.

Mao had tried to toughen up Anying, a sensitive young man, by sending him to aid in the land reform programme in Communist-held areas in 1948, where he had been shocked by the brutality he witnessed. 'After careful rehearsals, on the fifth day denunciations began . . . all the masses were told to raise their hands and shout "Kill! Kill! Kill!"' he wrote in his diary, 'Eight people were beaten to death.'[8] In order to prove himself, he volunteered to fight the Americans in Korea. There he would fight alongside many other 'volunteers' who had gone to the war to cleanse themselves of perceived bourgeois taint or Nationalist connections. He was killed in an American napalm attack, leaving Mao with a mad son and two surviving daughters.

Mao had a surrogate son, however, Mao Yuanxin, the son of his younger brother. Mao Yuanxin's father had been killed in 1943, when he was two, and his uncle had become his guardian. He'd risen to be one of the rulers of Liaoning, a small north-eastern province, where he was also a political commissar in the PLA. From the start he'd sided with the far left, cosied up to Jiang Qing, and run a grimly repressive regime in Liaoning. He had vigorously badmouthed Deng to Mao in the second half of 1975, helping persuade Mao to back the campaign against him. But he wasn't in the Politburo, had an abrasive personality, and was far too young to be a plausible candidate. Mao used him as a liaison to communicate with the Politburo from his deathbed, but wasn't prepared to commit China's future to him, though he envisaged it being a possibility in a few years' time.

With any likelihood of a family dynasty gone, Mao toyed with other heirs. The most obvious was Lin Biao, who was actually appointed Mao's official successor in a rewrite to the Constitution. After his fall, however, Mao became cagey about explicitly naming another pick.

For several years though, there seemed to be a clear front-runner. Wang Hongwen, the youngest member of the Gang of Four, had been transferred to Beijing from Shanghai at Mao's personal request in September 1972, and begun attending high-level meetings. It was an obvious grooming for power, and, indeed Mao made him, at the age of thirty-eight, a vice-chairman of the Party in 1973. Mao had picked him as a sop to the leftists, and because he was worried about preserving the spirit of the Cultural Revolution at the same time as circumstances compelled him to let Zhou restore Deng and other pragmatists to power. But Wang had proved yet another disappointment to the Chairman.

Although brash and forceful, he was both unnerved by working at such a high level and overwhelmed by the volume of bureaucracy and the weight of the decisions he had to make. He kept looking to Jiang Qing for advice and guidance, until he was soon perceived as nothing but her creature. Wang had lived for some time near Jiang at the Diaoyutai state guesthouse, another complex of old buildings built around a favourite fishing spot of past emperors, though he switched his home back to Zhongnanhai later. Mao frequently warned him off Jiang Qing: 'Don't form this little Shanghai clique!' Sometimes, talking to friends back home, Wang regretted how close he'd become to her, but then he'd go back and end up nodding along once more. He could yell at a political opponent or lead men into battle, but he lacked the grit or the wiles to run a country.

Zhang Chunqiao, another member of the Gang of Four, arrogantly expected to be promoted to Zhou's former role. He was among the highest-ranking Politburo members, and ran a tight organisational ship. His hopes were misplaced. Mao had a fine sense of balance and picking Zhang would have angered so many of the old guard that he never really considered it. Instead Mao started to favour another likely successor, Hua Guofeng, who was named acting Premier on 8 February 1976.

His appointment was announced in the first central policy document of the year, always reserved for a matter of serious state import. Hua, born in Mao's home province of Hunan in 1921, was already minister of public security and a Politburo member, but his appointment came as something of a surprise nonetheless.

It was certainly a slap in the face of the Gang of Four. They showed their feelings in different ways. Zhang and Yao started saying to each other whenever they met, 'Hey, the higher you go, the harder you fall,'[9] in reference to Hua. Wang Hongwen, on the other hand, bought a motorcycle and started driving around Zhongnanhai and Diaoyutai late at night at great speeds. It was a reminder of his relative youth compared to the rest of China's leadership; at forty-one, he was about twenty years younger than the average Politburo member.

It's still hard to know what to make of Hua. Some thirty-five years on, nobody seems to have really understood what exactly prompted Mao to elevate him to one of the most powerful positions in the country. Some experts on Chinese elite politics, such as Victor Shih, have seriously suggested that Hua was, in fact, Mao's illegitimate son, abandoned and then rediscovered in Hunan. The two had a certain family resemblance, both tall, good-looking men in their youth who lapsed into chubbiness in middle-age, but not an uncanny one.[10]

In fact, Mao first noticed Hua in 1959, when the latter was a Party official overseeing Mao's old home town. While on a visit, Mao was impressed both by Hua's efficient management and his building of a memorial hall commemorating Mao's early life. This mixture of talent, personal charm and sycophancy would be critical in Hua's rise to the top.

Hua had a respectable military background – he had served under General Zhu De as a regular soldier for twelve years – but had done nothing spectacular. Like a lot of people, he'd taken a patriotic name, replacing his birth name of Su Zhu. Hua Guofeng was an abbreviation of a wartime description for his unit – *Zhong<u>hua</u> kangri jiu<u>guo</u> xian<u>feng</u>dui*, 'Nation-Saving Vanguard of Chinese Resistance Against Japan'. He was a '38-er', someone who had joined the Party after the Japanese invasion, lacking the credentials of the old guard. (Admittedly, he hardly had a choice in the matter, since he had been only a child during the first struggle against the Nationalists, and had joined the Party at seventeen.)

It was Hunan that made him. He'd become provincial Party secretary in the early sixties, cannily sided with leftists in the chaos of 1966, and then been equally opportunistic in using the army to crush them in 1969. He first came to Beijing in 1971, to work with Zhou Enlai, but had returned to Hunan before being elected to the Politburo in 1973 and made minister of public security in 1975.

Most of all, though, he was all things to all men. It was rare for anyone to come away from a conversation with Hua without the feeling that he agreed with them. He could listen, which, at a time when everyone was shouting, was a rare gift. He was the kind of man who could have been a successful mid-level politician in any system, a well-liked MP, say, or a regularly re-elected mayor. People remembered him as modest, likeable and friendly. He had the same common touch that Mao liked to show, remembering children's names, family illnesses and nagging health concerns. He could visit a town and still be remembered with fondness decades later.

Hua's social skills didn't transfer, unfortunately, to dealing with foreigners. Singaporean dictator Lee Kuan Yew dismissed him as a 'thug', and one Australian ambassador saw him as 'wooden, forgettable, and not engaging with his visitor's agenda'.[11] Even in a Chinese context, he couldn't get on with everyone; Foreign Minister Qiao Guanhua, a veteran politician, complained when accompanying Hua to greet diplomatic visitors that his role was like 'the tutor looking after the ignorant crown prince'.

He got on with almost everybody else. Critically, he was seen as a moderating figure, somebody who could walk the fine line between right and left. He'd helped Zhou Enlai and Deng Xiaoping with various projects, but he was also on cordial terms with the leftists, and he'd managed much of the anti-Deng campaign of late 1975. As a relative newcomer to Beijing, he was not bound into the nets of old enmities and friendships as closely as the others, and his lack of a major political power base made him appear less threatening. He was probably closest to Wang Dongxing, Mao's security chief.

Born in 1916, Wang was a Long March veteran. An orphaned peasant boy taken in by revolutionaries, he was deeply loyal to

Mao. He controlled the powerful 8341 security unit, which was not only in charge of guarding the senior political leadership but had also taken over several factories and important institutions in Beijing. He had a long-standing enmity with Jiang Qing, and the two had a history of regularly sniping at each other. After almost tripping himself up by supporting Lin Biao when Mao was beginning to turn against him, he redeemed himself in Mao's eyes by doing everything he could to make sure that the supremo's needs were met – including the cover-ups of his sexual escapades.

Mao expected Hua to be discreet in a very different way. When he picked Hua, he had something more than just a political fix in mind. He was looking for someone who could ensure not only stability, but also that Mao's own legacy was never abandoned. He had been dwelling on this repeatedly for the last few years, calling meetings to discuss the Cultural Revolution's pros (ideological cleansing and revolutionary triumph) and cons (failure to keep up living standards), and who was to blame (people who weren't with him, but especially Lin Biao and his 'anti-Party clique'). The meetings saw little discussion as the last people to stand up to Mao, over the failures of the Great Leap Forward, had been swiftly disposed of.

A later Chinese joke captures Hua's devotion to Mao. 'Mao, Deng and Hua are crossing a bridge in the countryside when it collapses, leaving all three of them clinging on as the remains of the bridge dangle into the ravine below. The bridge is straining, and it's obvious that it can't bear the weight of all three of them. So Deng says: "Great Helmsman, the people cannot continue without your inspired leadership. China is nothing without Mao Zedong! I will cast myself into the abyss so that you may climb to safety." Hua is so moved that he lets go to applaud . . .' From Mao's point of view, Hua's sycophancy was just what was needed.

Mao was always keenly interested in the writing of history. When the historian and deputy mayor of Beijing, Wu Han, wrote his biography of the Hongwu Emperor, the first ruler of the Ming dynasty, Mao read it attentively and suggested numerous changes. Zhu Yuanzhang, who became the Hongwu Emperor, was a peasant who had risen to greatness by leading a revolutionary movement against foreign occupiers (Mongols, in this case). In power, though, he eliminated those who had helped him rise, purged officials in the name of popular discontent, and then been disappointed that the ones he replaced them with turned out no better, ran a ruthless secret police and reduced his reign to a byword for tyranny.

Mao was entirely aware of the parallels, and his changes offered justification for Zhu's actions in the name of political unity and national strength. His editorial concerns didn't stop him destroying Wu Han's entire family later, after the unfortunate scholar wrote a historical drama in which the dismissal of an upstanding official seemed to mirror Mao's own dismissal of the peasant general Peng Dehuai in 1959. Wu was beaten and humiliated by Red Guards. He died in prison in 1968, and his wife, who was sentenced to hard labour, a year later. Meanwhile Wu's daughter suffered a mental breakdown and then, in an act of utterly pointless vengeance, was arrested in 1975 and driven to suicide. A man who could set such things in motion had reason to worry what history might say about him.

Another reason for Mao's concern was Stalin's fate in the Soviet Union. Twenty years before, Stalin's successor, Nikita Khrushchev, had denounced Stalin's reign of terror and his personality cult in front of an audience of stunned Communist luminaries. The supposedly secret speech was soon widely leaked, and it deeply disturbed Mao. Mao had no particular liking for Stalin personally. The Soviet dictator had alternately patronised and bullied him, throwing the full weight of the USSR behind the Chinese revolution only when it appeared certain to succeed. What worried him was that Stalin's legacy could be jettisoned so soon after his death, culminating in the removal of his body from Lenin's tomb in 1961.

Mao believed that the USSR had abandoned basic revolutionary principles by denouncing Stalinism. Many parts of PRC's history had repeated the Stalinist experience, such as forced collectivisation resulting in famine, hasty industrialisation, frequent purges, show trials, the war against religion and, of course, the personality cult. The parties had common ideological motivations, and the Chinese had deliberately imitated Soviet policy. Even the idea of a 'cultural revolution' was taken from Soviet slogans, although the far more centralised, bureaucratic mode of Soviet repression bore little resemblance to China's years of chaos. After Khrushchev went off the beaten Stalinist path and tilted at reforms (which only half-materialised) Mao's suspicions were confirmed.

One of the favoured insults directed against Deng Xiaoping was to dub him 'China's Khrushchev', an epithet first applied to Liu Shaoqi. Mao and Khrushchev had never got along at the best of times, with Mao repeatedly challenging the portly Soviet leader to swimming contests and directing subtle conversational jabs against him. There had been a spectacular slanging match – 'Revisionist!' 'Adventurist!' 'Tyrant!' 'Deviationist!' – between the two before the Sino-Soviet split. Even after Khrushchev was unceremoniously bundled out of power in 1964, Mao argued that the Soviet Union had turned to the capitalist path, and that his successors were continuing 'Khrushchev-ism without Khrushchev'. Mao was obsessed with his recipe for the future of China and for preserving his own place in history: Zhou dead, Deng out, and Hua in charge, with the leftists hovering in the background. Deng's removal from power was not formally announced, but it soon became obvious, with the campaign against his reforms intensified and his failures explicitly touted. The process evoked a weary *déjà vu*. Posters went up on campuses across China again, followed by a blizzard of articles in the major newspapers, and drummed-up rallies to condemn Deng. A Western observer reported of one such meeting that it was 'predictable, boring, and repetitive. Teachers embarrassed by the low quality of the debate. Nothing at all spontaneous. Every contribution read in a monotone as the audience sleeps, knits, smokes, and chats. Fear and apathy are responsible.'[12]

The public didn't take this well. To begin with, many people were still smarting from what they saw as a gross lack of respect shown to Zhou Enlai. Although scenes from the funeral had been shown on TV, there had been no radio broadcast, whereas when other major leaders died the funeral had been on repeat for days. A central directive discouraging commemorative meetings and the wearing of memorial armbands – a hint that people should channel their grief into condemning the 'right-deviationists' – made people spit blood.

People were keenly interested in what was going on at the centre. With Mao gone from public occasions, it was clear that he didn't have that long left. Deng's reforms were popular because they promised a better life, although actual evidence of improvements was negligible. Public dislike of Jiang Qing and her allies, already strong, hardened as it became obvious that they were the leading figures in the campaign against him. Deng was increasingly and strongly projected as Zhou's true political heir, and many read the attacks on him as yet more attacks on the dead Premier and all that he stood for.

Kang Sheng, Mao's intelligence chief who had died the year before, once complained about people's habit of 'reading the newspapers like they were code'. Readers looked for subtle hints that pointed to a shift in the political wind or the fall of political figures both local and national. They pored over photos, wondering why X was facing towards Y, speculating on the order of Maoist quotations used in speeches, and arguing over why one politician's words had been given slightly more prominence than another's. Part of the reason for reading newspapers this way was because it was pretty pointless to read them for news or entertainment. Literally half of most articles was dedicated to hackneyed political phrases, with only minor divergences. With rare exceptions, they made stunningly tedious reading, and even interesting stories were intercut with variations on the current political line.

The Chinese language has a higher tolerance for cliché than English, but it was hard for anyone to believe that celebrations were always joyful, opposition always fierce, and masses always united. People needed only to look around to find a reality that clashed with the endlessly positive portrayal of life. Take a typical *People's Daily* editorial:

The people are overjoyed at these happy tidings. The capital is astir as is the whole country. Army men and civilians in their hundreds of millions have turned out to parade amid cheers and the beating of drums and gongs to hail the happy news. Grand rallies have been held in various parts of the country and messages sent to Chairman Mao and the Party Central Committee, warmly acclaiming and resolutely supporting the two wise decisions. A revolutionary scene of unity in struggle prevails throughout China, with the whole nation determined to carry through to the end the great struggle to beat back the right deviationist attempt.[13]

People knew perfectly well that if there was a revolutionary sense of unity, it was very well hidden, and that neither they, nor anyone else they knew, had felt particularly overjoyed that day. If there had been parades and drums, it was because the bosses had made them turn out early that morning to have a 'rally' where most had shuffled along shouting a slogan or two, before going off to start work. Their trust in the papers was no longer very great.

But, more than anything else, it was the fall of Lin Biao that had undermined public trust in official announcements. Lin had held such a prominent place in Party propaganda, second at points only to Mao himself, that his fall simply didn't fit into a believable narrative. If Mao had been able to undercut him over time, gradually working him away from power before a final fall, this might not have happened. But the sheer suddenness of the events of 1971 utterly threw people.

It was akin to the impact of the Hitler–Stalin pact on Western communists more than a generation earlier; it went so much against everything that the regime had said before that it took self-deceit of a high order to convince oneself of its truth. The pale spot on a hundred million Chinese walls between Mao Zedong and Zhou Enlai's portraits testified to the memories Lin's fall had left behind. Of course, there were always trusting souls willing to disregard the evidence of their memories in favour of whatever authority was telling them, but, even in the remotest countryside, such true believers weren't that common.

In the absence of a reliable media, rumours were epidemic. Everybody knew somebody who was 'connected', who they turned to when they wanted to know what was 'really' going on, whether an uncle in the city or a friend in the Party. Passing on rumours inevitably required a certain amount of trust, given the multitude of informers with which Party organisations and factories were riddled, but rumours still travelled with remarkable speed.

One of the best carriers of particular rumours, as well as a vehicle for cutting satire, was the form known as *shunkouliu*, 'slippery rhymes', little pieces of doggerel made up to mock the authorities. China didn't have the same wealth of jokes as the Soviet Union and its satellites, but *shunkouliu* were adequate substitutes. A good one made you laugh, or else nod in grim recognition, it was easily remembered, and was something that could be passed on to friends, a tiny piece of memetic warfare. They were sometimes framed as mock proverbs, as angry as they were witty. (One of this type was a verse from the starvation years – 'Flatter shamelessly – eat delicacies and drink hot stuff. Don't flatter – starve to death for sure.'[14]) They were often extremely local, attacking the foibles or crimes of village officials or local difficulties, such as the complex verse produced in Xiaojinzhuang, a supposedly 'model village' that satirised how tour guides received more money and acclaim than the farmers the village was meant to represent. Some, however, dealt with the very top levels, and they could travel surprisingly far. In Beijing, several would fly round every time a government minister fell until a new favourite emerged. Beijingers would then pass the rhymes on to their provincial relatives when they visited, with a conspiratorial and knowing grin.

Urban Chinese were surprisingly well travelled, even in those years, since families were often spread out across the country by work assignments. Trains were still cheap, even if it was no longer possible to ride free as the Red Guards had once done. China's gigantic train network played a vital role in spreading rumours, not just through transport but through the trains themselves. People would paint slogans on to the side of trundling goods trains, sending their arguments across the country. Or they would paint characters or slap a poster on a wall near where trains regularly stopped, so that passengers would see the information and pass it on when they returned home.

There's an oddly persistent myth in both China and the West that the Chinese are unusually passive, that they easily accept oppression or are naturally willing to bow down to power. It's never been true; open any chapter of Chinese history and uprisings, revolts and dissenting intellectuals leap from the page. (Thousands more rebellions that never made it beyond the local level have been lost, of course.) Even in the later stages of the Cultural Revolution, when the country was locked in stultifying political paranoia, a minority of people kept struggling even as most of the public, quite understandably, preferred to turn away from politics as much as possible.

One of the most common sources of complaint was the economy. With real wages having dropped by 20 per cent over the previous decade, factory workers blocked railways, ran go-slow strikes, and sometimes took to the streets. Protests were often tied to local factional struggles spilling over from the regionalised civil wars of the late sixties.

The surviving losers of those conflicts often stuck together, forming tight knots of resistance to power. Resistance could be surprisingly open, like when one faction in Nanchang challenged the leadership of the local Party committee by producing a referendum signed by 150,000 people. (One wonders, however, how many of them were signed with the Chinese equivalent of 'Mickey Mouse'.)

Protest was a far more charged and potent experience in a closed and oppressive society like Maoist China. Work is the closest that most people living in the developed world get to the experience of what living in an authoritarian society is like. I don't mean the effort or reward of work, the energetic joy of building something with others – though that too had its place in Chinese communism, especially in the early years. Even those sent to labour in far-off villages in the 1970s sometimes felt that same sense of comradeship. I mean working in a very bad office, run from some distant and uncaring headquarters, where you operate under an idiot boss and decisions are made from the top that you, and everyone around you, knows are dumb, but have to be gone through with anyway.

Most people who've had to deal with a particularly obnoxious workplace harbour the fantasy of some day quitting in style. Sometimes this is about grand (or obscene) actions, but more often it's about speech – about telling the boss exactly what you think of him, why the company is failing, what it's like working under an idiot or a sadist or a martinet. But for the sake of the mortgage or the rent or the kids, the vast majority of people bite these words back.

Having to hold one's tongue every day may be easier when one is likely to be harassed, imprisoned or killed for telling the truth, but the psychological effect is no less torturous. In China it was harder, too, to maintain the small sacred space of individual conscience, the knowledge that everything people were being told was nonsense, in a country where community was so strongly emphasised and the term for 'stand out in a crowd' carried a strong implication of being a fool. To find a chance to speak, especially in a crowd, was a vast psychological relief.

The great irony was that this was exactly how much of the Cultural Revolution had begun. Many of the protests that turned into violent 'rebel' movements had been sparked by genuinely bad and corrupt leadership. For a long time people had put up with the petty oppressions and the burden of little privileges usurped by bent cadres and rotten officials, and said nothing, because there had never been a safe time to speak. Protests and riots had still been frequent, especially in rural areas, but they had also been stomped on hard.

The first stages of the Cultural Revolution had broken a dam and let out a million complaints. That was one reason why it was such a fragmented affair: it was driven by intensely local grievances – 'The village head stole food during the Great Leap Forward', or 'Our factory boss sleeps with the girls' – and deep-rooted resentments against the stiflingly petty nature of everyday life. Perhaps, at another time, that outburst of popular feeling could have been channelled for positive ends but it was rapidly subverted by vengeance, fanaticism and a political cult far more rigid than ever before, while the leaders who had been pitchforked to power by this revolution within the revolution proved even more corrupt and inefficient than their predecessors.

Former Red Guards were always prominent among the protestors in 1976. When it came to notions of justice, social responsibility and political democracy, the inspiration for the vast majority of people was still derived from Marxism. The Marxist classics were so easily available; a Communist regime, after all, could hardly take *Das Kapital* off the bookshelves, however much the sarcasm and humanity of the book clashed with the callous humourlessness of official speech. There were other sources of resistance, such as traditional Chinese culture or, for the tens of millions of Chinese Christians and Muslims, the Bible and the Koran,[15] but they were far more directly and publicly attacked, while Marxism remained sacrosanct. (For some young people, however, the public criticism of the Confucian classics was their first chance to read and be inspired by them.) The revolution provided the seeds of its own opposition.

It was something far more local and traditional than Marxism that brought people on to the streets in 1976. It was three months before the public anger at the way Zhou's memory had been maligned burst out in full spate. Before that, there were small-scale protests in February and March, especially in Sichuan, Deng's home province. But the real spark was the arrival of Qing Ming, the 'Festival of Brightness', which fell on 5 April that year.

It was a day for celebrating the past. Before 1949, people would clean and decorate their family tombs and make offerings to their ancestors, sometimes travelling hundreds of miles to do so. As a result it was also known as 'Tomb-Sweeping Day'. The cataclysmic upheavals of the previous half century meant that many families no longer had any idea where their ancestral tombs were. Instead they would visit their parents' or grandparents' graves.

At the height of anti-religious sentiments in the Cultural Revolution it had, in places, been dangerous to do even this, as it could be seen as a sign of superstition or attachment to the feudal past. Elsewhere the festival had been co-opted into the Communist idealisation of revolutionary martyrs. Now it would be turned into a chance to give Zhou the respect that his enemies had stolen from him.

It was appropriate that the first wave of major protests started as a series of misreadings. Slips of the tongue or pen had endangered many lives in the last ten years, such as the village schoolteacher who meant to write 'use Maoist thought to criticise bourgeois thought' when marking up a student's essay, and instead wrote 'use Maoist thought to criticise Maoist thought', or the family that accidentally put a bust of Mao underneath a miswritten character in a slogan that made it look like 'idiot', or including in a poem the line 'the east is white'. (Guo Morou, an extraordinarily gifted poet, scholar and politician was attacked for precisely this in 1966, when he was seventy-four. He survived until 1978, since Zhou Enlai sent men to guard him, like other cultural monuments, but two of his sons were driven to suicide.)

In this case, the first misreading was of an action, not a text. On 24 March, a photographer went to take a picture of a wreath laid to honour Zhou Enlai in the Revolutionary Martyrs' Cemetery in the southern city of Nanjing. The wreath had a couplet praising Zhou on it, and, probably because it was interfering with the shot, the photographer removed it. When people saw the picture, however, they jumped to the conclusion that the couplet had been removed on purpose, as a deliberate slur on Zhou. They blamed Zhou's opponents, identified with 'the Shanghai gang' of Jiang Qing and her followers. An angry crowd marched to the cemetery, and these 'pilgrimages' continued for the next few days, despite official efforts to stop them.

A day later, on 25 March, *Wenhui Bao*, a major Shanghai newspaper, published a front-page article on the need to criticise Deng Xiaoping. It contained an incendiary sentence, which in saner times might have prompted a flood of letters to the editor: 'The capitalist roader inside the Party wanted to help the unrepentant capitalist roader regain power.' This was immediately read as being close to a blatant attack on Zhou's memory. He, it was assumed, was 'the capitalist roader inside the Party', while the 'unrepentant capitalist roader' he had been helping back into power was Deng. It didn't help that *Wenhui Bao* had deliberately – at least as far as the protestors were concerned – left Zhou Enlai's calligraphy out of a series of inscriptions in praise of Communist icon Lei Feng published three weeks earlier.[16]

The perceived slander prompted rage across the south-east, but especially in Nanjing, where, on 29 March, a copy of the article was pinned up inside a window-case at the university, with the offending line underlined and 'What does this mean?' written next to it. Soon copies of *Wenhui Bao* were being publicly burnt, and Nanjingers were shouting, 'We'll defend our beloved Premier to the end!' and 'We miss Yang Kaihui!' (an earlier wife of Mao's).

But the whole thing may well have been a mistake caused by a grammatical ambiguity. Plurals are barely used in Chinese;

singular or plural forms are largely derived from context. The sentence was supposed to be read as, 'The capitalist roader inside the Party wanted to help the unrepentant capitalist *roaders* regain power', with the first capitalist being Deng himself, and the unrepentant capitalist roaders being his political supporters throughout the country, the 'little Deng Xiaopings'. No insult to Zhou had been intended, but the damage had been done.

The Nanjing students were determined to spread their message to other cities, and about seventy of them marched to the railway station with pots and paste, ready to slather trains with posters. On the way there the bus driver, when he realised what they were going to do, told them they could ride for free, while the station staff happily provided them with train timetables, ink and refreshments. It became something of a party. Passengers came out to help them, while one of the station attendants commented that previous slogans had been washed off up the line, and they should try something more lasting. He produced a large bucket of tar, and the students daubed 'Somebody behind the scenes is responsible for the *Wenhui Bao* of 5 and 25 March, and that somebody is at the centre!' and 'Whoever pointed the *Wenhui Bao*'s spearhead at Premier Zhou on 5 and 25 March deserves to die 10,000 deaths' on the train. It must have livened up the day of anyone who saw the train as it trundled through the countryside later.

The mourning protests sometimes had a paradoxical joy about them. The teenage son of a Nanjing university professor remembered people coming to their house just to stare at his father, who bore some resemblance to Zhou.

A blue-collar worker in his twenties came out of the crowd. I heard him say:

'If you all want me to read aloud, I will do it.'

'Read aloud! Read aloud!' The crowd yelled. The man then started to read.

Sometimes he had to pause because the street light was not bright enough. Someone suggested that he use a flashlight.

'Who has a flashlight?' 'Who has a flashlight?' The words were repeated until someone said: 'I have one.' An even younger man stepped up. With the help of the flashlight the man read more fluently. The readings ended with slogans for the people to follow and repeat. The man read these in an even louder voice and the whole crowd joined in. We shouted as loudly as we could, and our voices burst out through the darkness and echoed in the freezing March air. I felt warmed up by the excitement as I joined in the yelling.[17]

Only a minority of the population was ever involved in the protests. Most of them preferred the solution exemplified in a popular saying, 'If the thunder of cannons comes from left and right, cower in the middle.'[18] But those willing to risk cannon fire were numerous, and angry. Over 660,000 people visited the cemetery in Nanjing, and nearly 40,000 marched directly in protest. Jiangsu and other provinces exploded in their own mourning fury.

In Guangzhou, villagers woke up to find the ground scattered with pamphlets condemning the leftists, airdropped during the night by southern military officers who, like their commanders, favoured Deng. In Changzhou, a city in Jiangsu, pro-Deng marchers shouted, 'We won't believe Deng's a counter-revolutionary even if we're beheaded for it!'

The protests scared the Gang of Four; they spent many hours that March reading detailed reports and telephoning provincial leaders and demanding action. They were convinced, as Yao wrote in his journal, that there was 'some underground capitalist force at work here',[19] a hidden hand coordinating the movements. The leftists were trapped in a worldview where any wrong decision 'the masses' made was inevitably the result of conspiracy and deceit; the idea that these might be genuine grassroots movements was unthinkable.

But as thick as the protests came in the south, they were nothing compared to the weight of events in Tiananmen that April. While in other cities the revolutionary martyrs were safely tucked in graveyards, in Beijing the Monument to the People's

Heroes was right in the centre of Tiananmen Square. It bore an inscription from Mao on one side, and from Zhou on the other. The first wreath to Zhou was placed underneath his calligraphy by a primary school on 19 March, and another one four days later.

Both were quickly and quietly removed, but between 25 and 30 March, a group of middle-school students left their wreaths, followed by a group of workers, then an army unit. None of them were taken away, and by 1 April the word had spread. Slogan-painted trains were arriving in Beijing so thick and fast from other cities that the railway workers couldn't keep up with washing off the offending characters, so word of the protests elsewhere was spreading quickly.

Everybody who could went to the square. Whole factories marched past the monument, hundreds at a time. 'My whole work unit went together,' one woman recalled, 'We were a long way away, but our supervisor was the one who took us to the bus. Everybody else there was carrying wreaths. When we got there it was like an army pressed into the square; we could barely find room to leave our tributes.' Real flowers weren't the usual form; instead people crafted home-made flowers from paper, with ribbons hanging down from each side recording the tribute to Zhou and the name of the makers. Something like *two million* people visited the square in a single day on 4 April, which was a Sunday and therefore most people's only day off, and perhaps as many as four million visited over a five-day period.

Scientific and technical institutions, such as the Railway Ministry, the Academy of Sciences, and the Seismological Bureau, were unusually ardent in getting their people into the square. They had a particularly strong investment in the kind of scientific modernisation process pushed by Zhou and Deng, and a strong dislike of the leftists. Technicians, engineers and intellectuals had all suffered over the past decade for being more 'expert' than 'red', forced to watch know-nothing ideologues promoted above them.

There were not as many students as in Nanjing, as the campus authorities barred the gates and patrolled the grounds to prevent their charges from getting into the centre of the city. But present, too, were hundreds of thousands of former Red Guards. Zhou had epitomised the old order they had once set out to attack; now they came to mourn him, and to protest the ideas they had once unwittingly supported. As Wei Jingsheng, one of present-day China's most famous exiled democratic activists, put it,

Many of those who in 1966 had stood in Tiananmen like idiots, with tears in their eyes, before that man who stripped them of their freedom [Mao], returned courageously in 1976 to oppose him in the same place.[20]

As the wreaths were placed, plain-clothes militiamen struggled to record the names of the people leaving them, and to remove the tributes at night if possible. Somebody scrawled a piece of doggerel on the monument on 26 March: 'I came to make trouble at Qing Ming; plain-clothesman is my name. I destroyed all the wreaths when it was dark; I am a ghost stealing the flowers.'[21]

Some of the poems were simple expressions of mourning and regret, like the disturbingly prescient:

As thunder shocked heaven,
As the earth broke the horizon open,
Silence over China, speechless are the tears,
Try to tell it but words can't be formed,
Try to tell it and tears run down again.
Heard it, but couldn't believe it,
Believed it and our hearts broke.

Even such lines were worrying enough, since they implied a lack of confidence in the government left behind after Zhou's death. Far more disturbing to Jiang and her allies were the numerous memorials attacking them. Jiang always bore the brunt of the attacks, with Yao and Zhang closely associated with her. Wang was a distant fourth, mentioned only in passing. The insults levelled at Jiang were sometimes blunt:

You must be mad
To want to be an empress
Here's a mirror to look at yourself
And see what you really are.
You've got together a little gang
To stir up trouble all the time,
Hoodwinking the people, capering about
But your days are numbered.[22]

Sometimes they were thick with historical allusion: 'We want Premier Zhou, we don't want Franco [Mao] and even less the Empress Dowager [Jiang Qing].'[23] Jiang received special abuse as a female ruler, with the protestors comparing her to Wu Zetian, China's only female empress, who had become a stock symbol of manipulative female power. Significantly, Wu had taken the throne following her husband's death – and had come in for a slating from traditionally minded critics, especially after her death, when she couldn't have them executed any more.

Jiang means 'river', which the protestors had fun with. 'Don't let the river waters wash away the memories of Zhou!' One poem included the line 'The swaying bridge over the Pu river' (*pu jiang yao qiao*), which could also be read as 'Arrest *Jiang*, *Yao*, and Zhang Chun*qiao*'.[24]

Other poems called directly for action.

I mourn but the ghosts are screaming,
I cry but the jackals are laughing.
Tears are shed, in memory of the hero,
Eyebrows are raised, as I take my sword from my scabbard.

But the mourners didn't just challenge Jiang and the jackals in her court. Some of them pointed to Mao, at least indirectly. One placard read 'The day of Qin Shihuangdi is done!' (Qin was the first emperor of China, famous as both a unifier and a tyrant; Mao had repeatedly praised him.) Across Tiananmen Square, protestors holding up pictures of Zhou directly faced the giant portrait of Mao under the gate itself. They pasted his photo on to

Chinese maps and flags, a collage previously reserved for Mao. Some people hung small bottles from trees, a punning reference to Deng, whose given name can be made to sound like '*xiao ping*' – small bottle.

Deng was rarely referred to directly, but the economic disasters that he had been trying to cure were. There were hard words for people who believed that the economy could be maintained through political campaigns rather than reforms. Posters called for a revival of Zhou and Deng's economic modernisations. 'We don't want all those other nice slogans any more! The troublemaking and the sabotage of those people are the reason why the economy is stagnating! The peasants do not have enough to eat, and the workers' lives are growing harder and harder.'[25] They didn't envisage the overthrow of the system but, like many reformists in the Eastern bloc in Europe, wanted a changed socialist system, one concerned with national well-being rather than ideological shibboleths.

The crowds did not limit themselves to poetry. They became impromptu discussion groups, talking about the high-level leaders, what constituted true Marxism, how society could be changed. Some stood on boxes and addressed the crowds, or led songs.

This was a million miles away from the regimented, ritualised politics of fear people had grown used to, a genuine expression of popular will, grief and anger. But also celebration. Like the other protests, it had an atmosphere of festive release about it, of speaking up for the first time in years. A revolution can sometimes be a party, and the psychological release of speaking their minds was enormous for many of the protestors. People linked arms and sang, not because anybody was telling them to, but out of spontaneous fellow feeling. The atmosphere of comradeship, joy and popular unity that state propaganda claimed was normal in China manifested itself for real.

Little 'fighting groups' formed, composed of young people who had only met each other a few hours before swearing eternal friendship. ('When the TV showed the Egyptian people in Tahrir Square, singing against Mubarak, I saw the same thing,' commented one veteran of 1976 to me in February 2011.)

People passed around poems they had long kept hidden, while amateur photographers snapped the crowds; 27-year-old Zhao Zhengkai, later to be famous under his pseudonym of 'Bei Dao', but then just an ordinary worker, read his poetic cry of defiance, 'The Answer', to a stunned audience.

Let me tell you, world
I do not believe!
If a thousand challengers fall under your feet
Count me as challenger a thousand-and-one.

I don't believe the sky is blue
I don't believe in thunder's echoes
I don't believe that dreams are false
I don't believe that death has no revenge.

Factories used their mimeograph machines to print out pamphlets, and people collected and read each one as eagerly as children devouring fairytales. As one visitor put it, through most of the seventies you 'felt lonely even in a crowd',[26] but here people came together. It wasn't all good; on the edges of the throng gangs of Beijing teenagers scuffled with each other, while a few pickpockets worked the crowds. But for many, there was a kind of magic about these days of relative freedom.

Late on the evening of 4 April, Hua Guofeng gathered the Politburo in the Great Hall of the People, the huge government building that overlooks the square itself on the east side. Deng and his allies were deliberately excluded. Wang Hongwen had made a late-night visit the day before, and reported on the disturbing slogans he'd read by torchlight, but the main speaker was the 63-year-old Wu De, the mayor of Beijing and Party vice-chairman, who commanded the capital's security forces. There had been deliberate attacks on the leadership and the Party, he complained, and it was clearly a pre-planned counter-revolutionary attack – led, no doubt, by Deng. They were getting word, too, of more protests in the provinces, prompted by news of the Tiananmen events.

They agreed the mourning was both unprecedented and dangerous, and dispatched Mao Yuanxin to his uncle's bedside to get approval to do something about it. Pitching the need for action to the Chairman, he emphasised that people were not commemorating Zhou at all, but using his memories to support Deng – and worst of all, to criticise Mao himself. He compared the situation to Hungary in 1956, claiming that it was clear the protests were being organised by some controlling hand – with the heavy implication it was Deng himself.

Deng had often been labelled 'China's Imre Nagy', a reference to the Marxist Hungarian leader during the revolution against Soviet rule in 1956. Memories of the Hungarian revolution terrified China's leaders. It was the first time a whole people had shucked off communism and abolished the one-party system. Despite Soviet propaganda about fascists, hooligans and counter-revolutionaries, the Chinese were bitterly aware of the truth: the people had turned on the Party with a vengeance. Of course, there had to be a sinister hand behind it, and the idea of a 'Petofi club', which in reality had been a gathering spot for young intellectuals in Budapest, became one of the great bogeymen of Party thought.

Mao agreed to action, but it had already been taken. Between 1:00 and 2:00 in the morning of 5 April, 200 trucks arrived to carry off the memorials. They were taken, like Zhou's body, to the Babaoshan Cemetery to be cremated. Police cordoned off the square, denying entry to the public.

Beijingers were furious. 'I heard about it from my workmate's brother,' one of them said many years later, 'He came up to me. "Did you hear? Those bastards won't let us mourn the premier!" I was so mad I wanted to smash something, but my mother found me before I could get into the centre of town. She was so scared something was going to happen she forbade me from going in.'

Other Beijingers didn't have such cautious parents. By 10:00, a crowd of thousands had gathered in the square, shouting slogans like 'Give us back the wreaths!', 'Down with those who oppose Premier Zhou!', 'Stamp on the cockroaches!' and 'Be ready to die in defence of Premier Zhou!' They scuffled with police and militia, manhandling them out of the square. The government troops had been cautioned against using force by their superiors, worried about the mood of the crowd if someone was killed.

Many of the militiamen present melted away, either out of sympathy or fear. Earnest students attempted to persuade them to join the crowds, reciting poems about how the army and militia served the people. When two loudspeaker vans started broadcasting against counter-revolutionary sabotage and class enemies, one of them was overturned and the loudspeaker smashed, and the other only allowed to drive away after it began broadcasting 'Long live Premier Zhou!'

Around noon, somebody noticed a small building on the south-east corner of the square, the joint command post of the security personnel, the police and the militia. The crowd began to sing the good old revolutionary songs – the 'Internationale', the 'March of the Volunteers' – and to head towards the security station. Surrounding it, they started to overturn cars and other vehicles parked outside – but over a period of some hours, with the peculiar caution of a mob that's not certain how far it wants to go; one person jumping in to kick a bumper or smash a window before others joined him, rocking empty jeeps and vans from side to side, then scurrying back as they were heaved over. Improvised Molotov cocktails were used to set the overturned vehicles on fire. As those in the crowd became more intoxicated with their own power, at around 5:00 they smashed the windows of the security station, bursting in to set it on fire as the terrified personnel escaped through the back door.

Zhang Chunqiao watched the crowds from behind a window in the Great Hall of the People. 'It was like watching the Hungarian uprising unfold. I could see it all clearly through my binoculars.

To his face, I cursed Deng Xiaoping, calling him Nagy. He stuck to his odious attitude but had no choice but to nod his head in silence.'[27]

Deng knew the protests put him in danger, especially if he could be blamed for them directly. He told his family to stay far away from Tiananmen, however badly they wanted to honour Zhou. If one of them was seen, it could be the end for all of them, he cautioned.

That morning the Gang of Four had held an angry discussion, with Zhang calling for more force, and the other three, nervous of the consequences, for relative restraint. 'No weapons?' Jiang sneered at Wang, 'Aren't you hindering our militia and soldiers in stamping out counter-revolution?' 'You can have weapons if you want!' Wang responded, 'You can open fire if you want too! But I won't be responsible for this crime!'[28] It was an odd restraint from a man who had happily led killing mobs in Shanghai ten years earlier. Perhaps there was something about the sincerity of the crowd, a reminder of his own heady days of leading protests, that touched Wang. Or, perhaps, like the others, he was just worried about the consequences of a massacre in the very heart of the capital.

In the end, restraint won out. At 6:30 that evening, the voice of Wu De came booming from the public address system, calling on the 'revolutionary masses' to leave the square immediately and not be duped by 'bad elements with ulterior motives'. He blamed the 'right-deviationist wind' – a reference to one of the common slogans in the campaign against Deng. It's unlikely that anybody had a sudden moment of revelation ('Why, yes, I *am* being duped by bad elements. Well, time to go.'), but it was enough of a warning for most people to leave quickly, nervous of what might happen if they stayed.

By 9:00, only a rump of a few hundred hardcore protestors was left, clustered in the dark around the Monument to the People's Heroes. At 9:30, the floodlights were suddenly turned on and over 10,000 militiamen, 3,000 policemen, and five army battalions poured into the square, carrying sticks, clubs and iron bars. Outnumbered by about 75 to 1, the crowd didn't even try to fight back, Instead they clung to the monument, shouting out revolutionary slogans, as they were dragged off and viciously beaten. The beatings went on even after the protestors were already shackled, mobs of militiamen taking turns to batter people, mostly young men, into unconsciousness. While bones were broken, it seems nobody died. In the end, only fifty-nine of those arrested were imprisoned, with the rest being dispatched, bruised and bloodied, back to their homes.

Despite the relative restraint, the crushing of the crowd stirred up many Beijingers' blood. The next day a crowd of several thousand people broke through the barricades erected around the square and milled around for a while, tutting at the still-visible bloodstains while the police eyed them warily. They cleared out soon enough, unwilling to risk pushing their luck.

On direct orders from Mao, *People's Daily* published a condemnation of the rioters on 8 April, composed chiefly by Zhang and Yao, entitled, 'A Reactionary Political Event in Tiananmen Square'. It blamed the events on 'a handful of class enemies' and 'a few bad elements wearing spectacles'. But it also unwittingly gave away the sheer size of the demonstration, and prompted people outside Beijing to try to find out exactly what had happened.

On 12 April, *People's Daily* received a letter in response from a worker who claimed to have witnessed the Tiananmen Square incident. Magnificently, it was signed 'To Mr Goebbels, Editor'. (References to the Nazis were surprisingly common among Chinese dissidents, for whom William Shirer's *Rise and Fall of the Third Reich* was considered a key text.) It cheerfully condemned the paper as a 'fascist mouthpiece', claimed that 'Jiang's little court' had deliberately provoked trouble in Tiananmen in order to create a 'Reichstag fire incident', and finished by calling for the overthrow of Zhang, Jiang and Yao. The letter was not published.

Jiang Qing informed Mao in person about the crushing of the 'counter-revolutionaries' on the evening of 5 April. Afterwards, she left his room jubilant, and invited his medical staff to join her in a celebratory toast. 'We are victorious!' she declared, 'I will become a bludgeon, ready to strike!'[29]

The reason for her cheerfulness was that the Tiananmen incident offered the perfect chance to intensify the campaign against Deng Xiaoping. Jiang and the others accused him of masterminding the crowds – they may even have actually believed it – and absurdly asserted that the mob had been planning to storm Zhongnanhai, seize Deng, and put him in power. Deng vigorously defended himself, but he was stripped of his Party and government posts. It was a much-savoured victory for the Gang and their allies; now, it seemed, Zhou's legacy was permanently done for.

For the Gang, the lessons learnt were clear. Staying up late on the night of 7 April, Yao Wenyuan wrote:

The three basic lessons learned from crushing this counter-revolutionary coup d'etat are to act in the interest of the proletariat, to smash all bourgeois democratic conventions and fetters (like convening a plenum and having an 'election', or obtaining the approval of the 'National People's Congress', etc.), and to take decisive organisational action to get rid of bad people.[30]

The fallout from Tiananmen wasn't anywhere near as beneficial for the Gang of Four as they hoped. Mao used Deng's expulsion from the Politburo to appoint Hua vice-chairman and Premier. In a conversation with Wang Dongxing, Mao noted Hua's breadth of experience, honesty, loyalty and generosity as reasons for his choice. 'Some people claim his understanding of political theory isn't great, but I'd rather have somebody who knows he doesn't understand.' According to Wang, Mao went on to slate the Gang of Four, noting Wang Hongwen's greed, Yao's inability to do anything practical, Zhang's reluctance to take responsibility and his being 'very active with his mouth but not with his hands' and that Jiang 'loves to purge people and give them a hard time'[31] but was ignorant of everything else.

And critically, the ultimate humiliation, on Mao's specific order, was spared Deng. His Party membership was not taken away. Indeed, the official announcement of his disgrace, issued nationwide on 8 April, specifically mentioned that 'on the proposal of our great Chairman Mao' the Politburo was allowing Deng 'to keep his Party membership so as to see how he will behave in the future'. In order to protect Deng from physically being seized by the radicals, Mao even acquiesced to Wang Dongxing's suggestion that Deng be secretly moved to a new location.

Wang shifted Deng and his family to an old embassy villa, and placed them under close watch by his men – both as a form of house arrest, and in order to protect them. He didn't tell the rest of the Politburo where they'd been shifted to, although the Gang spent a great deal of effort trying to find out, even resorting to tailing Wang himself. Many people became convinced Deng had been spirited away down south, under the protection of Ye Jianying.

The Gang of Four tried to associate Ye with the Tiananmen events too. In fact, they had rather more material to work with here than with Deng. While Deng had carefully stayed away, Ye had sent people, including his family, to go and check out what was going on in the square, and had even secretly driven down there himself, watching from behind dark glass. But the old marshal was too slippery, and could too easily plead age and infirmity, for any of the mud they threw to stick.

Why did Mao pull back from throwing Deng to the wolves entirely? Probably for the same reason he had half-protected him in 1966–8; Deng was simply too talented a man to be wasted. Sacrificing him would have taken a powerful potential playing piece off the board for good. Deng had never turned against Mao, and his loyalty over the Great Leap Forward still counted for something. It would also – and this was perhaps more important – have given the leftists the idea they could get anything they wanted, and risked alienating Deng's political allies. As his appointment of Hua showed, Mao was keen to make sure his ideological attack dogs had somebody to restrain them.

There are persistent rumours that Mao gave much stronger support to the Gang of Four than the record indicates – support later erased from the record by Hua and Wang Dongxing. He certainly seems to have envisaged the Gang as a support group for Hua's leadership, keeping him on the right track, and may have told Hua 'consult with Jiang Qing in important matters' and even that the Politburo should 'help Jiang Qing carry the red banner forward'. He probably suggested a leadership team with a heavy leftist representation, including his nephew Mao Yuanxin.

Visiting Mao on 30 April, Hua found he could barely understand the leader's slurred speech. Mao grabbed some scraps of paper and scribbled three lines on them – his previously elegant calligraphy was shaky, but just about legible – that would prove critical in Hua's career. They were 'Take your time, don't be anxious', 'Act according to past principles', and most importantly of all, 'With you in charge, I'm at ease'. Hua would pitch these as the Chairman's personal blessing and instructions to him for the future of China, a formal blessing in his last days. But it was far more likely that Mao was simply talking about the immediate subject of the conversation, Hua's work in calming down the south-western regions that, yet again, were resisting efforts to criticise local favourite Deng Xiaoping.

Hua's work in the south-west and elsewhere had some effect. A month after the Tiananmen incident, things appeared relatively quiet. There had been sporadic incidents of further protest across the country, and many provinces were still in a state of acute political tension. Local wars that had been running for nearly a decade had been fuelled by the new wave of protests. In Baoding, formerly the capital of Hebei province, a long-running factional struggle was still exploding in violence every few weeks, which was why the capital had been moved to the unlovely railway city of Shijiazhuang.

Compared to a few weeks beforehand, the authorities' efforts had done their job. There were no more gigantic protests for the moment, only the usual riots, strikes, factionalism, scandals, attacks, and the occasional murder. On 12 April Zhou Rongxing, the former minister of education removed from power as part of the anti-Deng campaign in late 1975, suffered a heart attack while being 'struggled' and died the next day. He would be the only high-level fatality of the movement.

The crackdown on the 5 April movement, as it was later known, had gone nationwide. The figures on how many were persecuted are even dodgier than usual, ranging from hundreds to millions, but an estimate of thousands arrested and tens of thousands more interrogated or criticised seems plausible. Being arrested usually meant being tortured too, most commonly through 'education by stick' or water-boarding. May began with a wave of executions, and anything from 500 to 1,000 people were killed across the country. Families were caught up in the arrests, with children as young as ten being imprisoned separately from their parents.

In Beijing, the public security forces, convinced that there had been 'wire-pullers behind the scenes',[32] went out looking for the authors of pamphlets, slogans and poems, as well as for the purveyors of counter-revolutionary rumours. The guiding principle for the crackdown, they were told, was 'Loyalty to Chairman Mao! Death to the enemy!' They put together a file of over 100,000 documents related to the Tiananmen incident alone.

Numerous mass rallies were held to condemn Deng. Normally these were a chore to be endured, or sometimes an opportunity for a group outing, but this time they took place, especially in areas that had seen serious protests, in an atmosphere of great fear and tension. In Nanjing, 50,000 people were forced on to the streets in one rally, surrounded by soldiers manning machine-gun posts on rooftops. Another 10,000 attended a rally to condemn six ringleaders of the protests, but the crowd thinned out halfway through, leaving behind only a few hundred to hear the litany of charges.

The investigators often operated on a favourite saying of the Cultural Revolution, 'Wrongly killing a hundred people is better than letting a single guilty one escape.' This was best exemplified in the crackdown in Niulang, a remote village in a Hmong minority area of Guizhou province. Niulang had been put on the political hit list back in January, after a spectacular fart among a group of workers. One of them was a shy young man called Long Zhengyun, from a 'landlord' family, and the others began to accuse him teasingly of having been the culprit. He started crying, and so they kept bullying him, until he suddenly burst out 'I'll kill two of you!'[33] This was reported to the village police head, Long Baoyin – Long was one of the village's clan names – who hung Long Zhengyun upside down and beat him until he wildly blurted out that his father, uncle and cousin were also planning to kill people. After they were arrested and beaten, they claimed that another distant relative was actually planning to lead 2,000 people in a mass riot against the Party.

It was obviously ridiculous, and the case was put aside for weeks, until Long Wenfei, the local Party secretary, wanted to prove himself during the anti-Deng crackdown. He announced that 'Deng Xiaoping's feet have stepped into Niulang!' and put Long Baoyin to work torturing more confessions out of random villagers, until the planned riot had expanded to 7,000–8,000 people, and forty-five villagers had been arrested as counter-revolutionaries. One of them named a farmer in a nearby town, and so Long Wenfei sent the local militia to expand the investigation there. They beat the farmer black and blue and then shut him in a barrel and rolled it around until he gave them more names, eventually implicating an impressive fifty-six counter-revolutionaries in the town.

With the campaign going so well, Long Wenfei was making a name for himself, and had no intention of stopping anytime soon. He put over 400 men from the police and militia on to the witch-hunt, setting up interrogation units which soon turned into torture chambers. Long Zhengyun's father was racked, but refused to give out any more names, until he grabbed a rock and smashed it against his head while crying out 'Long live Chairman Mao!' When his torturers found he wasn't dead yet, they buried him alive.

Another elderly farmer was burnt to death after he confessed to having destroyed a supposed list of counter-revolutionaries in order to save his son. Long declared an 8:00 p.m. curfew on pain of death and set up machine-gun posts around villages to fire on anyone seen moving in the fields at night. He threatened to turn his men on the local public security units if they didn't go along with him. The end result of one fart in a small village was 1,300 arrests, 32 executions, and 263 people left permanently injured by torture.

Yet elsewhere the authorities' efforts were met by an indifferent or actively hostile public. Poems, pamphlets and posters from the time were buried in the fields for safe-keeping or passed around *samizdat* fashion. In Beijing, there were more than a hundred incidents of protest against the persecution, and dozens more in other cities. Many individual areas went along with the crackdown for appearances' sake, but made no particular effort to arrest or persecute anyone. Outside of isolated cases like the sadistic ambition of Long Wenfei, there was little of the wild enthusiasm for persecution shown in the late sixties; people were simply sick of it, and of the kind of society it had created. They were determined to wait it out, hoping that something would change.

On 11 May, that waiting got a little shorter. Mao was in the middle of an argument with Zhang Yufeng, his ex-mistress and current personal assistant, when he started sweating and gasping for air. He had suffered a small heart attack. Hua took charge, designating himself, Wang Dongxing, Wang Hongwen and Zhang Chunqiao as the team in charge of Mao's health. In case of emergency, Hua was to be the first to be told.

Mao was soon stabilised, and remained conscious, but the paralysis of his throat was getting worse. His attendants could only get him to swallow very small amounts of thick broth. The medical team gave him glucose injections to compensate for his lack of food, but were worried about overburdening his heart. In a 15 May meeting with Hua, Zhang and the two Wangs, his doctors explained that the Chairman needed a nasal tube.

Everyone was hesitant about the idea. Sticking plastic up the Chairman's nose seemed inherently degrading, and it was unlikely that Mao himself would accept it. The four members of the health team agreed that they would undergo the procedure themselves, so that they could explain it to Mao and demonstrate that it was perfectly normal. All of them save Hua backed out of the promise. Hua went through with it, finding it uncomfortable but bearable, and appeared before Mao with the tube stuck up his nose to demonstrate the relative harmlessness of the procedure. But his attempts at persuasion were met with grumpy resistance.

Mao was equally reluctant to let his medical team run any tests save taking his pulse, dropping into the understandable unwillingness of an old sick man to be further prodded and poked. Unlike most dying pensioners, he still held absolute power over his medical team. After he fainted again on 30 May, the doctors quickly took the opportunity to run an electrocardiogram and insert a feeding tube, but he woke up to find them clustered around him, yanked out the tube, and ordered them out of the room, shaking his fist. They eventually persuaded him to let himself be fitted with an electrocardiograph, with three doctors monitoring his heart twenty-four hours a day.

By now, the Politburo was sending him only occasional reports, unwilling to stress him further. Mao passed most of his days watching imported movies. His favourites were Hong Kong martial arts flicks – it's somehow pleasing to imagine him curled up in bed, fixated on *Enter the Dragon*. There were Western movies too, but the Great Helmsman's opinion of *Love Story* and *The Sound of Music* has been lost to posterity.

Tensions around him were high. The doctors, the politicians and Mao's assistants continually snapped at each other, all of them worried about Mao's fragility and the chances of another heart attack. Mao had always been a mover, and he couldn't bear lying in one place for too long, so, on Jiang Qing's suggestion, another bed was put in his room and his attendants would lift him between the beds and the sofa whenever he felt restless.

Jiang's attitude towards her husband would be portrayed later as utterly callous, even jubilant at the thought of his passing. She actually seems to have been quite attentive, frequently visiting his bedside, going over his medical reports, and eventually moving back to Zhongnanhai to be close to him. Li Zhisui, Mao's physician, attributed sinister motives to her attempts to intervene in Mao's medical treatment by massaging him and administering traditional remedies. Many loving but stubborn Chinese wives still clash with their husbands' doctors over such practices today.

Jiang's concern was political play, too, since her entire claim to power rested on Mao's authority and her ties to him – which is what makes the stories of her indifference unbelievable. It would have been quite exceptionally stupid for her to show him anything but close attention. And, after all, they had lived as husband and wife for a long time. However thin a thing their marriage had become, perhaps there was still some real feeling there.

On 26 June, at 7:10 p.m., the doctors on watch saw Mao's heart rate spike, then drop dramatically. The whole medical team rushed to help, as the Politburo members milled around anxiously. By 4:00 a.m., they had him stabilised, but his condition was far worse. He was unconscious most of the time, despite moments of occasional lucidity and awareness. The death watch tightened, with an army of nurses and doctors on standby at all times.

Word of Mao's sinking condition soon spread. The government issued a notification to senior Party officials that he was seriously ill, but soon enough it leaked to the general public. (About two-thirds of those I talked to recalled knowing that Mao was dying.) With Zhou's death and the aftermath fresh in people's minds, the fear – of what would happen when Mao himself was gone – grew. Would Jiang take over? Would there be a fresh wave of persecution?

The sense of a bad year was worsened by yet another passing. On 6 July, Zhu De, another of the great revolutionary generals, died. It was hardly surprising, since he was eighty-nine, a former opium addict who'd nonetheless risen to become one of the country's foremost tacticians. He'd played no major role in politics for years, having been ousted in 1966 and protected by Zhou Enlai's support. His death aroused nowhere near the level of emotion felt for Zhou, but he was one of the founding figures of the PRC, and his death was widely taken as a bad omen. What disaster, people wondered, would strike the nation next?

4 Four hundred Hiroshimas

On the morning of 12 July 1976, China's foremost experts on earthquakes gathered in Tangshan. The administrators and scientists of the State Seismological Bureau were attending a week-long conference on earthquake preparedness, and to hear presentations on the disturbances in the region. It was a fairly routine affair. Seeing the signs held up to greet the arriving scientists, passers-by asked, half-jokingly, 'What's up? Is Tang-shan going to have an earthquake?'[1]

There was a shadow over the conference. On the same day, back in Beijing, the Party leadership of the State Seismological Bureau were holding their own meeting. It was part of the purge going on against Deng's supporters, in this case the unfortunate Hu Keshi, the Party head at the bureau. The conclusion was:

. . . keeping close step with Liu Shaoqi and Deng Xiaoping, Hu Keshi has persistently pursued a revisionist line; in this rightist trend to reverse verdicts, he is clearly acting as a capitalist roader. Hence it is no longer suitable for him to lead the bureau's Party leaders. He should be removed from his position as head of the leading group, write a self-criticism, and subject himself to mass criticism.

Hu wasn't formally removed from his post, but was immediately ostracised by the rest of the Bureau, eager to dis-associate themselves from a man who was now political poison. Liu Yingyong, the state head of the Bureau, commented later, 'Every day I was weighing what to say, what not to say, which document I had to read, and which I could pass on . . .'[2]

On 17 July, the Tangshan scientists began the 'Meeting for the Exchange of Ideas on Mass Forecasting and Precautionary Work', discussing upcoming forecasts for the north-east. A sense of political tension pervaded nearly every agency in China at the time, and the bureau was no exception. Today, the people involved prefer not to talk about it directly, instead falling back on standard circumlocutions. 'You know what the political situation was at the time . . .' News of Hu being ousted rapidly reached the scientists, who fretted about their own futures.

But they still got on with their work. Various predictions were discussed at the meeting, and everybody was concerned about the same possibility that had kept coming up since the start of the year: an earthquake in the Beijing–Tianjin–Tangshan area. Different teams concurred; the odds of an earthquake of magnitude 5 or higher were still high, some time in July or August.

One of the most fretful scientists was Wang Chengmin, the head of the Beijing–Tianjin section of the Analysis and Prediction department of the Bureau. He'd received a phone call from the Beijing seismic monitoring team three days before, warning of eight serious anomalies that could indicate a quake, including change in atmospheric electricity, drop in the water table, high levels of radon in the water, and deformations in the earth. He'd come to the conclusion that there was a serious risk of an earthquake in the next year or two, and, given the frequency of high-magnitude quakes worldwide in the previous year, it could be a big one.

Wang proposed intensive monitoring work, especially around Tangshan and in the nearby counties, which he considered the highest-risk area. Unable to find a place in the meeting's already tight schedule, he instead gathered people during breaks and handed out forms for them to fill in and report further anomalies.

Among those listening most intensely to Wang's words was Wang Chunqing, the young official who headed Qinglong County's disaster management team. He'd come on his own initiative, and he found Wang Chengmin's warnings deeply worrying. He went back to Qinglong, and took his worries to his immediate boss Yu Shen, the deputy head of the county's science committee.

Together they took the alert further up the political ladder, until it reached Ran Guangqi, the far-sighted local Party leader. His own obsessive interest in earthquakes made him all too eager to hear Wang's account, and he ordered him to check every one of the local monitoring sites and report back. When Wang returned on 23 July, he bore grave news – four sites showed signs of serious seismic activity.

Both of them agreed that the situation called for the same measures taken at Haicheng – intense monitoring and, where possible, complete evacuation. Ran was going to an agricultural conference, and so told Wang and Yu Shen to call a meeting the next day with the other important officials in the county. In this politically tense atmosphere they needed everybody on board when taking a step as big as this, especially since they were basing it on their own studies and intuitions about the earthquake rather than a direct warning from the Bureau of Seismology.

The 24 July meeting was heated, as the officials involved worried about loss of credibility, the possibility of public panic, and the reliability of the predictions. Yu and Wang argued their case strongly, backed up by Ran Guangqi's authority, but it was Document 69, the central government's earthquake preparation circular of 1975, that gave the committee the confidence to go ahead. The stamp of central government approval meant at least some political protection if their concerns turned out to be overblown.

The Qinglong team then went into a frenzy of work, mobilising local officials to press people to evacuate their homes, watch for signs of an earthquake, and set up basic warning systems. It was an example of the power of the socialist state at its rare best, using all the available resources of militias, committees, village heads and Party educators.

Ran set a personal example, moving from his office into a hastily erected plastic tent. Wang had sold the case well, working the committee members into a frenzy, especially as other possible signs of an upcoming earthquake – sudden changes in the temperature of well-drawn water, the stiflingly hot weather, nocturnal animals skittering around in the daytime – began to come in.

Some of them didn't sleep for three days, driving round the county and making phone calls – both activities harder than they sound, given the poor hill roads of the area and the terrible telecommunications network, where only the big villages had phones and misplaced calls were common. They evangelised lower-level officials with the gospel of the coming quake, telling them to send messages out by foot to remote settlements that couldn't be reached by car or phone. People were encouraged to evacuate if they could, and, if they had to stay indoors, to keep doors and windows open and place upturned bottles to warn them of tremors.

How seriously the warnings were taken varied from village to village. In one, every family kept somebody awake at all times, in another, the villagers moved into hastily built sheds in the fields, with tarp-drawn roofs designed to collapse easily and harmlessly. They set up patrols to prevent anybody sneaking back into the buildings – both for safety, and out of fear that the greedy or hungry might take advantage of the inhabitants' absence.

Back in Beijing, Wang Chengmin was so worried that he pinned two big-character posters to the door of the Bureau's managing director:

Hu Keshi had lost his authority. Wherever I turned to, nobody took responsibility. I had to do something, but I was young then and could not shoulder the burden . . . I didn't use any extreme language, I just wrote down what the situation was and hoped the leaders would take notice.[3]

Nothing happened as a result of Wang's warnings. Later, the Seismological Bureau would forthrightly accuse the Gang of Four of having interfered in their work, using the Qinglong measures as an example of what could have been achieved. A document issued by the Bureau on 8 November – well after the demise of the Gang – bluntly claimed, 'Because the Gang of Four interfered with the Seismological Bureau and with the forecasting work, it caused severe damage.'[4] This vastly overstated the case, and can be attributed to the general mood of the country at the time, when the Gang of Four made convenient scapegoats for every failure of the past decade.

The Bureau also wanted to cover itself, especially after having made such bold promises after the Haicheng earthquake. Personal clashes and differences of scientific opinion, such as those between Wang and other team leaders, also contributed to the atmosphere of recrimination. One side later wanted to claim that their warnings, issued in broad terms and covering a large area, had been fatally ignored; the other wanted to pretend the warnings had never existed.

The Gang of Four, unsurprisingly, had nothing to do with interfering with prediction work, though they were part of the political atmosphere that meant that what warnings there were went unheeded. Tangshan's name came up repeatedly in the predictions, but there's no evidence that the Tangshan political authorities, unlike the Qinglong team, actually looked at the information about possible earthquakes.

Qinglong was unusual in having both close cooperation between government agencies and local Party leaders keenly interested in seismology, which was the reason Wang Chunqing had been at the meeting in the first place. For the Tangshan authorities, on the other hand, reports from the Seismological Bureau were just more sheets in piles of paperwork, easily stuffed back into an in-tray or binned. Without the intense focus of the Qinglong staff, the Tangshan municipal authorities were distracted by a hundred daily worries, as well as by the political uncertainties of the time. The warning voices would have had to be far clearer, more certain, and backed by heavier political weight to gain attention.

The remarkable intuition of the Qinglong team aside, the evidence simply wasn't there to justify warnings of an imminent massive earthquake. The quake prediction teams were mostly predicting an earthquake of magnitude 5 or 6 somewhere in the region, over a timescale of weeks or months. The possibility of a high-magnitude earthquake was raised, but not emphasised. And nobody envisaged the apocalyptic potential of a quake directly beneath the centre of a major city like Tangshan.

Part of the problem was that Haicheng had inflated people's faith in the abilities of the Seismological Bureau. The public believed that the code of earthquakes had been cracked. The vague possibilities enumerated by the Bureau's scientists didn't match people's expectations of the miracles that socialist scientific development could deliver.

A document issued by the Kailuan mining board on 14 July 1975 captures the politically correct tone of earthquake prevention work well:

According to Document 69, earthquake work has to focus on taking preventative measures. Kailuan mine has taken this doctrine and criticised the theory that 'earthquakes are a mystery and anti-earthquake measures are useless' and set up a doctrine that 'earthquakes can be prevented and can be detected'.[5]

Yet even if a clear warning had been issued, it's uncertain just what the Tangshan authorities could have done about it, other than general earthquake-awareness programmes. The kind of evacuation carried out in Haicheng and Qinglong was unthinkable. Haicheng had the clearest warnings possible, and was a minor town. Qinglong was a political and industrial backwater, while Tangshan was the industrial crucible of the north-east. Shutting down production on the vast Kailuan mine alone would have cost the country 5 per cent of its coal, and brought numerous other factories to a standstill.

And if no earthquake came, what then? It would leave the local leaders critically vulnerable to attack, accused of being fools at best and saboteurs or traitors at worst. Much of the Tangshan leadership had risen to where they were by brutally purging the men there before them on the flimsiest of grounds; they were the last people to risk handing political ammunition to their many enemies.

The fate of one high-level politician illustrates the political dangers of a failed prediction. Qiao Guanhua was China's Minister of Foreign Affairs, but a relatively minor political player. After the Tangshan quake, he read predictions from the Seismological Bureau that Beijing might suffer severe aftershocks, and ordered the evacuation of many foreign diplomatic personnel. In the aftermath of Mao's death, while Qiao was struggling to keep his place, his enemies accused him of showing 'a reckless spirit and a lack of faith' in ordering the premature evacuation.

Back in Beijing, on the same day the Tangshan meeting finished, Hua Guofeng gathered Mao's medical team for a Politburo meeting. It had been three weeks since the Chairman's last heart attack, and he was stable, but critical. His heart, lungs and kidneys could all fail at any moment.

According to Li Zhisui, Mao's doctor, Jiang Qing was furious with the medical team, accusing 'us of exaggerating the gravity of Mao's condition in order to escape responsibility for our inability to treat him'. She insisted that Mao had just a case of bronchitis, that his lungs had been good, and that never before had he suffered kidney problems. 'You make everything sound so awful,' she said, 'I think you have not been properly reformed. In bourgeois society, doctors are the masters and nurses the servants. That is why Chairman says we should accept only a third of what doctors say.'[6]

The medical team were stunned. It was an extraordinary, out-of-the-blue attack, and it terrified the doctors. To begin with, it could be a set-up to accuse them later of failing to save Mao, or even deliberately poisoning him. They knew about the 'Doctors' Plot' in the USSR just before Stalin's death, where a group of prominent Jewish doctors had been accused of medically murdering Soviet leaders. But Hua stepped up to defend and praise the team. They'd been working very hard, all the Politburo had seen them doing so, and after all, what did politicians know about medicine? It was a typically affable Hua performance, and the medical team were deeply grateful.

Jiang's attack may not have been as menacing as Li feared. Doctors everywhere are used to the occasional accusatory outburst from families of the dying. She was watching a man die who was not only her husband, but her principal political support and protector.

When they were on a shift together later, Wang Dongxing, Mao's bodyguard and a friend of Li's, took the doctor aside and bluntly asked: how alert was Mao? Was it possible to move against Jiang Qing now? Hua was as fed up with her as anyone else, he said, and the two of them had been talking about arresting her, but were afraid that if she escaped, they could be in serious trouble. Li was cautious:

[I told him] Mao was ill, but he was still alive and very alert. His mind was clear. He was blind in his left eye, but he saw well with the right one. Nothing of importance could be kept from him, and it would be impossible to get rid of Jiang Qing without his consent. He would never agree to the purge of his wife.

Li suggested that they wait until after the end, though it would be a difficult process. Wang seemed more optimistic, and told Li that Hua and he had sworn to go to the ends of the earth to get rid of Jiang. In the meantime, they had to wait for Mao's death.

In Chinese folklore, omens attended the passing of an emperor. The same went for earthquakes. Nature, according to numerous accounts gathered *afterwards*, knew what was coming. Dogs bit their owners, or refused to go indoors. Chickens flapped their wings, trying to fly. Dragonflies flew in swarms a hundred metres long. Horses broke out of their halters. Cats clawed at mosquito netting, trying to wake their owners.

Some of the animal accounts stretch credibility. Did goldfish really jump from their tanks that afternoon, for instance, and scream when put back? Were rats found with their tails tangled together in the fields? (So-called 'rat kings' are a staple of disaster legends in Europe too.) Did a hundred weasels swarm into a village, with the old carrying the young on their backs? Probably not. Even the more plausible stories may have been the usual animal eccentricities, exaggerated in retrospect.

Still, there were signs, even though many of them remain mysterious, or may have had nothing to do with the upcoming quake at all. The Qinglong earthquake teams had seen them, after all, and made the right call. The first were in the sky. Earthquake lights are a well documented but almost completely unexplained phenomenon; the best theories involve magnetic disruptions, the release of gases from the earth or the creation of sudden intense electrical fields, but the possible mechanisms involved are little understood. Before the quake, farmers saw red lights and fireballs in the sky; when the earthquake hit, the flash over Tangshan was visible 110 km away. Near the port of Qinhuangdao, north-east of Tangshan, a swimmer saw a fantastic band of light under the water, 'like a procession of torches'. It was gone in an instant.

Radio stations nearby detected strange magnetic waves. Disconnected lightbulbs flashed to life. A pale yellow fog drifted over the mining district. Village ponds dried up overnight in some spots, and overflowed in others, or shot up water spouts. The fish in the Douhe reservoir, 15 km north-east of Tangshan, were so thick on the surface that local fishermen filled their nets with ease.

Some people heeded the warnings. Zhang Wenzhong was a 39-year-old barber, and father of seven, living in the city's eastern suburbs. He'd had a sudden urge for ice cream early in the morning, and went over to a neighbour's shop to buy some. His neighbour urged him on to the roof. 'Look at that,' he said, pointing out red flashes to the east of the city. Neither of them had any idea what they could be, but it disturbed Zhang enough that he was still awake when the earthquake hit, giving him long enough to grab his kids and get out of the house.

But for most people, it was an ordinary day. At 3:40 in the morning, most were still asleep. The weather was stiflingly hot, and many Tangshanese had been sleeping outside, a common habit in the summer, when people would stretch out mats and hammocks by their homes. A burst of rain at about 11:00 the previous evening put paid to that, and families hurried indoors.

There were already people out that early in the morning. Long-distance truck drivers were loading up iron, steel and coal. In the bus station, the militia was patrolling to keep out countryside 'vagabond criminals', *hukou*-less wanderers looking for a chance in the city. The buses and trains ran all through the night, and so did the little stalls selling cigarettes, booze and sweets to travellers. The mines ran twenty-four hours a day, and so did some of the factories where restarting a heavy furnace or a boiling cauldron of steel every morning would be a waste of time and energy. Food workers were preparing breakfast for the first shifts at the factories, while old men practised tai chi in the park.

A few farmers had come in early, getting ready to sell their products to eager shoppers. This kind of private trade was still a very grey area, if not a black one, but common nonetheless – many street corners had a straw-hatted hawker standing on them with a basket of eggs or a cluster of fish. Others were working within the system, hauling wheelbarrows to the government purchasing stations. It could be a long walk, and it was best to set out early in order to get back for other work later.

In the countryside, a few unlucky – or so they thought at the time – farmers were still working in the fields. One farming brigade had a recently promoted leader, and he was so taken with his new role that he kept them up all night, even after the electricity failed and the mechanical thresher gave out at midnight. He forced his team to sit around waiting till the electricity came back on at 2:00, grumbling and complaining.

At 3:42:53 a.m., the earthquake struck. At 3:43:16, it was over. For millennia, the rocks beneath Tangshan had been straining against each other, pushed by the westward movement of the

Pacific plate. Now, in one terrible instant, their built-up energy was released, a 150-kilometre-long faultline rupturing beneath the earth.

The 23 seconds of the earthquake were probably the most concentrated instant of destruction humanity has ever known. In Tangshan alone it did more damage than either Hiroshima or Nagasaki, more damage than the firebombings of Dresden or Hamburg or Tokyo, more damage than the explosion at Krakatoa. It took more lives in one fraction of north-east China than the 2004 tsunami did across the whole of the Indian Ocean. The actual strength of the earthquake itself was not remarkable – 7.8 on the Richter scale, terrifying but not that rare. It was the speed, timing and placing of the quake that made it so devastating.

Jiang Dianwei, an older worker at the Kailuan printing plant, was practising tai chi with his master, a pensioner who insisted on getting up every day at 3:00. They were in the public park at 3:30, getting ready to begin when they heard a loud roar and Jiang heard his master shouting 'Bad! Fire!' He turned and saw that the whole of the north-east was red. Then the earth started to shake, and he and the old man grabbed each other and clung on for dear life. As they were shaken up and down, the park walls fell with a crash, and a second later, the building across the street collapsed, filling the whole sky with dirt.

Li Hongyi was a nurse working on the late shift at the No. 255 hospital, the biggest in Tangshan. At 3:30, she decided to get some fresh air, and went outside to sit at a stone table underneath a large oak. Everything was unnaturally still, and she felt nervous in the dark on her own. Suddenly, she heard a shrill sound, 'like a knife cutting through the sky'.[7] Scared, she ran back inside, sat down and bolted the door. Then the sky turned a bright red, and there was another noise 'like hundreds of trucks all starting at once'. She'd heard the same sound before, because she'd been caught in the Xingtai earthquake ten years previously. As the building shook, she struggled to unbolt the door, but could only force it open a few inches. Squeezing out, she ran instinctively to the shelter of the tree as the hospital collapsed behind her, hugging on to the trunk with all her strength. The earth roared, and she and the tree both collapsed into an open pit.

For many unlucky people, the speed of the quake was overwhelming. Yang Zhikai, twenty-one, and Yuan Wuyi, twenty-seven in 1976, were both factory workers. Yang lived in a work dormitory, and was courting a young woman from another ceramics factory; they were about to announce their engagement. Yuan, like most young people, still lived with his family, walking every morning to the chemical plant where he worked.

Yang had come back late from a date with his fiancée, and fallen sound asleep in his workers' dormitory. The first impact of the earthquake shook him awake to find the whole building trembling 'like a birdcage suspended in the air'. He was about to run for the exit when the building came crashing down on him. 'You wouldn't believe how fast it was,' he said later, 'There wasn't even enough time to get from your bed to the doorway.'

Yuan was woken up by the sudden redness of the sky, just ten seconds before the earthquake. 'Like a fireball in the sky [but] by the time I opened my eyes properly, the house had disappeared. And then it was like somebody pushing me sharply from behind. Before I knew what was happening, the roof was on my back. I couldn't breathe. My arms and my legs were all folded together.'

At her parents' home, Zhang Daguang was working late, writing up her lab notes for the day. She was eighteen in 1976, and had been employed at a chemical plant for two years as an assistant technician. She was a bookish young woman who loved nothing more than reading and writing, and was even making attempts to learn English. If the university exams ever started up again, she badly wanted to enrol.

Both her parents were professionals, her father an engineer, and mother originally a teacher whose political canniness had 'helicoptered' her to the position of local Party leader by 1976. But her family was still dirt poor, and she and her little brother and sister skipped meals all too frequently. On 28 July, she'd just come back from a trip to Liaoning, another north-eastern industrial city, and was behind on her work as a result. She didn't notice the flashes, or feel any shakes. Instead, she heard a sudden cracking sound above her, and blacked out a second later.

'Little Red', He Jianguo's goldfish, proved singularly useless as an early warning device. Or perhaps he didn't – he could have been splashing furiously for all He and her roommates knew, as all eight of them were fast asleep. He's bed was nearest the window, and when the quake hit that gave her a few vital extra seconds to leap out. It took all the courage she had to jump, as she was a small, slight girl and they were on the first floor, but she did, landing well enough to get away with bruises and cuts. When she rolled over and looked back, the top of her dorm had caved in, bringing the whole building down. Of the eight girls, she was the only survivor

Earthquakes are the most unnatural of natural disasters. They turn the world upside down. The ground beneath your feet disappears. One Tangshan survivor described the sensation of running as the earth moved as 'like being beaten repeatedly on the soles of your feet'. Another likened it to being 'a pea on a drum, bounced around when the sticks hit', while one young girl described it as 'like being on a ship crashing into the rocks'.

The urban landscape was wildly distorted, as streets were torn apart, landmarks shifted willy-nilly and roads and rails twisted like noodles. Tangshan's roads, built in the grid pattern of post-war planning, were ruined beyond recognition, covered with rubble, asphalt ripped asunder, once straight streets bending like rivers. At the heart of the earthquake zone, the earth moved with such speed that the sides of trees facing the fault were burnt by the friction. The panic was absolute, especially for those, like the vast majority of Tangshanese that day, who had never experienced even a small earthquake. There seemed to be no refuge; wherever they moved, the earth rejected them.

Paradoxically, the further away they were from shelter, the safer they were. The few who were lucky enough to be out in open fields at 3:00 a.m. were in far less danger, however terrifying the experience, than people indoors. The worst threat they faced was falling trees, torn up by the roots as the earth pushed upwards, or the tiny chance of being caught in one of the massive cracks that scarred the landscape. The danger zone outdoors was in the hills, where people were buried in tumults of dirt, or killed by rolling stones flung down the hillsides. Near the quarries to the north of the city the mountainous slagpiles slipped, burying houses as they tumbled down the slope.

In the Tangshan train station, nearly 200 people were about to catch the early morning trains, or had come in on night trains and were waiting for the bus into town. When the quake hit, the lights in the waiting room went out, and it became a madhouse of yelling, screaming, panicked people desperate to get out. The station chandeliers fell into the crowd, smashing in showers of glass, and then, with a great rumble, the whole frame of the station collapsed inward.

Ironically, the safest place to be by far was underground. Of the roughly 10,000 miners beneath the earth when the quake hit, *seventeen* died. Earthquakes are less intense deeper underground, and Tangshan's eight major coal mines were dug deep.

The mines were professionally and thoroughly constructed, building on the experience and skills gained from the European investment and technical advice of the past and maintained by men and women proud of their work. (Today, older coal miners frequently talk of the safety standards of the 1970s highly favourably in comparison to the infamously deadly private mining industry in China today. Seventeen dead in a coal-mining accident nowadays barely makes the papers – at the nadir of the industry in 2002, nineteen coal miners were dying a day.) The solidly built home and office of the Belgian mine owners was among the fraction of buildings left standing after the quake.[8] 1975 had also seen substantial reinforcement of the mine's anti-earthquake measures after the issuing of Document 69. Handrails were repaired, buttresses strengthened, and the safety of tunnels and shafts double-checked.

As a result, the damage done to the mines was far less than to the buildings above. But it was still terrifying. Tunnels shook, frames collapsed, lights went out. Water burst through fresh cracks, dark floods cutting off familiar exits. Workers scrabbled up ladders or were yanked up by rope as the waters rose behind them.

The mine staff did everything they could to guide the under-ground miners. With the air ventilation system gone, they opened every possible vent by hand, hoping to give the miners fresh air. Below, groups of miners converged on familiar roadways, vast processions following the bobbing helmets of the men in front through the dark. In the Tangshan Mine, 1,600 people gathered on a surviving route, forming a line over a kilometre long, and following the long, winding path back to the surface. Miners made epic climbs, pressed against freezing cliff faces on rickety ladders, or winched heavy steel ropes by hand to pull up platforms full of stranded colleagues.

But, for many, there was no comfort in their arrival into the light. Miner Zhai was in his forties, with six girls and two boys. His team had been guided back to the surface by the beating of drums and the scent of fresh air. When he emerged, he ran straight to his home, only to find the entire row of buildings obliterated. Of 400 people in his village, eighty had survived. None of his family were among them.

Above ground, houses were suddenly deep in liquid earth. The quake churned sandy soil and subterranean water together to create a kind of quicksand, swallowing building foundations. Some houses folded inwards, all four walls falling together to crush anyone left inside. Flaky, poor quality brick crumbled into fist-sized chunks. In large buildings, pillars deformed, then cracked under the weight.

In the countryside, houses built of mud and adobe disintegrated in seconds, and their heavy roofs, built to weather the tough northern climate, slammed down like 'a great hand slapping the earth'. Traditional village wooden houses were among the best places to be, not because they survived better but because, although heavy beams and roofs could be fatal, the impact was far less than that of stone, steel and cement, and rescuers had an easier time digging the survivors out. Across Tangshan and its suburbs, there were nearly 11 million square metres of living space; 10.5 million square metres of it collapsed. In the centre of the city, less than 3 per cent of the buildings survived.

Salvation was random. One Christian survivor turned to St Matthew's description of the Second Coming when describing it:

It was so sudden. It just depended on where you were, or where your bed was. 'For in the days before the flood, they were eating and drinking, marrying and giving in marriage . . . and they knew nothing until the flood came and swept them all away . . . Then two will be in the field: one will be taken and one will be left. Two women will be grinding meal together: one will be taken and one will be left.' It was just like that.[9]

Mrs He was the chair of her neighbourhood committee, a matriarchal widow in her forties with three children. She'd just had one of the walls of her two-room house mended. When part of the roof fell on her, she couldn't move, but was able to grab her daughter and pinch her thigh to wake her, shouting 'Earthquake! Run!' At the same time, her two sons, wearing nothing but their underwear, ran into the room. Her daughter stayed calm, and pushed the rubble off her mother's legs so she could move. As the walls shook, Mrs He saw that the mended one was still standing, and pulled the children against it as the rest of their house collapsed. Another family's roof was thrown clear off into the street, so that they were left standing between the four walls of their house.

Guan Wen, in his late forties, was a food station worker, distributing supplies from the countryside to the collective kitchens. It was a reliable job, especially for a man with eight children to feed, but it kept him busy, and he hadn't taken any notice when his children had told him of seeing fish swimming along the top of the river the previous morning. The side wall of their house fell in on the bed first, and then the steel supports hit his back. In the darkness, underneath the rubble, he tried to breathe deeply, though his lung was damaged. At first he could hear his wife breathing nearby. After a little while, she stopped making any noise, and some time later he saw light, as two of his older children dug him out of the rubble. One of them supported him while the other tried to give mouth-to-mouth to Guan's wife, until blood spurted out of her mouth and he knew it was too late.

Yao Cuiqin was a 23-year-old, formerly an actress in an army propaganda troupe, and now a bank clerk. She couldn't remember the collapse of her dormitory, only how:

> . . . when I came to, I was lying on top of a pile of rubble, groaning. I thought it was a dream, and really tried to wake from it, but I couldn't; even when my mouth and nose were blocked with dust and earth and my body felt as though it was wedged on to the edge of a knife. I was sure it was going to crack open, still I thought it was a nightmare I was having.[10]

Many people weren't capable of feeling anything – not even sorrow. Although there were howls and screams and wild weeping, many wandered about in a flat stupor. Ordinary feelings were blunted to nothing. On the outskirts, a female driver had been bringing a supply truck into the city when the earthquake hit, knocking the truck to the side of the road, where the engine caught fire. She was trapped in the cab, banging desperately against the window. Some other survivors watched her as she burnt to death, but they did nothing. This wasn't callous indifference, but a stunned inability to act.

Elsewhere, survivors were frozen, caught between one world and another. A mother looked dumbly around, ignoring the dead child at her feet; a farmer clutched the chickens he was taking to sell in the city that morning. One survivor was running from the ruins of his house when he realised something was wrong, looked down, and found he was running along a rooftop, torn off and thrown to the ground. Almost as soon as the quake subsided, a freezing rainstorm began, drenching the survivors and covering the city in a wet mist, mixed with the dust of crumbled buildings.

The sensation of utter powerlessness is so overwhelming [wrote one Victorian student of earthquakes] that amid the crash of falling houses, the cries of entombed victims, the shrieks of fleeing multitudes, the rumblings of earth beneath, and the trembling of the soil like that of a steed in the presence of a lion, the boldest and bravest can but sit with bowed head, in silent, motionless despair, awaiting whatever fate a grim capricious chance can provide.

The journalist Qian Gang described the ruins:

There was an old woman whose life was spared on Xiaoshan Street [Tangshan's main shopping area] in Lu'nan District. What she saw after she struggled up through the rubble left her dumbstruck and speechless. The old street, that ancient street, that street once so busy – where was it now? Where was the 'Great World' market? The theatre? Where were the playgrounds? The bathhouses, the drugstores? And what about the fabric shops, the seal-engraving shops, the consignment shops? And the little stands that sold sesame cakes and Kaiping crullers and Tangshan smoked chicken? And the women who used to go shopping together each day, baskets in hand? Where had they gone? Dead silence. The street gone.[11]

For the first hour after the earthquake, the city was still shrouded in darkness, lit only by quake-started fires among the rubble. People scavenged for candles and torches – fortunately, every household had some, electricity being unreliable even in those areas that had it. Some trapped survivors had been burnt to death, and the smoke mixed with the dust. 'I was breathing in the ashes of the dead,' one survivor, then a boy of twelve, commented to me, 'But thank heaven I didn't think about it at the time. On top of everything else, it would have been too much.'

Dawn brought no comfort, but rather made the scale of damage plain. Chang Qing, then forty-two years old, was a professional photographer, working for the Tangshan government. He had swapped apartments with a workmate nine months beforehand. 'I was so lucky,' he said, with a touch of survivor's guilt, 'Mine was one of the few buildings that survived intact. My whole family lived. His didn't.'

When I talked to him, he was not only an exceedingly gracious host, but one of the most emotionally open and empathetic of survivors, perhaps because, unlike most, he hadn't had to shut down to cope with his own losses. After making sure that his family and neighbours were safe, he went out into the streets with his camera, determined to record the damage done. Much later, looking through his photos with him, I asked him why there were no pictures of the dead. 'They were everywhere,' he said, 'but I couldn't bear to look at them. So many . . .' He began to cry softly.

The sight of the dead was inescapable. Bodies dangled out of windows, caught as they tried to escape. An old woman lay in the street, her head pulped by flying debris. In the train station, a concrete pillar had pinned a young girl to the wall, impaling her through the torso. At the bus depot, a cook had been scalded to death in a cauldron of boiling water. Looking at any collapsed building, you could make out fragments of corpses mixed in with the rubble. As the rain slanted down, blood oozed out of the ruins, forming hideous red puddles on the street.

The living looked half-dead, an army of dazed victims wandering the streets in shock. Many were still naked, covered only in dust and blood. Children howled for their parents, parents for their children. They wore whatever they could find – wrapped bedsheets, swimming costumes, kitchen aprons, European-style bathrobes and dressing gowns, made for export and plundered from the garment factories. One group of survivors turned to the theatre, coming away wearing opera costumes, from diaphanous dresses to Japanese Army uniforms intended for the villains.

The wounds inflicted on buildings were as varied as those on flesh. Many collapsed inwards, while in others, the top floors slid off, as though they'd been neatly sliced by a knife, or a whole face of the building was torn away. On some the damage looked oddly rounded, as if a scoop had been taken out of them with a spoon. Factory chimneys broke into multiple pieces, or had their top and bottom halves twisted in different directions. From others, surviving supports stuck out mockingly, or one stray corner remained standing, a bed or a bath hanging incongruously in the sky. Broken floor slabs hung down from half-crumbled floors, 'crooked teeth in ruined mouths'. The Chinese use *dofu*, 'bean curd', to refer to anything weak that can't bear stress, and from the sky the buildings looked like *dofu* smeared across a plate.

In the countryside in particular, many people died because the quality of the buildings had been fatally weakened by the Great Leap Forward and the village chaos six years beforehand. Buildings had been cannibalised to provide soil nutrients during a fertiliser campaign in 1958, and in 1959–60 people had been so starving that they had torn out bricks from the walls to sell, or in some cases literally *eaten their own homes*. (To the hunger-crazed, even thatch and mud looked like food.)

Between 30 and 40 per cent of all housing in China had been destroyed in 1959–61. And during 1959–61 and 1969–70, village militias had rampaged through houses, looking for signs of hidden grain or counter-revolutionary feeling; they often hammered through walls or tore down parts of buildings to punish political deviants.[12]

In urban Tangshan, new buildings had been put up to house workers at the vital coal mines and factories, but in the countryside, where there was a huge shortage of building materials, many families were still living in jerry-built homes that were even more vulnerable to earthquake. They were also cramped together, making escape harder as panicked roommates scrambled over each other to get to the door, since the number of people sleeping in a single room had often doubled as a result of housing shortages.

The energy released by the seismic wave was equal, it was said afterwards, to 400 times that of the atomic bomb dropped on Hiroshima.

Unsurprisingly, the first thought of many was that it was a nuclear war. Tensions with the Soviets had eased somewhat since the war panics and murderous border skirmishes of the late sixties, when a Russian first strike had, at one point, seemed a real possibility. Tangshan, with its heavy industry, was an obvious target. The fear lurked in people's minds nonetheless, reinforced by air-raid drills and the building of fallout shelters – at least for the leaders – as well as by endless anti-Soviet propaganda.

Exactly what a nuclear war would entail was unclear, though, especially since a much-repeated slogan was that the imperialist powers, especially the Soviet revisionists, were mere 'paper tigers' over which China could easily triumph. The first question of one survivor, pulled out of the rubble in the early morning, was 'Did we win the war?'

Even after it was clear what had happened, people's thoughts kept turning back to Hiroshima. 'In the first few days after arriving in Tangshan,' one soldier later recalled,

I used to have a nightmare of Hiroshima every night. I'd seen a documentary on it in the army. It was a catastrophe – the whole city wiped out by an atom bomb, nothing but rubble everywhere, people burned so badly you couldn't recognise them. But our Tangshan was much worse than Hiroshima. In one morning, several hundred thousand people gone, finished![13]

Zhu Yinlai, the 26-year-old mining student, also mistook the earthquake for a nuclear explosion at first. Then, as he saw his college dormitory shaking, he realised what was happening. Still befuddled by sleep, he didn't realise how strong and sudden the quake was. He was putting on his shoes when he saw the ceiling begin to buckle, and threw himself to the floor.

Students enjoy a summer day at the Tangshan Public Library, 1962.
Tangshan City Museum

Tangshan's railway station, among the first in China, in the 1930s.
Tangshan City Museum

Left: A clock at the Tangshan Coal Power Station shows the exact time the earthquake hit. *Chang Qing*

Right: Local Party committee members hand out food, July 1976. *Chang Qing*

Below left: Ruined factories in Tangshan, July 1976. The bottom of the picture has been cropped out to remove piles of corpses. *Chang Qing*

Right: A political message survives atop the damaged sailor's club in Qinhuangdao, August 1976. *Tangshan Earthquake Museum*

Bottom left: Aerial view of the ruins, August 1976. *Chang Qing*

Below: Tangshan's rail track was the first in China. It was destroyed by the quake, August 1976. *Chang Qing*

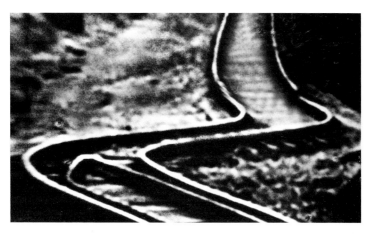

In these two photos, one probably real, the other clearly staged, PLA soldiers hurry to aid the stricken city, July 1976. *Tangshan Earthquake Museum*

PLA soldiers haul rubble in Tangshan, July 1976.
Tangshan Earthquake Museum

Tangshan residents make their way through the ruins of Xiaoshan,
once the city's major shopping district, while rescuers work to the side,
August 1976. *Chang Qing*

The People's Liberation Army struggles to recover survivors,
August 1976. *Chang Qing*

Survivors walk through a cleared path in early August 1976.
Tangshan Earthquake Museum

Children study in an open-air classroom among the ruins of Tangshan,
October 1976. *Chang Qing*

Clothing hangs among reconstructed houses in Tangshan,
October 1976. *Chang Qing*

In an improvised classroom in autumn 1976, Tangshan students learn
'Father is good, mother is good, but Chairman Mao is best.'
Tangshan Earthquake Museum

Hua Guofeng is applauded by city officials on a visit to Tangshan, 1978.
The photographer was reluctant to give me images of Hua's visit in 1976,
as they show too many officials who were later purged. *Chang Qing*

He curled up in a ball as the building fell, leaving him trapped in a space little more than a metre high, but with enough room for him to turn round. It took him a few moments to recover, but all he had were a few bruises. Remarkably, he didn't panic. His rural years had taught him the value of improvisation. The boy above him on the bunk bed, already dead, had been a smoker, and Zhu dug into the desk drawer to find his lighter, which gave him just enough illumination to get to work. He drew on memories of mining engineering classes and built a support frame around himself, using the shattered remnants of his wooden desk and parts of the bed.

As Zhu waited in the darkness, he could hear the sounds of his roommates dying under the rubble nearby. One boy was badly wounded, his chest crushed. Zhu could hear him calling for help at first, then saying, to nobody in particular, 'I can't breathe . . . I can't breathe.' A few minutes later he spoke softly again 'Dying, dying, dying.' Another classmate, Lin, had been hit on the head and was delirious, mumbling about problems with his homework before fading off into nothingness.

Thirty-three years later, when I asked him how he had coped mentally, he sighed. 'We were all very naïve then,' he said. 'You know, we believed in Mao, and we believed in the Party. And I had faith in the Chairman and the Party, that they would save me.'

As the earthquake hit, the Chairman needed saving himself. The tremors reached as far as Zhongnanhai, nearly 200 km away, where Mao's bed was vigorously shaken and the whole building trembled. After pulling Mao through two heart attacks and maintaining a twenty-four-hour medical watch for months, Li Zhisui was utterly exhausted, and, despite the building shaking, he didn't want to shift from his bed until his telephone rang and he heard Wang Dongxing shouting at him 'Hurry! This is a huge earthquake! Why aren't you here yet?'[14]

Mao was aware of what was going on, and after a brief discussion between Wang Dongxing and Wang Hongwen, he was wheeled through the pouring rain to Zhongnanhai's Building 202, his medical team clustered around him. The building had been put up in 1974 and was considered quake-proof.

Other emperors were disturbed by the quake. At the Ming tombs, the 500-year-old burial chambers of China's former rulers outside Beijing, roofs shook, ridges fell, shrines collapsed and the guardian statues at the entrance fell over. Closer to Tangshan, ancient pagodas and temples, too isolated, too old, or too treasured by the locals to have drawn the attention of the Red Guards, crumbled. Farmers in Wen Quan, a northern village, saw centuries-old sections of the Great Wall slide down the hillside.

The impact went far beyond Beijing. Seismographs across the world picked up the quake. At the Palmer Observatory in Alaska, the tremors from Tangshan triggered an alarm on the seismological warning system, forcing four scientists out of bed. Checking the results, they found that Alaska had moved an eighth of an inch.

The damage to Tianjin, 100 km away to the south-west of Beijing, was so bad that, in any other context, we would still speak of the 'Great Tianjin Earthquake'. Tens of thousands died; 10 per cent of the buildings in the city collapsed, and another third were critically damaged.

Gough Whitlam, the former Australian Prime Minister, was staying with his wife in Tianjin at the time; they were woken sharply as great cracks appeared in the wall of their hotel. (A cartoon in *The Age*, a Melbourne newspaper, the next week depicted Whitlam asking his wife 'Did the earth move for you too, darling?' It's hard to imagine the same joke being published so soon after the death of a quarter of a million Westerners.[15])

The worst damage was in an area of around 47 square kilometres in downtown Tangshan, centred neatly on the Hebei Mining and Metallurgy Institute, underneath which Zhu Yinlai was now buried. On the Mercalli scale used to measure the intensity of earthquake damage, the shaking of the ground there reached an 11. At points it hit 12, the top of the scale, where the ground shakes so vigorously the course of rivers is distorted and people are thrown metres into the air. The great San Francisco earthquake of 1906 reached, in the very worst spots, intensity 9.

Beyond the epicentre was an area of around 320 square kilometres, swallowing up all of Tangshan and its neighbouring villages, where the quake measured at intensity 10. Within this zone, 46.9 per cent of houses collapsed, dropping to about 40 per cent in the intensity 9 area beyond, which covered another 1,430 square kilometres. Further on, an intensity 8 area covered another 5,470 square kilometres, with a quarter of all homes destroyed. Finally, serious shaking – though only enough to destroy a 'mere' 5 per cent of houses – extended across a rectangular area of 26,000 square kilometres. In British terms, it was as though an earthquake centred on Birmingham were to bring serious damage to London and Leeds.

But each zone contained pockets of miraculous salvation, and reaches of utter destruction. The Hebei countryside is crowded, with villages pressing up against each other, but the vagaries of the land left even close neighbours with wildly different fates. In one village, well within the intensity 10 zone, the only known casualty was a young woman killed by sliding tiles, and half the buildings survived intact. A kilometre or so away, their neighbouring commune was utterly annihilated, without a single room left standing, and a third of the villagers killed.

Yu Xuebing's 'black' family was lucky in natural disasters, if not political ones. Her mother yelled 'Earthquake' as soon as she felt the first tremors. She, her parents and her cousins ran to the door, only to find it blocked, and so scrambled out the window. As she jumped, her mother pulled the washing line strung across the central room, out with her, rescuing their clothes. One wall of their house fell a minute after they were out, bringing the roof down and smashing everything else inside.

The strangest case of survival was the No. 40 train, which had set off from Qiqihar, a distant north-eastern city, the previous morning. It was ten minutes out of Tangshan station at 3:42, packed with 800 passengers. As the quake hit, sleepers were hurled from their berths, passengers thrown from side to side as the train rocked. The train derailed, smashing through concrete barriers and narrowly avoiding being overturned. As the passengers poured out in panic, the train crew assumed that it was a regular accident, caused by some unknown obstacle on the tracks, and began to run down the line to put warning lights out in order to stop any other train smashing into them. The lights were not needed; every rail line going into Tangshan was bent useless, and every train within 200 km derailed. The crew and passengers had no idea what had happened, but none of them were seriously injured, and the darkness hid the full extent of the damage.

As the engine car went up in flames, panic began to spread. The wind was blowing fiercely back from the engine towards the passengers. In a burst of activity, the passengers grabbed mattresses from the sleeper compartments, smearing them with churned up mud and sand from the nearby fields and using them to build a protective firebreak. It wasn't until injured villagers arrived from nearby, drawn by the lights of the train, that the passengers realised what had happened. They found an iron cauldron along the track and began preparing breakfast, stirring together food scraps from the train with potatoes dug up from nearby fields.

Eight-year old Zhang Youlu's village was not spared, though he was. He'd spent the day playing with his friends, and was sleeping so deeply that the first shakes didn't stir him. Instead, he was woken by his older sister. 'Hurry! Hurry! Go! Go!' As she pulled him from his bed, objects were crashing around him – books, bowls, the ordinary mess of a cramped house. As they ran outside, the house fell. The two children huddled outside as it started to rain. They could hear their mother crying for them under the rubble, for a while. Like a vast number of the survivors, they were naked, and Zhang's sister ventured back into the ruins to find something to cover them from the cold rain.

The summer heat was bad enough that most people slept without clothes, even in the crowded three-to-a-bed rooms. It was a startling sight for some teenage survivors. 'All those naked girls everywhere, and I didn't even have eyes for them!' one man recalled. 'In all that dust and filth, it wasn't like they were even people any more.'

Back in the city, Mrs He found a neighbour, Old Zhang. He was holding his naked daughter, who was clinging to him in shame. It was her period, and she was bleeding badly, and Zhang had no idea what to do. Mrs He found a cotton quilt, which she wrapped around the girl, rocking and comforting her.

Others were not so kind. There were stray reports of rapes among the ruins, usually in villages rather than central Tangshan itself. Some of them were individual cases, but others were gang rapes carried out by packs of young male survivors. The details were, understandably, never released, but a few perpetrators would later be tried and executed.

Qinglong was ready for the earthquake. It even came as a relief, after days of tension, waiting for disaster and with the region's officials mindful of the political consequences if no quake occurred. Families fled their homes at the first sign of shaking bottles. Those already outside had to endure, at worst, collapsed tents. In the hospitals, every doctor and nurse, in a fantastic feat of organisation, had been assigned specific duties in the event of a quake. Less seriously injured patients were given the task of tending to weaker ones, carrying them outside as soon as the shaking started, one man holding on to an IV drip as four others shifted a bed.

But the Qinglong evacuation was not as extensive, thorough, or life-saving as claimed by the officials involved, who assert that, 'Save for the very remote villages, everybody knew that an earthquake was coming.' When I travelled around the county, I found that, other than very close to the county centre and in the largest villages, people had no memory of any training or evacuation programmes. They had reacted to the earthquake spontaneously, fleeing their homes at the first sign of shock, but had still not suffered significant loss of life. The officials involved, whatever their successes, had obvious motivations for exaggerating their achievements afterwards. (As, indeed, do the experts in the US who use Qinglong as a positive example of disaster preparedness today – usually in contrast with disasters like Hurricane Katrina – and are eager to swallow stories of success.)

The Qinglong team's efforts were still an act of considerable bravery, hard work and remarkable prescience. The preparations saved some lives, but even in completely unprepared villages, nobody died. The figure of 180,000 'collapsed' buildings but no deaths sometimes gets bandied about, but this is based on a very simple mistake – 180,000 was the number of *damaged* buildings in Qinglong, not collapsed ones, and that damage could be as small as a few tiles shaken off a roof.

In one typical village, Changguo, which had never heard of any evacuation, the damage was limited to sliding roofs, collapse of free-standing walls, and the shattering of large mirrors. Qinglong's neighbouring counties, an equal distance from Tangshan, suffered a small number of deaths at worst. Qinglong was simply too far from the earthquake's epicentre for the disaster to have been that devastating even without any precautions being taken.

Another life-saving struggle was taking place only 15 km away from Tangshan. As the rain swept across the region, the water level in the Douhe reservoir was rising rapidly. Ordinarily, this wouldn't have been a problem, but the earthquake had left the reservoir's dam looking as if a giant claw had scraped across it. As the water rose, the dam strained, water leaking through the worst cracks. Local villagers panicked, abandoning rescue efforts to run for high ground. If the dam broke, a wave of water ten metres high would smash down upon Tangshan, drowning the already devastated city.

The army saved the day. An artillery regiment was stationed nearby. After rescuing what they could, they'd been immediately deployed to protect the dam. The reservoir's floodgates had to be opened and the water let out into the spillway before the dam gave out under the strain, but the electricity that fed the dam's controls was dead. In an astonishing feat of physical endurance and communal spirit, the artillerymen seized the winding mechanism that controlled the floodgate, never designed to be moved by hand, and began to lift the fifty-ton gate millimetre by agonising millimetre. Teams of four worked in ten-minute shifts, chanting work rhythms, their hands still covered with blood from digging out bodies at the barracks. It took eight torturous hours to lift the floodgate and release the water, sparing Tangshan from a second disaster.

Back in Beijing, the staff of the Seismological Bureau ran to work. Like most people with government positions, they had free housing near their offices. Their office was covered with shattered glass and smashed plates. Hu Keshi, still the nominal head of the Bureau, had come in as soon as he heard, but stood in a corner uselessly, ignored by the frantic scientists as a political unperson. The Bureau staff didn't know it yet, but they'd lost colleagues in the quake; a team of four scientists sent to observe Tangshan's seismic monitoring had been crushed in their beds. They still had no idea where the epicentre of the quake was; their communications setup was far too primitive even to pinpoint the direction. Instead, they sent four teams out by car to cover every point of the compass, interrogating stunned locals and glancing at crushed buildings to estimate where the damage was worst.

As the scientists fanned out in search of the quake's centre, a van sped towards Beijing from Tangshan. Four men, two of them, Li Yulin and Cao Gaocheng, officials attached to the Tangshan mines, and the other two, Cui Zhiliang and Yuan Qingwu, ordinary miners, had commandeered an ambulance, determined to get word to higher authorities. After crawling out of the ruins of their living quarters near the mines, they'd headed straight for the local Party offices, only to find them annihilated. They grabbed the ambulance, and set out looking for a phone.

The ambulance sped through the streets, ignoring desperate survivors trying to flag it down, who threw bricks after the vehicle when it failed to stop. They moved in fits and starts, veering past new potholes in the roads and stopping to shift fallen trees. Searching for a phone, they tried county after county, trying large factories and government offices that might have phones. At one point they were stopped by a Party official who demanded to know their work unit, names and political status – then interrogated them about the collapsed Party offices in Tangshan, where his family lived. None of the places they stopped at had a working phone.

In Jixian county, north of Tianjin, they ran into one of the seismological teams dispatched from Beijing. They swapped people, Yuan Qingwu heading back to Tangshan with the scientists while one of them jumped into the ambulance with the miners. Eventually they came to a factory twelve miles outside Beijing, and hammered on the door, only to have the gate porter tell them, 'You're phoning Beijing? In the time it'll take to put the call through, you'd be there in that ambulance of yours!'[16]

Flipping the siren on, they sped into Jianguomen, Beijing's central avenue, looking for the State Council. They could see people in shock in the streets, and shaken buildings, but nothing nearly as damaged as Tangshan. As they arrived at the State Council, they told the soldiers on guard where they'd come from, and, together with two air force men who had just flown in from Tangshan, they were rushed to Zhongnanhai at 8:30, and hurried into a pavilion in which a number of important leaders, including Chen Xilian, the Beijing area military commander, and Wu De, who had brutally crushed the Tiananmen protestors, were gathered around a large map. None of them were dressed for the visit; Cao Gaocheng was wearing nothing but a long undershirt and a helmet, while Li Yulin was clad in a pair of swimming trunks and a miner's jacket. Looking at the assembled officials, Li stumbled out words. 'Vice-premiers, there's nothing left standing in Tangshan!'

Three of the ministers gathered round Li, holding him. 'Don't get upset . . . take your time.' He began to cry. 'Vice-premiers, a million people in Tangshan; at the very least 800,000 of them are still buried.' Several of the officials began to weep, as the others interrogated the miners as to the extent of the damage and what was most urgently needed. Wu De, who had been a Party secretary in Tangshan at one point, asked after a particularly sturdy building constructed by the British for the Kailuan mines, and Li told him it had already collapsed. Wu sighed. 'Tangshan is gone, just gone . . .'[17]

5 Everybody saved me

Tangshan saved itself. It's a phrase you hear so often from earthquake survivors that it seems clichéd, but it's true. 'I was rescued by my neighbour.' 'Somebody pulled me out of the ruins that morning, I don't know who.' 'I never met the people who rescued me, but I will never forget them.' On that grey, deadly morning, the people of Tangshan – and the countryside around it – turned to each other for salvation.

The impulse to rescue is universal. It can override even the most extreme of hatreds. In the fighting around the ruined monastery of Monte Cassino in 1943, one of the most intense and gruelling battles of WWII, a damaged wall collapsed, burying two British soldiers. The Germans immediately put down their weapons and went to help, hauling rubble alongside their foes to rescue men they had been trying to kill a few moments before.

Mencius, the greatest and fiercest of Chinese philosophers, pinpointed the impulse to help. 'Suppose a man sees a child about to fall down a well,' he wrote, 'He will be moved to compassion, but not because he wants to get into the good graces of the parents, nor because he wants to improve his reputation among his friends and fellow villagers, nor because he dislikes the cry of the child.'[1] The instinct of benevolence is always there, though it may be stifled.

Mencius' words were proven in Tangshan. Whatever condition they were in – terrified, grieving, wounded, widowed, orphaned – people went to help others. They worked with nothing. The closest thing the city had to rescue equipment was mining gear. Thus, rescuers moved iron bars and fallen stone with their bare hands, impromptu teams forming to shift pieces too heavy for one man to clear alone. Across the city you could hear the chants of 'One-two-three, lift! One-two-three, lift!'

Many people lost all their fingernails tearing through the rubble. As soon as a family had finished looking for their own, they went to help neighbours. People were drafted in wherever needed. Often, the rescued plunged right in to the work of saving others. One man would dig another out, and then the two of them would find a third, and thus the chain expanded, the bond of mutual salvation pressing them on to help others.

In places, the rescue work started within minutes of the earthquake; in others, the coming of dawn gave people courage to move beyond their own terrors and help others. Saving others was so normal that survivors only casually mention it in their testimonies. 'After I got my cousin, then I went and pulled my neighbour's children out, and old Meng from across the road . . .' Somehow between 80 and 90 per cent of those rescued were dug out in those first few hours.

On the morning of 28 July, Tangshan was the most truly communist place in the world. Food, clothing, blankets – anything people had – were shared freely, even with strangers. Shop managers guided people to their surviving stocks, handing out clothing, shoes, coats and socks to half-naked survivors. A farmer grabbed He Jianguo and pressed half a watermelon in her hand, telling her 'Little sister, eat!'

They did this in spite of the sheer scale of their own loss. Across Tangshan, somewhere between a fifth and a quarter of the population was dead. About 6,000 households – around 30,000 people – had been wiped out entirely, from grandmothers to infants. The rest of the casualties were fathers, mothers, husbands, wives, children, gaping wounds torn out of families. When friends met, after the initial sharp burst of joy at finding each other alive, the first thing they asked was, 'How many lost in your family?'

In their home village, Yu Xuebing's family did what many others did, pulling rescued bedsheets down from a ruined wall to form an impromptu tent and cooking whatever food they could find to give to the just-rescued – sometimes the same people who had labelled them 'black' and ransacked their houses in past years. Later, theorists would describe what occurred as a form of 'primitive communism' similar to that shared by soldiers in wartime. It seemed to work rather better than the advanced kind.

Later propaganda would naturally emphasise the role of the Party leadership in the rescue efforts, and that was often true. The Party pervaded every aspect of life and Party officials tended to be more assertive and have at least some leadership skills. They also provided a reassuring hierarchy; they were the first people everyone looked to in a crisis. In the same way as survivors or mourners of disasters in the US cluster round local churches, people in Tangshan gathered at Party centres.

It was a profound shock for many survivors when, after instinctively heading to local Party headquarters to report, they found the buildings flattened. Where there were no Party survivors, people turned to other forms of authority instead. In villages deep in the hills, half-educated schoolteachers co-ordinated rescue efforts, drawing on vaguely remembered lectures at teachers' college on geology and engineering.

People also went to their elders, in a sharp contrast with the contempt for the old shown during the Cultural Revolution. 'Old' is an affectionate and usually respectful epithet in Chinese – 'Old Wang', 'Old Liu' and so on – and every community, even in those times, had its respected elders. By the standards of rural China, that could mean being in your late forties.[2]

In the thick of the disaster, the young looked to the old for direction, not least because the accumulated wisdom of living through decades of disaster had left them better able to cope with trauma and to improvise solutions. What to do about a broken limb with no doctor within a hundred miles? How to get a bull driven mad by fear back behind a locked gate? How do you move a broken bedstead out of the way to reach a trapped child, when the bedstead may be the only thing keeping the mound she's buried under from collapsing? With the well blocked, where's the nearest source of clean water? What's the strongest wood to be found within carrying distance? What do you feed a three-month-old orphan when there are no other nursing mothers in the village?

There were many examples of selfishness, greed and cowardice to be found that day, but they pale beside the extent of generosity, selflessness and courage. Across Hebei, hundreds of thousands of people were dug from the rubble. The rescuers knew the risk of aftershocks, and what these could do to already wrecked buildings. Whatever their fears, they climbed into half-destroyed houses, clambered over piles of unsteady rubble, and pressed into narrow cracks to save people.

The first and most severe aftershock came late the next afternoon. It hit far to the north of Tangshan, but the city was shaken again. Thankfully, there were very few new casualties, although many of those trapped were crushed or further injured as the debris shifted. Further small aftershocks continued to shake the ground for nearly a day afterwards, but didn't deter rescuers.

Yet, amidst this bravery and determination, the story that the state media chose to publicise was quite different. The front page of *People's Daily*, two days after the earthquake, told the heroic story of Che Zhengming, a senior cadre in Tangshan who had been helicoptered up during the Cultural Revolution. When the quake hit, his house had been shattered, burying his sixteen-year-old son and thirteen-year-old daughter. His daughter cried out 'Dad, save me!' His priority was not to save her, but to retrieve the local Party chairman from the ruins of his apartment nearby. While he was digging him out, his own children died. The article praised his political commitment, noting approvingly that he 'felt neither remorse nor sorrow' for the death of his children, but had shown 'a willingness to benefit the majority at the expense of his own children', which was an example to everyone.

Other published stories talked of people risking their own lives or ignoring the plight of family to rescue busts or paintings of Mao Zedong, but these may have been outright fiction; it was a well-developed trope in Communist disaster stories, perhaps copied from similar stories in Japanese papers of the 1930s about the much-venerated imperial portrait. Identical stories regularly appear in the North Korean media today about the portraits of the two Kims each family is supposed to hang on an otherwise blank wall.

There were other stories that were never going to make it into the Chinese papers. For two days after the earthquake, the sound of gunfire could be heard across the ruins of Tangshan. The people's militia were opening fire.

The militias had been established in the 1960s, as part of Mao's vision of a politicised, ideologically fervent military of 'men over weapons'. They were envisaged as the building blocks of a vast insurgent army that would swallow up potential invaders while the PLA itself retreated and regrouped. China's leaders remained worried about the possibility of invasion long after securing the country.

The militias had a touch of Dad's Army about them, as, at their peak, they included a quarter of China's population, regardless of age. Those who turned out regularly tended to be young men, thrilled at playing at war. The same people often made up the militia and the village Red Guard. They drilled with wooden rifles or spears most of the time, and when they were given live ammunition for practice proved likely to be more dangerous to each other than to the enemy. Trained to fight Japanese, Americans or Russians, they never saw combat against foreigners but, instead, were turned against their fellow Chinese in internal battles or to suppress protestors.

One of the most common phenomena after natural disasters is panic, not among ordinary people, but among leaders, soldiers and police. Disasters bring out the worst beliefs and fears of the elite, the fear that the mob is one step away from chaos, looting and murder. In reality, destructive panic among ordinary people is rare, and scavenging generally aimed at the necessities of survival rather than a greedy picking-over of corpses.

In other catastrophes, elite panic has been linked with racism and scapegoating, such as the shooting of black 'looters' by white vigilantes and New Orleans police during Hurricane Katrina, or the murder of Korean workers accused of pillaging the dead after the 1923 Kanto earthquake in Japan. (Kanto was an unusually thorough case of politicised murder linked to disaster; not only did vigilantes set up roadblocks and lynch any unfortunate soul who couldn't pronounce a Japanese shibboleth, but the Japanese military seized the chance to dispose of inconvenient leftists who, they claimed afterwards, might have used the disaster to overthrow the government. Since their victims included a six-year-old boy, this was unconvincing.[3])

There was no convenient minority group to blame the Tangshan earthquake on, but that wasn't a problem. Over the last seventeen years, after all, it had been possible to brand just about anybody a saboteur, a traitor or a 'bad element'.[4] Fearing your fellow countrymen was not only common, but positively encouraged.

The aftermath of the quake turned many of the militia into petty tyrants. They swaggered around bare-chested, rifles strapped across their backs. Anybody they didn't know, or who they found holding valuable equipment, or whose family had a bad reputation, was likely to be interrogated, beaten up or shot on the spot. They were trigger-happy, cheered on by slogans like 'Fire with hate in your heart, and you cannot miss!'

He Jianguo saw two militiamen hitting a young man found going through a ruined shop, beating him with the butts of their rifles even after he was on the ground. At first, most militiamen fired warning shots, but soon switched to killing on sight. Like bad police everywhere, they took running as a sign of guilt; one survivor recalled being told a few months later, in conversation with a doctor, that the majority of victims had been shot in the back.

There were genuine cases of looting. Watches were particularly common targets, being portable and expensive. But pre-existing prejudices played a strong role in picking out 'looters'. The division of city and countryside was still strong, and Tangshan residents set up roadblocks to interrogate and search peasants from nearby villages, who they suspected of wanting to pillage the rich ruins of the town.

Looters caught by angry neighbours, or by the more restrained militia units, were tied with steel wire or rope to whatever was still standing, or harnessed together and made to kneel in the gutters until they could be handed over to higher authorities. Families or individuals suspected of hoarding food were sometimes pulled out of their paltry shelters and roughed up.

Some forms of collective justice were far more brutal. Military commissar Chi Haotian came across a mob beating a man to death. He couldn't see the victim, who was buried amidst a mass of rising and falling cudgels and bricks, but he was told by onlookers that the man had been caught with no fewer than thirty-seven watches, scavenged from the ruins of a hotel. It was a cunning choice, since anybody who could afford to stay in the hotel would be far more likely to own a watch. (But not as clever as the old woman seen going through the streets, collapsing over bodies, and wailing 'My son! My son!' as she removed the watch from the corpse's arm, a trick she pulled off several times before being caught.) When Chi reported it to his superiors, he was told not to investigate any further cases of the same nature – the people were maintaining their own form of order.

Looting and the role of the militia has always been a deeply sensitive subject in Tangshan. Although several people boasted of having protected their neighbourhoods from 'looters', and talked about beating up or imprisoning suspects, they rapidly clammed up when asked about actual killings.

In his book on Tangshan, written in the mid-1980s, Qian Gang displays a mastery of irony, allusion and suggestion, in which he goes along with claims of looting on the surface while simultaneously demonstrating the violence of the militias, and then concludes:

There had been no mention of such incidents [in previous earthquakes]. Even though the records of natural disasters do frequently mention things like 'robbers rising up in swarms', people always considered them *abuse directed by the ruling classes against resistance shown by the common people* [my italics]. I struggled to understand it all. Then it suddenly occurred to me: if the Tangshan earthquake had taken place in 1956 or 1965, would there have been this outbreak of criminal activity?

The worst conflicts were near the state-run granaries. It might seem strange that people were so desperate for food so soon after the quake, but many people were living on the brink of starvation even in ordinary times. The Banqiao disaster, where tens of thousands had perished within a couple of weeks as a result of the government's inability to deliver food aid, demonstrated the fragility of a malnourished population.

Memories of the Great Leap Forward, when the government had failed utterly to deliver on its promises of food security, were still strong among anyone over thirty. The survivors had gone less than a day without food, but they had no trust in the ability of the government to provide help. Instead, they set out to seize the means of survival themselves.

The state was used to protecting its precious food from the people. Mobs of starving farmers had frequently attacked granaries during the Great Leap Forward, sometimes successfully. In a single county, for instance, thirty out of 500 state granaries had been attacked over two months. The army and specially raised militias had to be deployed to protect granaries, as well as guard railway lines where hungry gangs would blockade the track and overturn rail cars transporting food.

Now, as crowds threatened the granaries, the militia mounted machine guns and menaced the survivors in turn. Surviving local Party leaders instructed them that not a single grain should be given out; weakness would only spark more 'looting'. But raids on purchasing depots and elsewhere led to the 'loss', according to official records, of over 335 tons of grain. They did not report the number of people shot while trying to get it, but hundreds were arrested.

People who did believe in the government were looking to the sky. Tangshan had one of the biggest military air bases in the north-east. In ordinary times, jets zooming overhead were common enough that local children made a game of trying to name the type of plane. Now the air base was the city's only lifeline. The first plane from Beijing landed there at 10:00 a.m., carrying an advance group from the Beijing military command, and then, throughout the afternoon, planes began to trickle in, carrying military medical groups and mine rescue teams. The latter were barely needed, thanks to the sterling work of the Tangshan miners, and so they used their skills above ground.

Long before they saw planes, a vast procession of survivors trudged along the 9 kilometres to the airfield, pilgrims seeking miracles. Word had quickly spread that the airfield had the only functioning medical centre in the city. The injured were slung in improvised hammocks made from bedsheets and screen doors, carted in wheelbarrows, or leant on crutches formed from broken tree branches. Dozens died on the road, unceremoniously rolled into the ditches. People paused to help those who had fallen from exhaustion or shock, bearing strangers for long miles on their backs. Some drove cars half-wrecked by the quake, and with windows gone. These were soon flagged down and crammed with the severely wounded.

The airport's medical team was utterly overwhelmed. The airport buildings were solid, single-storey affairs, built with Russian aid in the 1950s, and very few of them had collapsed. At first, the staff had no idea of the scale of the earthquake, and so they dispatched their only ambulance into the city bearing more severely wounded patients, sending them to hospital. It came back a short while later, loaded with wounded picked up along the road and bearing the grim news that every other hospital in the city was flattened.

With forty nursing staff and two doctors, the air base medical team was used to treating countryside injuries and sick airmen. Before long, there were hundreds of wounded dotted around the airfield, blood pooling underneath them in the rain. The doctors were forced to perform ruthless triage. 'He's too far gone, put him outside.' Mothers, crazy with grief, brought in children who had died hours before.

The doctors were working at the most basic level of battlefield medicine, at which the PLA excelled. They amputated thousands of limbs, throwing severed arms and legs into a pit outside. The reed mats underneath their feet became splattered with blood. They rapidly ran out of morphine, sawing off limbs and cleaning bloodied flaps of skin with no anaesthetic for the patient other than a rag to bite on and a hand to hold. With no normal water supply, surgical instruments and gloves were cleaned in water taken from the air base's swimming pool and boiled.[5] With blood supplies destroyed in the quake, doctors drew it for immediate use from volunteers, and in some cases, even from themselves.[6]

On 29 July, the airfield got hold of a large truck, and sent the worst injured over to an army hospital in another county, which they'd heard was still operating. Zhao Fu, a male nurse from the No. 255 hospital who had broken his arm in the quake, was among them:

There was one man who had lost his foot [he told Qian Gang]. The skin had curled back and you could see the bone; a sickening white colour . . . He was crying out piteously the whole way; his throat sounded as if it had been ripped out. Then there was a girl in her twenties, who had something wrong with her abdomen. I think her spleen was ruptured, and every time the truck jolted a bit she would cry out . . . She clutched at my hand and said, 'Please, comrade, I beg you. Please knock me out, please, please, knock me out. It hurts. I can't bear it. Really, I can't.'[7]

When they arrived at the hospital, the courtyard was thick with bodies, festering in the heat. Zhao begged a doctor to operate on him. 'Operate? How can we operate here? Just yesterday we lost 1,400 people. We can't manage, we just can't manage.' Across

Tangshan and its surrounding counties, 86 per cent of medical facilities had been utterly destroyed, and the rest badly damaged. Zhao lay in the courtyard, surrounded by the dead, for two more days before being treated.

As aid converged on Tangshan from the rest of China over the next three days, the airport grew busier, and there was some relief from the chaos in the hospital. All manner of aircraft, from bulky transporters to tiny two-man props, most of them Russian gifts from the fifties and sixties, had been commandeered. In total 1,364 landings were made between 28 July and 2 August. Other airborne relief efforts were less successful; helicopters dropped crates of food and medicine among the ruins of the city, but so many people gathered as the packages were dropped that they became something of a safety hazard. At least one man was killed when a crate fell on him.

The most common planes used were the Tu-104 and the Il-18, two sturdy Soviet passenger jets, but the airport lacked proper boarding equipment for such large aircraft and so the wounded had to be hauled up into the hold by rope and pulley, a difficult and slow operation that meant it could take an hour to load 200 wounded. Medical teams from elsewhere arrived, setting up their own hospital tents, and from 30 July the worst injured were evacuated, 2,000 a day flown to other Hebei cities. At one point, the slew of planes was so thick that the time between one taking off and another landing was 26 seconds.

The air control team, working with little more than hand signals and a few radios, coordinated a miraculous aerial ballet, without a single accident. Young soldiers ran up and down the length of the runway, sweating profusely as they waved planes in, some of them covering the equivalent of 50 km in a day. Chang Qing photographed them. 'They were astonishing,' he said, 'That small airport saved so many lives. I believe it saved a hundred thousand lives.'

Zhang Daguang spent a week drifting in and out of consciousness in one of the new hospital tents. It took her some days to realise exactly what had happened, and that her parents were dead. 'I never knew who pulled me out of the rubble,' she said. 'I never knew who saved me. Everybody saved me.'

As the skies started to buzz with planes, a vast army of rescuers was tramping across land to Tangshan. China had no professional earthquake rescue teams. Instead, it had the People's Liberation Army. The PLA had a long history of dealing with rural catastrophes, having started as an insurgent force for which the trust of the people was absolutely essential to survive. Taking in the harvest, digging wells and saving people from floods became a regular part of their work. Even after the foundation of the PRC, PLA units often helped with the harvest, and in rural areas military doctors were often the only help available for those with serious injuries.

The PLA took its own name seriously. In contrast to the traditionally low status of soldiers in Chinese culture, the PLA saw itself as the embodiment of popular strength and national will, a guardian against foreign invaders constantly looking to divide China, and against 'tigers and wolves' who would gnaw away at it from the inside. PLA officers had a strong idealistic streak. 'Our job was to protect the people,' one of them told me. 'We weren't like Western armies, used to invade and conquer others.' (Tibetans, Mongolians and Uighur might differ on this particular point.)

The PLA never conscripted, but it didn't lack for volunteers. A military career was one of the few ways a bright young boy – or girl, as the PLA had many female soldiers – from the countryside could make a name for him or herself. It helped recruitment that children's toys and books were massively militarised,[8] something the PLA played up with posters showing adorable infants clutching assault rifles.

Officers usually rose through the ranks, in stark contrast to the practice in Western and Western-inspired post-colonial armies, and were then sent for advanced training, rather than being picked out from the start. Many soldiers' motivations were not as ambitious or as idealistic, naturally; they were in the PLA for three square meals a day and a roof over their heads. (Recruitment slogans in the 1930s were blunt about this. 'Do you want to eat rice every day? Do you want to kill Japanese? Do you want to sleep with the landlord's little wife? Then join the Red Army!')

The Cultural Revolution had left the PLA deeply entangled in politics and the economy. The dual command structure had been copied from the Soviet Union, with each commanding officer matched by a commissar. In practice, though, the commissars tended to be military leaders rather than, as in the Soviet Army, mere political mouthpieces, and they usually worked well with their counterparts. Mao had deliberately held the PLA back during the worst periods of civil war in the late sixties, though it had inevitably been drawn into fighting in various areas.

After 1969, when it was deployed to clean up the Red Guards, the PLA moved to take control of vast swathes of administrative and economic duties, seconding hundreds of thousands of men to civilian tasks. The Lin Biao affair had dealt the military a serious political blow, since Lin was the country's foremost general, and the subsequent purge of his supporters implicated senior military figures.

In general, the PLA tended mildly to favour political pragmatists, rather than ideologues, but provincial commanders had a wide range of loyalties. The removal of Ye Jianying from the Central Military Commission as part of the anti-Deng campaign had put the bulk of regional military power into the hands of Chen Xilian, the commander of the Beijing Military Region. Chen had come up as a commissar in the 1930s, proved himself in heroic small-scale actions against both Muslim warlords and the Japanese (Deng was his commander at one stage, and had praised him as 'The only one of us who really knows how to fight!'), and continued his military rise after Liberation, growing comfortably fat.

The start of the Cultural Revolution had seen him attacked by students, but not severely, and by 1976, at the age of 61, he was surprisingly cosy with the leftist faction, despite being to some degree a protégé of Deng's. Mao's high opinion of him helped; even before Ye was removed he'd been talking about giving Chen a higher command role. Now he was coordinating the rescue efforts at Tangshan – he'd been among those who'd seen the three miners arrive that morning.

As soon as the earthquake's epicentre was pinpointed, over a hundred thousand troops began to converge on Tangshan, some coming from the Beijing military group, and others from Shenyang to the north. With the rails destroyed, the vast majority of them came by foot, undergoing a gruelling twenty-four-hour march across the broken countryside to reach the city. There were trucks, cars and jeeps with them, but the obstacle course created by the quake was easier for men on foot to cross.

It was blazing hot, and the men were already exhausted. Their sleep the night before had been shaken by the earthquake, and some had worn themselves out in other rescue efforts. Forced marches were a regular part of PLA training, thanks to the army's background as a guerrilla force and its lack of mechanisation, but this was a harder and longer one than most.

They marched across a landscape remade overnight. Fields had flooded, water bubbling up from underground to drown crops. Sand boils and craters had erupted, leaving the ground scarred like an adolescent's face. Sandbanks had slid into rivers, silting the water. Cornfields had been knocked flat, as though a hurricane had blown them down. Wells were choked with sand, new lakes made from sunken ground and fresh islands formed in rivers. Highways were lifted up, one side now nearly a metre above the other. Three-metre-deep sinkholes caught careless marchers, while some giant pits reached thirty metres deep and ten metres across.

Everywhere the soldiers looked there were cracks in the earth, like struck glass. Telegraph poles had blown down, blocking vehicles and leaving tangles of wire along the side of the roads. Some areas looked as if a giant worm had slithered across them, breaking the earth as it went. Others seemed to have been ploughed up by artillery, creating swathes of no-man's land broken by quake-formed trenches. 'One of our officers had been a volunteer in the Korean War,' a soldier recalled, 'He said it looked just like a battlefield that had been bombed by the Americans.'

The heat was killing. A few soldiers fainted and had to be carried by their companions. None of the troops received anything to eat until they arrived in Tangshan, whereupon the mess orderlies began to cook up basic meals of rice gruel. Water was in such short supply that parched troops drank from stagnant pools tainted by oil or coal runoff. As they marched, villagers ran towards them, desperate for aid. Small groups of soldiers broke off to help the worst-hit, but officers urged them not to be distracted, to keep going for Tangshan. The countryside was not the priority.

Indeed, outside the centre of Tangshan, it would be a long, long time before anyone saw the PLA, or any other form of government relief. The first troops made it to the city by the early morning of the 29th, but there were villages only a couple of hours away that didn't see any sign of the army for a week or more, if at all. Up in the hills, the army never came.

The generous interpretation of the decision to concentrate solely on the city is this. The PLA and the central authorities were working with limited resources, and facing a disaster of vast magnitude. They needed to perform what was, in effect, a form of triage. The infrastructure of the region had been wrecked, and it would take hours or days to reach even nearby villages and towns. Central Tangshan had the highest population density and was, after all, the epicentre of the earthquake; it made sense to save lives there as quickly as possible, and only after that to spread out and concentrate on the countryside.

But the reality is that the countryside simply didn't matter to the central authorities. The quake victims there were only farmers, and the country had hundreds of millions of them. Nor were the northern Hebei villages and small towns important political battlefields.

Tangshan, in contrast, was a critical industrial centre, a mining powerhouse that couldn't be lost. Industry was far more important than agriculture, as had been demonstrated during the Great Leap Forward, where basic agronomy was neglected in favour of frantic industrialisation to 'catch up' with Western nations. And while the PLA eventually fanned out from the city centre into the counties close to Tangshan, great swathes of the region, and many individual villages in the areas the military did reach, saw not a scrap of disaster relief for months. Some never saw any at all.

Hundreds of thousands of rural Hebei residents were left to cope with the catastrophe entirely by themselves. Their fields had been destroyed, and the state granaries that could have supplied them were cordoned off by local militias and the army. Food aid took weeks to be delivered, if it ever came. In a previous era, they would have spilled down from their homes into the big cities, looking for work or charity. But it was bitterly hard to leave your home without proper registration, and especially to move from the countryside into the city.

Those who tried, unless they had relatives elsewhere willing to sponsor and help them, were rounded up and shipped back to the quake-struck area like any other illegal migrant. Even in the wake of the disaster, the residence laws were enforced as inflexibly as ever; maintaining proper order was far more important than helping suffering farmers. Indeed, given the vigilante mobs guarding their ruined towns from the peasants, flight had become even riskier.

The concentration on the city was also a simple case of panicked and inadequate planning and communication. After it became known that Tangshan was the earthquake's epicentre, it was the natural destination for every battalion commander. Nobody could risk not going to Tangshan. Heading into the countryside, away from the rest of the army, would have left them open to accusations of exploiting the situation for counter-revolutionary ends.

A better plan would have spread men across the region, focusing on important towns and establishing relief centres to help the areas around them. But with no planning in place for an event of this scale, and poor communications between different units, it was unsurprising that all the soldiers ended up in the one spot, and that it was days or weeks before the military authorities got their act together enough, and received approval from the higher political leaders to dispatch men to the countryside.

One political decision was later universally admitted to be a mistake, the refusal of aid from foreign nations. Upon hearing of the quake, Japan, the UN, the EEC and the US had immediately offered help, including dedicated technical teams, helicopters, rescue tools, blankets and food. China turned them down flat. Foreign help was inconceivable because 'imitating foreign devils' was one of the cardinal sins during the Cultural Revolution. Only two years before, Jiang Qing had used the building of the SS *Fenging*, an ocean-going freighter constructed as part of a campaign of vigorous self-reliance, as yet another opportunity to attack Zhou Enlai through allusions to foreign ministers of the past who had sought help for China's navy overseas.

Chi Haotian, then a deputy political commissar for the military in Tangshan and later PLA deputy chief of staff, cheered the decision at the time but, like many others, was to regret it later:

A sympathy delegation headed by one of the leaders from the Party Central Commission came to the disaster zone and . . . said to us 'Foreigners want to come to China and provide us with aid, but this great and powerful country of ours . . . does not need the interference of others and does not need anyone else coming to our assistance!' At the time, listening to him, we all got very excited and applauded and wept and yelled out the same kind of thing. So many years went by before we realised what a stupid thing we'd done![9]

The refusal of foreign aid is still a sore point in Tangshan. It didn't escape local notice that an unusually high percentage of foreign-built buildings, both from the mining companies and from the period of Soviet aid, had survived the quake. It's uncertain how much foreign expertise could have helped, given the timescale. Even if the regime had accepted aid, it would have been days before it could have reached Tangshan, especially in view of the constraints and suspicions foreigners would have been operating under.

Ironically, the only three non-Chinese to die in the Tangshan earthquake had been there to teach the Chinese how to imitate foreign devils. They were Japanese engineers, working in Tangshan as part of an under-the-table deal struck between the Japanese and Chinese governments in the early 1960s, brokered by Zhou Enlai. Japan provided extensive technical aid, support and funds to China in return for China waiving any claims for wartime compensation, but neither side would mention it in public – the Japanese weren't keen to admit any kind of guilt, and the Chinese didn't want to broadcast that they had received foreign aid.

The Japanese had been working to help build the Douhe power plant for over a year, as part of a team of nine technicians. At the Spring Festival in February, they'd celebrated with their Chinese counterparts, with whom they'd been working closely, and one of the Japanese suggested that they all sign their names in a small book as a memento of their time together. The Chinese stared blankly at each other, and then walked en masse out of the room and called the mine's political officer, in a panic. Who knew what the foreigners were up to? The political officer told them firmly not to sign – maybe it was some kind of cunning Japanese ploy.

By the time the troops arrived in the city, Tangshan stank. The quake had torn up the sewage system, wrecked the public toilets, and left piles of shit to rot in the hot sun. Bodies were already bloating, and maggots squirmed in corpses and garbage as black clouds of flies fed on the human debris. Like the troops, the survivors were desperately thirsty, and drank whatever was available – from broken public toilet bowls, swimming pools into which sewage pipes had burst, canteens of stale tea two days old. People filled cups and thermoses with the green rainwater that had collected in the newly cratered ground.

Without any professional expertise in rescue work, the PLA, at least at first, amounted to nothing more than strong backs and willing hands. That helped, of course, though the vast majority of the easier rescues had already been accomplished by Tangshanese. Since the soldiers were worn out, hungry and thirsty themselves, in some areas the influx of men was at first a burden rather than a help, although the troops were consistently generous in giving their food and water to survivors, especially children. But they were also relatively well-fed, and generally extremely fit; wiry-bodied tough young men trained to work in teams. They saved, according to the official figures, 16,400 people from the ruins, a fraction of those recovered earlier, but still a heroic and exhausting effort.

The army had another task besides rescue. The excesses of the militia soon became obvious, especially to the relatively well-disciplined professionals of the PLA. On 1 August the army issued 'General Order No. 1', both forbidding looting and noting that, 'Effective today, members of the People's Militia are forbidden to open fire without due cause.' The army had forcibly to disarm some of the militias, drunk with their own power. The militia members were never officially prosecuted, though at least one case of gang rape was rumoured to have been committed by the members of a militia brigade, subsequently executed or sentenced to hard labour.

When it came to rescue work, within a few hours, one of the most critical shortages became obvious. The heavy relatively modern buildings of central Tangshan offered a surprising obstacle to rescue efforts: wood was very rare. Timber is desperately important in any disaster that involves collapsed buildings, and sturdy four-by-fours have saved many lives. It is needed to stabilise shafts and hold up tunnels; without it efforts to dig in to save the buried become even more grindingly slow and risk further collapses. The troops did their best with wood scavenged from other buildings, but there was never enough. Nine million planks would eventually be shipped to Tangshan, but far too late.

On top of that, there was no heavy rescue equipment. The PLA had no more way to break through the wreckage than the initial rescuers had that first morning. With few combat engineers in the first battalions to arrive, when it came to shifting rubble without crushing the people below, they went mostly by guesswork and luck. They were an army without weapons, forced to resort to sawing through steel rods with nothing more than hacksaws, or using blasting caps from the mines to blow holes through fallen walls and hope they wouldn't bring the whole structure down. Astonishingly, rescue equipment didn't arrive until 7 August – ten days after the quake.

Those still trapped tapped out messages to the soldiers, or called out weakly – sometimes no more than a metre or two away from the men trying to save them. The soldiers stuck food on bayonet blades and lowered them down on string through thin cracks to try to give those trapped a little more time, but often it was hopeless, and agonising scenes played out across the city as a baby's crying stopped, or a voice heard calling 'Save me, soldiers, save me' gave out at last.

The soldiers remembered the children and the women most of all:

There were three young women we couldn't reach [one former soldier said later]. I kept talking to them, trying to give them hope to hang on just a little longer. None of them were Tangshanese; they had all come from other provinces, and I kept thinking how awful it was, that they had come to this place to die. They told me about their families, and I told them about my sisters and my mother. I kept talking, even after they stopped answering. When we brought their bodies out of the rubble they were all so beautiful.

But some were saved. It was Zhu Yinlai's third day underneath the rubble when he heard the sound of soldiers moving outside.

He had had no water, and when he tried to call to them his mouth was dry and cracked and at first he could barely force a sound out. He banged on stones, wondering how they couldn't hear him. It was so quiet, and they were ignoring the noise! He reasoned it must be deliberate, that they must have heard him but were afraid of being blamed if they couldn't save him. And then, as he heard more people, he realised that it might be quiet for him, but not for them.

It took him another full day before anyone heard him. The soldiers kept coming past, because there was a ruined swimming pool nearby. They were so thirsty they were refilling their canteens from the stagnant water. When they heard him at last, they dropped everything. They started to yell to him. 'Be quiet! Don't waste your energy!' but he wanted to talk, to hear a response from them.

The soldiers began clearing the fallen stone, until a chink of sunlight appeared above Zhu. As the light fell on his face, the first he'd seen in four days, he felt an immense sense of salvation. But the soldiers were then confronted by a tangle of metal, and had to wait for a cutter to be brought up. Zhu tried to direct them as best he could based on his mental image of the dormitory, but it was so wrecked his efforts were more hindrance than help.

Zhu wanted water desperately after they pulled him out, but the soldiers were worried he might die if they gave it to him straight away. Eventually they threw a nutrient bag over a nearby tree and hooked it into his arm. He passed out then, but not before seeing another classmate of his, Chen Yi-Hui, carried out of the ruins, only just alive, his face swollen purple and black from numerous bruises. They were two survivors out of ten in his department; his other fifty comrades were dead.

Zhu's four-day ordeal was not unusual. Survivors were still being found, pulled up alive after five, six, seven days in the darkness. The most remarkable was Lu Guilan, a 46-year-old housewife who was pulled out on 9 August, after thirteen days underneath the wreckage of her house. She had slipped into a coma, but recovered, although lame in one leg. Perhaps, like many others, it was the toughness of her previous life which gave her the strength to last through those days, in which 'my tongue got so dry in the end it was like a clod of earth banging away inside; I tore off a bit of the skin and the blood started dripping out, at least it felt a bit moist that way'.[10]

She lost her third husband in the earthquake, having first been widowed at seventeen. 'The Japanese bullets had as good as taken my head off; they'd killed my first man.' She'd had to look after her parents-in-law after losing her first husband, and would walk a dozen kilometres to bring them firewood, but 'I was that strong then, I'd get a thirst on doing all that work, and then I'd drop down into a ditch and drink the cold water there, never got ill from it once.' She married another man at twenty-two, only to have him die when she was twenty-five, leaving her 'without a pair of shoes to my name'. It was memories of how she'd survived previously that gave her the strength to keep going, singing revolutionary songs in her head and thinking about how much she despised her next-door neighbour.

Many attempts at rescue ended tragically. Feng Chengbo was a young nurse in the No. 255 hospital, a twenty-year-old girl known for her gentle nature, but who suffered frequent criticism for her 'love of beauty'. By the standards of 1976, this meant that she styled her fringe, and that she liked to wash her face with scented soap.

She was on the first floor with patients when the building collapsed. The next day rescuers broke through to find her trapped in a small cavity, caught at the waist between a huge concrete slab and an iron hospital bed, her legs buried in the ruins but her top half free. The rescuers struggled for over a day to find a way to remove her from the rubble, but the concrete slabs were too heavy to shift. Without cranes or drills, there was no way to save her. They considered amputation, but without transfusion facilities, she couldn't survive the massive blood loss.

By now most of those trying to save her were young soldiers, looking down into the cavity from above, and they couldn't bear it. Feng kept standing there, leaning her head on her elbow smiling weakly up at the men around her as they wept. The soldiers took it in turns to climb down and be with her. One crushed up half a watermelon he had with him and fed her spoonfuls.

She'd had a shower just before going on her last shift, and her hair was fluffy and tangled. A friend of hers arrived at last, asking 'Little Feng, is there anything I can do?' Feng was trying to speak, but was too weak, yet her friend understood. She picked up a comb and began to go through Feng's hair, cleaning out the tangles, until her eyes closed. The slab still couldn't be shifted, and so she was left standing there as if still alive, her head resting on her arms and her hair combed.

Goods as well as people needed to be saved from the rubble. Many of the survivors had been left with almost nothing, and were desperate to save some fragment of their old lives, especially rare and precious items like sewing machines and radios. One man picked through his old home to find every last scrap of his sewing machine, broken into seventeen pieces, which he then rebuilt. In the factories, workers and soldiers tried to salvage valuable industrial equipment – in some cases nearly irreplaceable, given China's lack of imports and the paltry state of technical knowledge after a decade of closed universities.

In Tianjin, the writer and teacher Feng Jicai found himself dealing with a particularly tricky rescue operation. For years he had been collecting stories from victims of the Cultural Revolution and storing them in cracks in his house. His house was shattered by the earthquake, and he dreaded rescuers or clean-up crews coming across his works. In the days after the quake he 'carefully rummaged through the ruins to look for my writings. In the end, I collected a whole bagful of small pieces of paper.'[11]

Apart from rescue operations, the troops' main task was to dispose of bodies. The journalist Qing Gang, who had arrived alongside the army, watched:

. . . some soldiers coming down from the ruins with a corpse. The body had been wrapped in an old piece of cotton and tightly bound at either end with wire; it was hanging from a steel support bar . . . The two soldiers were so small and thin, with the faces of young boys. Their army caps were tilted to one side, and their sleeves hitched high up their arms. Fluid was dripping down the corpse on to their trousers where damp patches had already formed.[12]

Tangshan residents had already done their best to clean up the carrion fields, stacking bodies in basketball courts and lorry parks. Now the army dumped bleaching powder on the tens of thousands of remaining bodies, then moved them to graveyards five kilometres outside the city, where they buried them a metre deep. Rightly fearful of disease, sterilisation teams spread out throughout the ruins, gas-masked figures in sealed white coats spraying powder from tubes like scenes from a science fiction movie.

To combat the hordes of flies and mosquitoes, planes flew across the city, dousing it with pesticides, while thousands of pest sprays were distributed to ordinary soldiers who lost their concern for good karma and set out on a happy programme of insect genocide. They hated the mosquitoes, in particular, with the fury of the extremely itchy. The efforts succeeded, and there was no epidemic, though flu, encephalitis and dysentery were common among the survivors. (According to one doctor, the rates of certain types of cancer today among those alive at the time of the quake are unusually high, around double the normal rate for China. Given the amount of heavy industry in the city, blaming this on the pesticides may be a stretch.)

As news of the quake spread, tens of thousands of desperate Tangshanese working elsewhere began trying to make their way home. Mr Zhang had been working on the railways in Shanxi, normally a twelve-hour ride from his home and his wife in the town of Fengnan, near Tangshan, when a workmate woke him up with the news. He jumped on a train to Beijing with another Tangshanese comrade. This was normally an easy journey, but it took them a whole day and night just to reach the capital on a clogged rail system. Arriving in Beijing, they were told that there were no trains to Tangshan. Some people were even saying that Tangshan didn't exist any more, and that it had been drowned by flood waters from broken dams.

They took a train to Chengde, and from there walked for three days to his friend's home village, which had been relatively unaffected. Exhausted and terrified at the thought of his family's fate, he borrowed a bike and pressed on without rest. All along the long road to Fengnan, he saw bodies on both sides, and when he got to the village, there was nobody there, only flattened remains. The only thing left standing in Fengnan was a red police box.

He wandered around for several hours, convinced that everybody had died, until two young women who had come back to find water told him that the survivors had taken refuge in a large temple near the village – which, like many old buildings, had weathered the earthquake. There he found his children and his wife; she'd been badly hurt by a falling tile, but the local doctor had used his last bandage to bind her wound before he ran to check on his own family.

Pockets of survivors like this were common. With government efforts entirely concentrated in the city, the countryside had to fend for itself. Temples, schools and hospitals became common focus points for shattered communities. One of the strangest was formed around the derailed No. 40 train. It was the only remaining shelter in a devastated countryside, and the 800 passengers huddled inside for three days, living off unhusked rice scavenged from the fields. They sent rescue teams out to help dig through the ruins of nearby villages and improvised a bathhouse by draping a sheet over a culvert near the tracks with a stream in it.

At night, the train's electric lights, powered by the surviving engine, were a small beacon of hope and life in a black landscape. It was three days before the passengers were picked up by coaches driven from Tianjin and put back into the railway system to continue their brutally interrupted journey. The train staff stayed, and when the rails were mended, cleaned the train and drove it back to Qiqihar

But the experiences of one middle-aged teacher working away from home were, sadly, more typical of the grim end of return trips to Tangshan. 'The train couldn't get through, and I had to run a dozen or so miles to get home. By the time I got there, our village was rubble and corpses. The corpses were all relatives and friends. I knew them all.'[13]

More corpses were being added to the pile. Two weeks after the earthquake, the army conducted its own tribunal, sentencing 367 'guilty of the most heinous crimes'; twenty-six of them were executed on the spot by military firing squads, while the rest were sent to hard labour. Army statistics, admittedly incomplete, recorded a total of nearly 10,000 crimes, while the people's militias recorded the theft of 67,695 items of clothing, 48,638 metres of cloth and 1,149 watches.

Individual institutions also dispensed their own forms of popular justice. Zhu Yinlai, freshly recovered from his four-day ordeal under the rubble, took part in one such trial. Out of the ten girls in his class, only two had survived. One of them had been caught by the army stealing watches and clothes from the dead. They had tied her to a tree while they carried on searching for survivors. Afterwards, the surviving members of the university gathered to 'criticise' her. Unlike most public criticisms, there was little violence, just a relentless barrage of insults. She wept in the middle of the circle as they flung accusations and ripped up her student papers. At the end they shouted at her 'Go! Get out of here!' 'Where shall I go?' she asked, 'Where shall I go?' In the end she walked the 800 miles back to her home town of Handan. There, Zhu heard later, she became a policewoman.

Those areas reached by the PLA were genuinely grateful to the army. The efforts made to restore some kind of normal life in the days and weeks after the earthquake were astonishing. The roads between Tangshan and Beijing, which normally saw around 3,000 vehicles a day, were now carrying 20,000 vehicles daily as water tanks, food trucks, bulldozers, mobile power generators and cranes moved to help rebuild the city. Traffic jams became common as trucks tried to force their way through the ruins.

Some 75,000 tons of food was shipped to the city over the next four months, along with vast quantities of other goods – 40 tons of steel piping, 2,620,000 reed mats, 410,000 pairs of shoes, 6,110 cases of matches. Goods were given to survivors for free, leading some in Tangshan to speculate that this was, in fact, a preparation for a new stage of communism to be implemented across the rest of the nation, although the reopening of small stores and the banks might have been a clue that this wasn't the case.

Unsurprisingly, little of the aid made it to the countryside, although some trickled through or was requisitioned by ingenious local leaders. When aid did come through, the distribution was often caught up in local politics. One survivor remembered how the emergency rations – a few bags of crackers – were given out. 'Everyone went to stand in line, but the production brigade said the crackers were only to be given to the poor peasants.' These were not the poorest people in the village, but those whose families had been labelled 'poor' and therefore deserving twenty years or more earlier, in contrast to the 'rich peasants' whose tainted background made them untrustworthy:

People like us who had 'problems' were not allowed to receive any crackers. My wife went, but they sent her home empty-handed . . . Such a simple thing had clearly divided people into two classes. Villagers who had crackers would never give you any; you had to slink off to one side like a dog. But neither would they eat them in front of you. Why do you think that was? Because they were afraid you'd ask for some if you saw them eating? Or because they were afraid they wouldn't be able to withstand the urge to share a little with you, and would therefore be punished by the production brigade?

Many of the goods that arrived were donations collected by individual provinces, cities and factories. These 'donations' involved a large element of coercion. In many cases, how much each work unit was expected to donate would simply be decreed from the top. (Social pressure still plays an important role in modern Chinese disaster relief; after the Yushu earthquake my office displayed a list of the donations made by each staff member – in order of size of donation and rank, which magically corresponded. Each section chief, for instance, had spontaneously decided to give exactly 400 yuan.) But the public also felt genuine empathy and horror at the earthquake. Although official media played down the victims' suffering in favour of stories of socialist triumph, ordinary Chinese knew all too well what it was like to live in the aftermath of disaster.

With all the rhetoric of triumph and struggle, there was very little room for grief. No national day of mourning was announced, and no real acknowledgement was made of the dead. Survivors were left to cope with their losses on their own amid devastated communities where, with losses in every family, comfort other than shared grief was in short supply. People numbed themselves. 'It was six months before I cried for my roommates,' said He Jianguo. 'Before then, that part of my heart was closed off.' Contemplating the sheer scale of loss was too much for most people.

The language of struggle did comfort some. It gave a purpose to the tragedy, made it into part of China's long battle towards self-reliance and perfect communism. As sketches of a rebuilt Tangshan were drawn up, the new landmarks were named 'Anti-Earthquake Square', 'Anti-Earthquake Boulevard'.

The press to get the mines and steel factories back up and running began within a couple of days of the earthquake. It showed the regime's priorities: industrial production, or at least the appearance of industrial production, came before everything else. Tangshan mattered because of the mines and factories, not because of the people.

But restarting work was an important psychological lift for many Tangshanese. It might seem inhumane, but, with the industrial mania and Stakhanovite cults of China, work was vital to people's sense of self. Besides, it was a mining city, and their civic pride was rooted in their ability to produce. Thirty years later, it still stirred former miners. 'Three days after a 7.8 magnitude earthquake, and we were working again! They couldn't do that nowadays!'

Tangshanese and outside engineers alike worked twenty-hour days to get the mines – so critical to the industrial functioning of the region – up and running again; on 9 August, the first reopened, and within another week seven of the eight major mines were functioning, albeit with drastically reduced production.

It was the reopening of the mines that saved the last survivors of the earthquake, five miners who had been wandering in a closed mine, gradually working their way back towards the surface and surviving on the water that had flooded in, when they stumbled upon the lights of a team returning to the coalface. 'Two bloody weeks!' their rescuers exclaimed. 'We figured you'd died a long way back.'[14]

One of the few beneficiaries of the disaster was Hua Guofeng, who played the situation like a master. He was the only high-level figure to visit Tangshan, and pictures of him meeting earthquake victims were widely publicised. Chang Qing, the photographer, was one of those snapping him, and praised him for his kindness, engagement and ability to connect with ordinary people.

'He was easy to get along with. A little soft, not a hard man like many of the politicians. And he never insisted on the official tunes being played when he arrived; he just walked into the room and started talking to people.' Chang watched him as he left Tangshan, taking a picture of him waving goodbye to eager crowds from the door of the train. 'When he came,' he said, 'it was the first time I really felt hopeful about the future of our city.'

6 You die, I live

For months after Tangshan, people lived in fear of another quake. As far away as Anhui, villagers slept in tents outside until winter made it impossible. (Geographically, this is akin to people in London abandoning their homes after an earthquake in Inverness.) In Beijing, people rigged plastic shelters over beds out in the street, now packed with families. Space was so scarce that people had to take turns sleeping.

Deng Xiaoping's family built a shelter in their living room, placing the wooden frames of their beds on the tables to create cover and sleeping on mattresses underneath. But Deng's prostate meant he had to get up often in the night, and he kept bumping his head, so they moved out to a courtyard shelter, two heavy tarpaulins over the family's beds. Lights were rigged up, along with the family's television set.

Even under house arrest, that was a pleasant lifestyle compared to most people. In the ruins of Tangshan, the army shipped in immense quantities of tarpaulin and wood, and people improvised shelter around the ruins of the city. There were fights about who got to use the remaining walls as one side of a home. Did they belong to the people who lived there before (and if so, which floor had priority?) or to those who had camped there first?

Tangshan itself, oddly enough, ate better than most of the country. The food distribution teams meant that people were getting enough to eat, while, for the rest of the country, it was a hard autumn. The good done by Deng's previous reforms and the rapidly improving state of agricultural science was counteracted by a growing population and the political turmoil of the summer. Eggs were in particularly short supply, and city-dwellers made trips out to the countryside just to buy them.

The Seismological Bureau worked overtime, setting up new local monitoring teams and jumping at every report of a plague of frogs or a boiling spring. The same list of tricks Qinglong had given out was distributed across the nation; families everywhere watched upturned glasses nervously for a sign of imbalance.

With the anti-Deng campaign still being drummed into people at every opportunity, the quake fears added another layer of tension to an already stressed society. These worsened after another, much smaller, earthquake hit a remote part of Sichuan on 16 August, killing forty-one people. China's mountainous southern belt often suffered such quakes, but the timing naturally unnerved the public even further.

Sichuan was dominated by Zhao Ziyang, another survivor of the mid-sixties purges who had been rehabilitated by Zhou Enlai in 1972. He was one of the most radical reformists in the Party, and was already experimenting with the market economy in Sichuan, as a result of which agricultural production in the province had soared. After he went up into the mountains to oversee the disaster relief efforts that August, landslides blocked the road down and he spent a week in the wrecked highlands coordinating aid. Unsurprisingly, he was another bitter enemy of the radicals, who spread rumours that he was 'hiding in the mountains' in order to avoid taking part in the anti-Deng campaign.

Apart from fear of earthquakes, the other public obsession that summer was the dying Mao. It was a gross faux pas to talk openly about the Chairman's impending death, though everyone knew it was coming. The official announcement that he was seriously ill had gone out, and those who had this 'secret' information were busy spreading the news among their friends and relations. Others traced his physical condition through pictures; months had gone by without a photo of the Chairman – the last one issued had appeared in May 1976, showing him slumped in his chair during a visit by Kaysone Phomvihane, the Laotian Communist Prime Minister.

Mao was drifting in and out of consciousness. He could still be remarkably focused, but only when he cared. Jiang Qing tried to bring him anti-Deng documents to sign, but he showed no particular interest in them, or her. Appropriately enough, the last official document he read was a report on the Tangshan earthquake, delivered to him by Hua Guofeng on 18 August. Otherwise he spent his time sleeping, watching movies and being fed pap by his attendants. Zhang Yufeng, his ex-mistress, was on hand to translate and attend to him, faithful to the last.

Mao was off the political board, but he still dominated it. Nobody was willing to move while the Chairman was still on the scene, even bed-ridden and half-conscious. For thirty years he had built a system that centred around himself, smashing any challenger and pitting potential successors against each other. Everyone around him was still caught by his power. Hua and the others had considered doing away with the Gang of Four long before Mao's death. But even half-comatose, Mao's disapproval was too awful to risk. The danger that he might rise from his bed and condemn whoever acted too rashly hung over all their heads. The government was in stasis, waiting for the heart of an 82-year-old man to fail. Wang Hongwen passed his time riding his motorcycle, shooting rabbits in the fields and watching imported Hong Kong movies.

On 2 September, at 5:00 p.m., Mao went into convulsions as he was hit by another heart attack. The doctors, monitoring every bodily fluctuation, saw instantly that it was worse than the earlier two. They rushed to start emergency treatment, pounding a few more days of life into him. He was awake throughout, and kept asking whether he was in danger, getting only reassuring lies from the doctors. Nobody wanted to be the one to tell the Great Helmsman that his journey was coming to an end. He tried to talk to his doctors, but could only get out choked sounds. On 7 September, his heart started palpitating wildly; the end was close. The Politburo members started a death watch, taking turns by his bedside.

Jiang Qing was in Xiaojinzhuang, the 'model village' in Hebei she had carefully cultivated as a political example, when the news came, on 5 September, that she should return to Beijing immediately. She'd spent the past few days ranting about Deng to farmers: '[He] wants to consign me to hell! He's far worse than Khrushchev ever was! The man wants to get himself crowned, to declare himself emperor!'[1] She rushed back to Beijing, shouting at the Zhongnanhai staff with frantic concern for her husband. She set herself up in the offices of the Xinhua official news agency, calling reporters and editors to prepare to spin the news, then made herself a nuisance for Mao's medical team. The official accounts talk constantly of her callousness towards Mao and her belief that he was the last obstacle to her power, but, yet again, this is rubbish; Mao wasn't the obstacle to her power, but the bulwark of it.

During the deathbed vigil, there was a moment when Mao seemed to recognise the names of his colleagues, but was unable to speak. As Ye Jianying was about to leave the room with other leaders, Mao gestured for him to come back, then grasped his hand and stared intensely into his eyes. Ye believed Mao was trying to communicate something to him, but couldn't tell what. He decided afterwards that Mao had been saying 'I entrust Hua Guofeng's well-being to you.'

Just before midnight on 8 September, the doctors gave Mao an injection of ginseng to stimulate his heart. It gave him a temporary boost, but he was sinking fast. Mao's chief doctor remembered the scene:

Hua Guofeng pulled me aside after we administered the injection. 'Dr Li,' he whispered as . . . Zhang Chonqiao and Wang Dongxing strained to hear, 'Is there anything you can do?' . . . The air was frozen. The whirring of Mao's respirator was the only sound in the room. Then I shook my head. 'We have done all we can,' I whispered hoarsely.[2]

In those last moments, virtually all of the senior leadership was crowded into the room, pressed up against the medical team. The doctors and nurses hadn't slept properly for days, and the politicians weren't in a much better state. At ten minutes past midnight, Mao exhaled deeply, and the line on the monitor went flat.

Jiang Qing clutched at the body. 'Doctors! Quickly! Save the Chairman! Why can't you save him?'[3] She then turned to comfort Zhang Yufeng, who was bemoaning her fate with Mao gone. Mao's two former lovers embraced each other. 'You can work for me now,' Jiang Qing told her. Then she turned conspiratorial, 'From now on, don't allow anyone else into Chairman's bedroom or living room. Collect all the Chairman's documents, keep them in order, and deliver them to me.'[4]

Wang and Hua gathered the Politburo for a meeting in the swimming pool building nearby, where Mao had been housed until the earthquake. Not much could be accomplished, since the members kept breaking down, weeping openly. In the face of such grief, they managed to agree on the official announcement of the death, but little else.

The public reaction to the news, which went out at 4:00 that afternoon, was muted. People mourned, but not with the same depth of feeling as for Zhou. One observer described it as, 'Many people only remembered the disasters he had caused. The prevailing feeling throughout the nation was more one of concern than sorrow.'[5] One Beijinger put it bluntly: 'I didn't give a fart when Mao died. It wasn't like the premier. He never cared for us, so why should we care for him?' In Tangshan, the reaction was mixed. 'Some of the kids cried more for Mao than they did for their real family,' an orphaned survivor reported, 'Maybe they really loved him. But some of the people looking after us didn't like it if you cried for your real family too much, and the kids would pick on you. But you could cry for Mao, because everyone was crying.'

Adult survivors remember a more subdued response. Most Chinese can tell you where they were and what they were doing when they heard of Mao's death. It's the Kennedy assassination or 9/11 of their era. But among Tangshanese, who were still traumatised by the earthquake and struggling to find basic necessities, the memories are much less clear.

Many people elsewhere felt a sense of affected grief, of tears being shed because everyone else was crying rather than out of real feeling. Everyone was given ample opportunities to cry. Daily rallies were held to mourn and honour the Chairman, and tears were virtually compulsory, at least if you wanted to keep up appearances. Several dissidents write of forcing themselves to tears, and then wondering whether those around them were doing the same.

Even though the personality cult had been toned down in the last few years, Mao's death brought back a resurgence of that personal faith for some. This is always a minority, as in any country, for whom whatever the authorities say is true, and whose faith in the righteous leader can't be shaken by mere reality.

Women tended to show the most intense personal grief for Mao, including some who had always projected distinctly non-political feelings on to the Chairman. I was once invited to listen to Mao's poems by a devout, unmarried Maoist in her fifties, who would have been a young woman when the Chairman died. She put on a cassette for background music and began to sing a setting of one of Mao's poems in a high tremble, her eyes closed and her face contorted in an expression half-religious and half-erotic. Stalin used to receive explicit letters from Russian women looking to bear his child; there may well be a similar cache of epistolary erotica somewhere in China's central archives.

Even among the disillusioned, many felt some sense of loss. Whatever else he had done, Mao had, at one stage, been a genuinely unifying figure. People still remembered the sense of swelling pride when the new republic was declared and the excitement of the early years when everything was in flux and a renewed, modern and socialist China seemed within reach. The image of Mao on top of Tiananmen, proclaiming the new republic, resonated with many who could recall the years of chaos, division and bloodshed that had preceded it. It was a shame that years of chaos, division and bloodshed had followed.

The media – newspapers, television, radio – were full of Mao. A series of impressive lies about his personal life accompanied the reiteration of his political achievements. He had kept blankets, cups and shoes, the public was told, worn thin from use. During the 'difficult period' of 1959–61 he had eaten nothing but simple food. The only parts of this hagiography that were true were his occasional acts of thoughtfulness for his guards and personal staff – a hallmark of most dictators, who tend to be the kind of people who can congratulate themselves over giving somebody a week off to see their family at the same time as they sign the death warrant for an old comrade. Mao, unlike Zhou, had never shown even a trace of regret or guilt over any of the numerous past allies and friends he had disposed of, or for the millions of people his politics had destroyed.

Mao's doctors struggled with an unexpected decision by the Politburo. Mao was to be preserved, for eventual placement in a mausoleum of his own. It went against years of Chinese Communist tradition, where deceased leaders had been cremated, a decision intended to set an example in a country burdened, as the Communists saw it, by the weight of the dead, where cemetery space was in short supply. Cremation was also seen as scientific and modern, in contrast to the superstitious funeral rites of the past. Mao himself had said, in 1956, when approving the cremation policy, 'After people die they shouldn't be allowed to occupy any more space. They should be cremated. I'll take the lead. We should all be burnt after we die, turned into ashes and used for fertiliser.'

Mao had not been joking. During the Great Leap Forward, the bodies of famine victims had been boiled down and sprinkled on the fields. But nobody felt comfortable using Mao's body like nightsoil. The closest models they had for what to do with a deceased revolutionary hero were Lenin and Stalin, both of whose bodies had been embalmed and put on display – though

Stalin's had since been quietly removed, and his remains buried. But the techniques used for both had been experimental; and embalming hadn't been taught at any of the foreign medical schools Mao's medical team had mostly attended.

At first they tried injecting Mao with a massive dose of formaldehyde, using a formula found in a Western journal, but all it achieved was to make his body puff up, so that he looked like a drowned man, his arms and head bloated and his skin shiny. They massaged his limbs, hoping to force the liquid back down into the body. Eventually they got him looking acceptable, but left bruises on his arms and legs that had to be covered with make-up. With the formaldehyde squeezed into his chest, however, it was so swollen that they couldn't button his jacket, and had surreptitiously to slit it and his trousers to fit his deformed size. It would do for the moment.

The formal funeral arrangements were far more elaborate than for Zhou. Mao's body lay in state in the Great Hall of the People, in a glass-topped coffin with a red carpet before it and white memorial wreaths to either side. Foreign and Chinese dignitaries alike lined up to pay their respects, greeted by a reception line of the top leaders. The diplomatic editor of *Time* magazine, Jerrold Schecter, was among them. He noted of Hua that 'the immensity of the challenge he faces was etched into his features, lines of tension and shock betraying deep emotion and pain', and was more impressed by Wang Hongwen, who – judging him in fine journalistic style through a five-second handshake – he described as 'radiating the charisma of a leader; he moves with flowing, athletic grace and there is the feel of fine steel and energy in his handshake. He seems ready, even eager for the challenges and testing of power.'[6]

Some time that summer, Mao had summed up his life's work to Wang, Hua and Jiang:

I have accomplished two things in my life. First I fought Chiang Kai-Shek for a few decades and drove him to a few islands. After eight years of war against the Japanese, they were sent home. We fought our

way to Beijing, at last entering the Forbidden City. There are not many
people who do not recognise these achievements . . . The second matter
you all know about. It was to launch the Cultural Revolution. On this
matter few support it, many oppose it. But it is not finished, and its
legacy must be handed down to the next generation.[7]

It was true that nobody would doubt his first accomplishment,
though future Chinese generations would place more emphasis
on fighting the Japanese than fighting Chiang. Yet Mao was right
to stress the former. In the later years of the war, after Pearl
Harbor, he'd called off major operations against the Japanese.
With his eye for the long-run, he recognised that the US entry
into the war meant that Japan was doomed, and that using
Communist soldiers and resources against them would leave him
with fewer forces to confront the Nationalists after the war.

Having won the country wasn't enough; he was determined to
leave his own stamp on it for good. Mao had wanted, above all,
to preserve the legacy of the Cultural Revolution. Yet his final
political moves had set up the game board in such a fashion as
to make that impossible. His vision seems to have been of Hua
Guofeng at the head of a leadership group in which the leftists
played a major role, with Deng sidelined and eager to be brought
back to apply his skills after he'd shown due repentance.

But Mao was the only factor keeping the leadership together.
After ten years of mutual hatred and purges, did he seriously
expect it to be sustainable? Or was the very instability of the
arrangement deliberate? Mao had always thrived on chaos,
upheaval and tumult. He loved to turn things upside down,
even those of his own creation. Maybe the idea that after he was
gone there would be another period of chaos, giving birth to yet
another new order, pleased him.

For the moment, the leadership was determined to send out
a message of unity. The top leaders posed together for photos
around Mao's body, and for one long photo, with heads bowed,
at the funeral service in Tiananmen Square. The square was
packed with crowds again, but carefully selected this time.

Hua Guofeng's funeral address was not destined to go down in the annals of rhetoric, not least because it had been written by a committee two days before. It started with the usual lies:

It was under Chairman Mao's leadership that the Chinese people who had long suffered oppression and exploitation won emancipation and became masters of the country. It was under Chairman Mao's leadership that the disaster-plagued Chinese nation rose to its feet. The Chinese people love, trust and esteem Chairman Mao from the bottom of their hearts.

(There's always something desperate about the overstatement in communist rhetoric. Imagine having to hear this kind of thing day in, day out, for forty years.)

His conclusions for the future were equally banal. 'Deepen the struggle to criticise Deng Xiaoping and repulse the right deviationist attempt to reverse correct verdicts, consolidate and develop the victories of the Great Proletarian Cultural Revolution, combat and prevent revisionism . . .' Hua's words contained no hint of change. He did place unusual emphasis, though, on another instruction from Mao Zedong. 'Unite, don't split. Be open and above board, don't intrigue and conspire.' These were the words Mao had used when chastising Jiang and the others the previous year.

After the ceremony, Mao's doctors kept puzzling over how to handle his body. They looked for clues in ancient Chinese and Egyptian tracts, and even sent a team from the embassy in London to Madame Tussauds to study the wax figures there. (They were decidedly unimpressed.) They badly wanted to ask the Soviets how they had managed Lenin, but relations were so poor that it was unthinkable. The closest example they had was the Vietnamese, who had preserved Ho Chi Minh after his death in 1969. The two doctors sent to Hanoi were stonewalled, however, until one of the Vietnamese shamefacedly confessed that Ho was already beginning to rot, and his beard had fallen off.

They eventually settled on a variation of ancient Egyptian methods, removing all of Mao's organs save his brain – they were fearful of cracking open his skull – then filling the cavities with formaldehyde-soaked cotton. Just in case something went wrong, a perfect wax duplicate was made by the Institute of Arts and Crafts, and kept close by the original corpse. The work was done in the vast catacombs built beneath the city in case of nuclear attack from the Soviets – in, naturally, the special section reserved for the leaders, which came complete with a four-lane underground highway and a full hospital. There, deep underneath the capital, Mao's body rested in a cold chamber.

Above ground, things were heating up. Two days after Mao's death, Hua was already looking to build his alliance against the radicals. His fears that they were plotting something themselves had started upon hearing news that Wang Hongwen had asked the provincial authorities throughout China, during the funeral, to contact his office directly when they had questions about directives from the Party centre. He hadn't cleared this with Hua, and Hua saw it as the first step towards undermining his authority.

Hua's main priority was to reach out to Ye Jianying, but he had do so as quietly as possible, since being seen with Ye would raise the suspicions of the Gang. Phone calls had to go through a central operator, and were all recorded, so everything had to be done face to face.

He picked another Politburo member, Li Xiannian, as his go-between. Li was another grizzled survivor of the attempt to stop the Cultural Revolution in 1967; unlike Ye, he'd actually had to do hard labour for four years at a timber mill near Beijing. On 11 September, Hua said he was feeling ill while he was supposed to be keeping vigil at Mao's coffin, and claimed he had to leave. Li had pled sick to avoid the morass of Politburo struggles, and was taking refuge at his house. Hua visited him there and asked him to reach out to Ye.

Li agreed, but he was nervous of being spied upon. He concocted a plan whereby he would go to the Fragrant Hills botanical garden three days later, ostensibly for sightseeing, and if he was certain he wasn't being followed would then be driven to Ye's residence nearby. The gardens were quiet that day, and on 14 September he met Ye for the first time in months.

Both were tense, and fearful of being bugged, and the conversation was conducted mostly by writing notes to each other. Li passed Ye a list of possible conspirators, and Ye scribbled a question mark next to both Wu De and Chen Xilian, cautious of their previously good relationships with the radicals and the fact that, despite their shared military background, he had no real connections with them. Li assured him that both were trustworthy. No definite plans were made, but a vital link between Hua and Ye had been established.

Coups featured strongly in communist historical memory, both public, glorified seizures of power, such as the October Revolution in Russia, and the quieter, deadlier backroom coups pulled off in internal Party struggles. The type that preoccupied the plotters was definitely in the second category. It concerned the career of the despised Khrushchev – in fact, it was his moment of greatest triumph. (His final fall had also involved a coup, but one conducted with such simple efficiency and total complicity among the rest of the leadership that it hardly set a good example for Hua's schemes.)

In the struggle after Stalin's death in 1953, Khrushchev had seized power through two brilliant moves. The first was the arrest and rapid execution of Beria, Stalin's secret police chief, who had energetically positioned himself as the frontrunner in the succession stakes. Khrushchev had spearheaded the plot against Beria, in conjunction with the army, represented by the war hero Marshal Zhukov. Khrushchev had kept Beria convinced he was on his side even as he schemed against him, right up to the moment Beria walked into a meeting to find a gun against his head and a stone-faced committee of five, led by Khrushchev, reciting his crimes against the Party.

The second move had been Khrushchev's gradual undermining and final dismissal of his surviving chief rival for the leadership, Malenkov. There had been no sudden strike this time; instead Khrushchev had gradually built up his own power base in the wider Party, allowing him to override his relative weakness in the Politburo, and eventually, again with the support of the military, have Malenkov humiliated and demoted.

In a meeting between Hua, Li Xiannian and Wu De on 27 September, they mulled over Khrushchev's example, wondering whether the Gang could be eliminated through something as simple as a vote in the Politburo. They speculated on the likely votes, but decided that the result they wanted was probable, but not certain. They worried about the possibility of the leftists stirring up support in the lower Party ranks. So soon after Mao's death, getting rid of his wife would require more than just a vote. Her elimination had to be more decisive, a clear-cut message to her supporters elsewhere that their time was over.

Where was Deng in all this plotting? The official accounts, particularly his daughter's, go to such lengths to deny any involvement or even knowledge on his part that it's tempting to assume the opposite. There are stories of him meeting with Ye, Li and others to give advice. It certainly seems very unlikely that he couldn't have known something was going to happen, given his closeness to Ye in particular. So, if he did play any role, it was a minor, advisory one at best. He couldn't risk putting his head out of hiding. Mao, who had repeatedly condemned him, had also been his shield; ultimately it had been his hand that stopped the attacks on Deng from turning physical. Now he had to rely on Wang Dongxing and his men for protection.

The circle of those involved was relatively small. The chief players were Hua and Wang Dongxing, with Ye acting, in the marvellous phrase of Frederick Teiwes and Warren Sun, as '*consigliere*' (like Tom Hagen in *The Godfather*) to the pair. They were backed up by Chen Xilian, Li Xiannian, Wu De and a few others. Only about half of them, such as Ye, were clear enemies of the leftists in the past; many had, in fact, allied with them at various times. (Hua, Wang Dongxing, Chen and Li had all pushed for the line about 'Don't intrigue and conspire' to be included in the funeral speech, which should have been more of a clue to the Gang about who was out to intrigue and conspire against them.)

In the small world of Chinese elite politics, personality mattered. One factor that can't be overstated in the decision of many leaders, including those, like Chen Xilian and Wu De, who had not suffered politically from the leftists' manoeuvres, was just how *irritating* Jiang Qing was. Robert Muldoon, the Prime Minister of New Zealand, had sat beside her at a football game once, and afterwards commented, 'It was easy to see where Jiang Qing got her reputation as a "nagger".'[8] Even the other members of the Gang would sometimes advise people quietly just to let her finish.

She had a habit of suddenly turning on people, even those relatively close to her, with great vehemence. She would carry on about ideological or personal failings, and toss out wild accusations of people being Nationalists, spies or counter-revolutionaries. When Hua took over leading Politburo meetings, she undermined and jabbed at him at every possible opportunity, despite Hua not even being a political enemy as such. At the least provocation, she'd launch into strident feminist rants, mixed with attacks on her political opponents – 'Men are simple. All they have is sperm. When I talked this way at the Politburo, they laughed at me. The Politburo members are influenced by Deng Xiaoping's male chauvinism.'[9] Amid a political elite still nearly entirely dominated by men, many of them born at the turn of the century, this was never going to be popular.

It had been Jiang's status as Mao's wife that protected her. With him gone, she was an obvious target. But the plotters were more than happy to take the other three out with her. Some of them had maintained relatively cordial relations with the rest of the Gang, if not Jiang, but they were political parvenus, catapulted to power by the Cultural Revolution. They hadn't put in their time at the coalface of the revolution. Without Mao's blessing, Zhang and Yao would have never been more than Shanghai scribblers, and Wang nothing more than another petty provincial firebrand.

Those involved were conscious of another possible benefit from the purge of the Gang. The last decade had broken the country; if there was to be any kind of recovery, somebody had to be found to take the rap. It couldn't, for obvious reasons, be the actual instigator of the chaos, Mao himself. The Gang of Four were not only political enemies, but also splendid potential scapegoats for everything that had gone wrong.

This was the reason Hua was so crucial to the coup: he offered a direct link to Mao's legacy, and the claimed continuation of his policies, while at the same time being able to disassociate himself from the damage these policies had done. He had come to the centre when Zhou and Deng were trying to put the country back together, after the worst period of the Cultural Revolution was already over. If the plot had just been made up of the 'old revolutionaries' like Ye and Li, it would have seemed like a challenge to the whole premise of Maoist succession. Hua's legitimacy made him the pivotal figure; with him in play, the coup could be spun as a righteous cleansing rather than an outright attack on the system.

It seems astonishing that none of the Gang of Four recognised the precariousness of their position. Their sole source of authority had just disappeared, and the public mood had swung against them long ago. Jiang was especially blind to this, claiming, in the wake of the Tiananmen incident, that the public was 'happy, elated, and feel that Deng should have been dragged out long ago'.[10] Zhang had got an inkling of public feeling as he watched the crowds in Tiananmen from the safety of the Great Hall of the People, but he still blamed the usual 'counter-revolutionary forces' and 'Petofi clubs' rather than accepting the obvious: people no longer wanted what the Gang of Four were selling.

With Mao gone, their only chance of continuing in power was to claim the legacy of the Cultural Revolution. They were ideologically committed to the vision of constant, purging revolution as well – or at least Zhang and Yao were – but by now that was, perhaps, less important than ensuring the safety of their own positions.

In politics in any society, the higher you climb, the narrower your vision becomes. Washington insiders stop believing in a world outside the Beltway, while French politicians barely acknowledge the existence of anyone but the Parisian elite. As responsibilities widen and reach increases, the ruling elite's contact with everyday reality diminishes rapidly. The members of the Gang of Four had almost no contact with the everyday realities of Chinese life.

Chinese politics suffered from an extreme case of this syndrome, for several reasons. One was the size of the country, and the appalling communications infrastructure. It was touch-and-go whether any phone call would get through to its destination, and the countryside, as seen during the Tangshan disaster relief effort, was another world entirely. Then there was the insular nature of Beijing politics itself, where the elite lived cheek-by-jowl with their allies and enemies, went to the same few places for entertainment, and their whole lives revolved around Zhongnanhai and its environs. Some leaders, like Ye Jianying, were able to escape tunnel vision by keeping up their own regional connections, returning regularly to cultivate local alliances. But the Gang of Four suffered from being connected only to Shanghai, China's other great metropolis and a peculiar political realm of its own.

The worst problem was that the political atmosphere they created was at odds with reality. Shooting the messenger is a danger in any hierarchy, but literally so in Maoist China. Nobody wanted to say that a programme didn't work or a policy was causing riots when it had been put in place with the centre's approval. During the early stages of the Great Leap Forward, this kind of delusion was pervasive. Staged photos were published of fields of wheat so thick that children could stand on them; and wildly exaggerated numbers were sent up to the centre at the same time as harvests failed and people starved.

Albert Speer, Hitler's architect and a man who knew something about self-deception, described the phenomenon perfectly in his memoirs:

In normal circumstances, people who turn their backs on reality are soon set straight by the mockery and criticism of those around them. In the Third Reich, there was no such corrective, especially for those who belonged to the upper stratum. On the contrary, every self-deception was multiplied as in a hall of distorting mirrors, becoming a repeatedly confirmed picture of a fantastical dream world, which no longer bore any relationship to the grim outside world.[11]

*

Tangshan showed how removed the Gang was from the concerns of most Chinese. Later accounts claimed that, in private, they made remarks like, 'The earthquake in Tangshan affected only one million people, of whom only a few hundred thousand died. It's nothing compared to the criticism of Deng, which is a matter of eight hundred million people.'[12] Yao supposedly improvised a poem that proclaimed, 'Mountains topple and the earth cracks. These are but ordinary happenings. The more hardships we endure, the stronger is our will.' But these are probably just part of the black legend that accumulated around the four ideologues later. However, it was certainly the case that, while Hua Guofeng was visiting the disaster site and building his image as a national leader, the Gang took no such steps. It made it easy for their opponents to suggest that they cared as little for Tangshan as they did about the rest of China.

What the Gang didn't expect was that Hua would play so critical a role in moves against them. He wasn't an obvious enemy, like Wang Dongxing or Ye Jianying, men with whom Jiang, in particular, had been clashing for over two decades. They saw him as essentially a placeholder, a nonentity pushed by circumstances to the top who could be manipulated or ignored.

Jiang, backed by her supporters, had alternately patronised and sniped at him in Politburo meetings. Hua hid his own feelings about the Gang of Four well, placating them at meetings and appearing as a willing peacemaker between the two sides. He gave no inkling of having already cast his lot against the leftists weeks before Mao's death.

In the closed meetings and whispered conspiracies during those tense weeks, one phrase occurred again and again on both sides. It was, as Zhang and Yao reassured each other, 'kill or be killed'. Hua said the same words to Wang Dongxing. In Chinese, it's very blunt: 'You die, I live. I die, you live.' The game was being played for the very highest stakes. And, the plotters had a crucial advantage over the Gang of Four. They were cohesive, knew their enemies, and had a clear goal. The leftists, on the other hand, were scattered and lacked a single-minded aim.

The narrative of the Gang of Four's actions put forward by their enemies later goes like this. After Mao's death, the Gang immediately moved to try to seize power. Jiang, mad with ambition, was convinced that she could now wield authority as her heroine, Wu Zetian, had done after the death of her husband. They began plotting before Mao's body was cold, and it was only the heroic actions of Hua, Wang Dongxing and Ye that nipped their plot in the bud. It bore an obvious parallel with the accusations levelled against Lin Biao in 1971, save that the chances that Lin actually *was* putting concrete plans for a coup in motion are much higher.

It's true that Jiang may have been thinking in those terms, at least on occasion. She loved grandiose language and fantasies about being an empress, after all, even if it seems inconceivable that she didn't recognise how hugely unpopular she would be as a leader. For the moment, the Gang seemed to be moderately content with the idea of a pliant Hua in charge, allowing them to work towards long-term control. They backed him from the start in meetings of the leadership, and, even among themselves, talked about him with condescension, not enmity. In their discussions, such as they were, they obsessed yet again over getting Deng Xiaoping thrown out of the Party, ignoring the threats much closer to them.

Even the earthquake was turned to political ends. 'Be alert to Deng Xiaoping's criminal attempt to exploit earthquake phobia to suppress revolution! Solemnly condemn the capitalist roaders who use the fear of an earthquake to sabotage the denunciation of Deng!' A 200,000-strong rally was held in Chengdu to 'condemn the capitalist roaders who try to hamper the criticism of Deng Xiaoping under the pretext of engaging in earthquake relief work', while a *People's Daily* editorial warned that disasters were often an excuse for counter-revolutionary forces to attempt to topple the righteous government.

The Gang of Four still weren't thinking in terms of seizing power, but intended to purge critical long-term opponents like Ye Jianying, and dispose of Deng Xiaoping for good. They intended to work through Party institutions, not midnight seizures. Ten years of being on top, shielded by Mao, had made them soft, and only half-aware of the danger they were in.

It didn't help that the Gang wasn't much of a gang at all. Wang was convinced of his own revolutionary integrity and the loyalty of his supporters in Shanghai. Jiang was a flailing hysteric certain she was the true inheritor of her husband's legacy, and the tightly knit duo of Zhang and Yao were simultaneously fanatics and opportunists. While they were closer to each other than to anyone else at the centre, and Jiang, in particular, could exert a hypnotic grip over Wang, they actually met, with the exception of Zhang and Yao, relatively rarely in those days.

The narrative put forward later by Hua and his collaborators wasn't entirely self-justification. They genuinely believed, it seems, that the Gang were planning their own coup. After all, it was how Wang, Zhang and Yao had climbed to the top in the first place, seizing the grand chances offered to them by the chaos of the Cultural Revolution. And, as Hua and the others knew, the leftists' position at the centre was dangerously weak.

A seizure of power would be their only chance. Political signals were so confused in China at the time that the appearance of control would have made a huge difference. Even if the majority were against them, the possible consequences of acting, without having any way of knowing that others would back you, were so dire that even an unpopular faction like the Gang could have taken the reins of government, at least for a while. But this would have required an immediate and theatrical seizure of power, not the bureaucratic manoeuvring that the Gang seemed convinced still mattered.

To the Gang's opponents, it simply made no sense that the leftists *weren't* plotting. As a result, Hua and Wang Dongxing became locked into a paranoid interpretation of the Gang's actions. It was like a chessmaster playing a vastly inferior opponent he thinks is ranked at the same level. Small events and petty political moves were elevated into grand plots, ready to be sprung at any moment.

The irony of the Gang's incompetence was that a spectacular coup had propelled them to power in the first place. Wang Hongwen had come to power during the January Storm in Shanghai, when his faction, backed politically and intellectually by Zhang and Yao, had seized power from the old guard of officials, ruthlessly eliminating both them and other radical factions that threatened their power.

The heady rush of that Shanghai winter was a long way away, though, and it had been chance and charisma, rather than scheming, that had left Wang Hongwen, rather than any of his numerous competitors, sitting on top. Zhang and Yao, meanwhile, still longed for the rush of having the crowds on their side. They dreamed of a popular uprising, but 1976 was very different from 1967. There were no crowds waiting to hurry to their side, no hordes of Red Guards looking to overthrow the old order. In their conversations, they kept going back to the Paris Commune, when the citizens' militia had seized power in Paris in 1871 and established a radical government. But the Beijing crowds, as the events of April had so vividly shown, were sick of radicals.

There are three stages to a successful coup. The first is secrecy and intelligence-gathering. The second is seizing the centre and eliminating opponents. The third is presenting the outcome as both inevitable and a moral imperative. A failed coup leaves its forces reeling and vulnerable, able to be rolled up with perfect justification by the putschists' foes.

When it came to intelligence, the Gang failed miserably. The Gang's chief mistake here was failure to identify Hua as their enemy. They were also blind-sided by the involvement of Chen Xilian, with whom they had no particular quarrel, and whose own rise in the military had been helped by stepping on the backs of purged leaders. Nor had they any strong differences with Hua. They supported his confirmation as leader-for-the-moment, even if they thought of him as a figurehead. There were plenty of clues that Hua was pushing for his authority to be more clearly recognised, though, such as his quarrel with Jiang Qing on 21 September over her attempts to claim Mao's papers for herself. He told her clearly that they belonged to the Party, not to her, and had them put under lock and key protected by Wang Dongxing's men. This wasn't enough to put the Gang on guard against him.

The Gang of Four's inability to sniff out the plot against them was quite remarkable, especially given that rumours of it seem to have leaked widely. In Anhui, for instance, one formerly high-ranking Beijing doctor, exiled deep in the countryside in the Anti-Rightist Campaign, received a letter from an old friend in early September, advising him not to worry overmuch, as the leftists would soon be arrested.

The man they had most clearly identified as their enemy was Ye Jianying. He had been a political opponent of the radicals since 1967, and his staged retreat from Politburo affairs in support of Deng only worsened their mistrust of him. Their attempts to keep tabs on him largely consisted of Wang Hongwen moving to a house in the Western Hills that overlooked Ye's residence. For several days he peered down whenever he had a chance, trying to see who was visiting Ye. Then he discovered that in fact Ye had moved to a different home as soon as he had heard about Wang becoming his neighbour. Most of the other spying attempts were similarly clumsy, a case of leaning round doors or interrogating drivers as to where they'd taken their bosses.

Both sides worried about bugs. (As far as the record goes, there's no sign that they were ever justified in doing so; most of the intelligence-gathering seems to have been based on simple questioning and gossip. But the side most likely to use electronic methods would have been Wang Dongxing's men, and they would have an obvious interest in leaving it out of the story afterwards.) They ran showers to cover up discussions, wrote out conversations on paper and burnt them afterwards, or traced characters on each other's hands. Standing over Mao's deathbed, Chen Xilian had apparently communicated to Wang Dongxing 'via hand gestures' that they should arrest the Gang of Four immediately, prompting Wang's reply that they should wait until Mao's death; they must both have been fantastic at charades.

It was in matters of simple physical security that the radicals botched things worse. Unit 8341, the elite guards controlled by Wang Dongxing, ran every aspect of security around Zhong-nanhai and the other imperial buildings. They controlled the gates, chauffeured the leaders and provided the bodyguards. Wang Dongxing, although not politically opposed to the Gang, was a bitter personal enemy of Jiang Qing's, and had been for decades. Entrusting every aspect of their lives to a group run by him was ridiculous.

They were exposed, too, by their dependence on Shanghai as a power base. Shanghai was a long way from Beijing – a two-hour flight or an overnight train ride. And any time they visited there to butter up allies or prepare the military, they risked losing touch with goings-on in the capital. Their very absence could be turned against them, making it seem they were scheming to build their strength in the provinces – the same thing they had accused Zhao Ziyang of doing in Sichuan.

Given their fundamental weaknesses at the centre, the most sensible move would have been for at least one of the Gang to shift permanently to Shanghai. There they would have been shielded by a circle of political allies and a workers' militia primed to follow them. Holding Shanghai would have left them with a valuable bargaining chip in any political negotiations, allowing them at least to maintain some place in whatever new political order now emerged. However, doing that would have required a degree of self-awareness of their situation, of their basic problems in Beijing, and of the hatred that so many in the Politburo felt for them.

Instead, they gave the worst possible impression, flying down to Shanghai to talk to leaders there for a day or two and then back to Beijing. With the Shanghai Revolutionary Committee, mostly sycophants of Wang Hongwen, they talked vaguely about the danger posed by rightists, and about counter-revolutionary forces that threatened the centre. Wang even stated outright that, in the event of a rightist coup, the Shanghai leaders might have to take to the hills and fight as guerrillas.

Zhang may have made a particularly feeble attempt to reach out to the Shanghai military leadership. He approached one of the garrison commanders, and showed him some positions on a map, which he suggested the Shanghai troops should occupy in case of 'invasion'. Well, invasion by whom, the commander wanted to know. Foreign imperialists, Zhang replied. Then why, the commander asked, were the positions all so far from the beaches where the imperialists would be landing?

The biggest military assets of the leftists were the late dictator's son Mao Yuanxin, with his army position, and the people's militia in Beijing. But Mao Yuanxin was travelling about the north-west, organising relief efforts around Tangshan, and they never made proper use of the militia. Zhang was the only one who even put together a bodyguard of his own, assembling some of the biggest and brawniest of the militia into a personal unit he named 'the Bears'.

The plotters around Hua, meanwhile, expected far more concrete action from the Gang of Four than they actually took. Ye Jianying used his extensive network within the PLA closely to monitor potential military moves near the capital. Tangshan was a particular concern. The continuing disaster relief efforts meant that army units were constantly moving in and out of the region. Hua's allies watched the situation carefully, concerned that this could be used as cover for an assault on the capital, only a day away. There was a story told that Mao Yuanxin had tried to shift an armoured division from Shenyang to the capital, commanded by an officer with ties to Wang Hongwen, and that Ye blocked this. But this seems to have been nothing more than rumour, as were stories that Mao had tried to gather support among troops in Tangshan where most of the forces were indeed still tied up in quake relief. A more plausible threat seems to have come from the 6th Tank Division, stationed in a county on the edge of Beijing, which was receiving regular visits from Zhang Chunqiao's younger brother, Zhang Qiuqiao.

The possibility that the Gang might be planning a military advance on the capital disturbed Ye enough for him to warn Hua about it. Hua then consulted with Wu De and was reassured that the Beijing garrison commander was reliable, and that, if necessary, a loyal tank battalion could be brought into play. But Zhang Qiuqiao was a commissar in the PLA, and the visits were a routine part of his job; there would be no epic tank battles for the capital.

Everything was delayed until after the National Day holiday on 1 October. The holiday, commemorating Mao's declaration of the People's Republic from Tiananmen Square in 1949, was marked by vast meetings in memory of Mao. It would have been both logistically nightmarish and politically inappropriate for either side to act while these were going on.

Across the nation, people's nerves were stretched to the limit. 'Even as a child, I knew something was wrong,' one woman recalled, 'Nobody wanted to talk about it, but my parents kept saying things to each other in private about what could be happening in Beijing. My father read the newspaper from cover to cover every day, looking for information.' Like seismologists poring over charts of ground anomalies, the Chinese public looked for signs of the political earthquake they feared was coming.

The atmosphere of fear was particularly strong in Tangshan, although it focused on the possibility of both natural and political disasters. As usual, 'bad elements' were blamed for 'rumour-mongering', specifically the spreading of 'reactionary and superstitious remarks'. Spreading 'false rumours' remains a criminal offence even today in China, often used as an excuse by local authorities to crack down on protestors. It was of particular interest in 1976 when, as the protests in March and April had shown, rumour could be a tremendous political weapon.

In Tangshan, the first thing the authorities were keen to crack down on was any claim that the disaster somehow foreshadowed the fall of the government or future calamities. With Mao dying and Zhao Enlai and Zhu De dead, the earthquake was rapidly worked into a narrative of a 'disastrous year', which implied more disasters to come. It was a direct challenge to the Mandate of Heaven, a blow struck at the very heart of the government's legitimacy.

The most persistent rumour was that the government had known about the quake, but failed to act. They didn't care about Tangshan, or they were caught up in their own power struggles, or it was a deliberate attempt to engineer a disaster that would allow a coup. The government's own insistence on the Haicheng prediction as a miracle of scientific socialism, submissive nature bowing before Maoist ingenuity, came back to haunt it. The idea that there simply hadn't been enough evidence to make a strong prediction was unthinkable, especially as word of Qinglong's actions began to spread among the survivors.

When the men of the Seismological Bureau arrived, people spat at them and threw bricks and stones at their van. They were turned back from food lines. An injured scientist was taken to a medical station, but when he gave his profession, the crowd turned against him. 'Don't treat him, doctor! Let him bleed to death! Why didn't the earthquake get him?' Rumours of future earthquakes were passed on in whispers, most frequently that disaster was going to strike at the government's heart in Beijing – a story told with the occasional hint of vengeful wish fulfilment.

In response, hundreds of propaganda teams were sent across the region to remind people of the government line, going from tent to tent 'expressing the sympathy of the Central Party Committee', and 'to explain the incomparable superiority of the socialist system, explain the great truth that "man can conquer nature", and explain scientific knowledge about earthquakes'. Cars drove through the rubble proclaiming Mao's deep concern for the victims. A new poster showed a worker with his hand thrown up and scenes of disaster relief behind, proclaiming 'Earthquakes don't frighten us! The people will surely vanquish nature!' Meanwhile, higher-level Hebei officials visited Qinglong, already being touted within the State Seismological Bureau as an example of successful prediction, and quietly ordered the leaders there not to publicise the evacuation.

On 5 August, *People's Daily* published a poem reinforcing these themes:

The mountain collapsed and earth cracked but there is no fear
We swear to win victory over the disaster.
When Taishan [a famous mountain] falls on our heads we will not bend
Fighting earthquakes is like forging our red heart.
When the earth sinks we fix it.
When the heavens collapse we hold them up.

The reaction the authorities were looking for is expressed in a wonderfully stilted quote from the official Chinese history of the disaster:

People in the disaster area said with deep feeling, 'In the old society, when a disaster occurred the local authorities and profiteers took advantage of the people's misfortune and the labouring people became destitute and homeless. Today in a socialist society the Party and government have shown the utmost solicitude to people in the disaster area. We have been hit by a natural disaster but are not in distress. Truly, the old and new societies are two different worlds!'[13]

Tangshanese would have been surprised to find that they were not in distress. Howsoever extensive the disaster relief effort, the city had become, in effect, an enormous refugee camp. Ruined houses were cleared and tarpaulins draped over what walls were left to create shelters. The army threw up temporary wooden buildings for the administration of the stricken region, and erected tens of thousands of tents for homeless survivors.

Throughout those weeks, the conspirators continued to see signs that the Gang was planning a counter-coup. One of the most ridiculous centred on the differing interpretations of Mao's final instructions. He had told Hua to 'act according to past principles', but after his death Jiang and the others started to promulgate a different version, that he had instructed his successors to 'act according to the principles laid down'. After reading Jiang's version in several articles published in late September, Hua angrily crossed them out of a document he was sent on 2 October, noting, 'I am striking this out to prevent the wrong version being spread.'[14]

The distinction between the two was, even in the nuance-driven linguistic paranoia of the time, minimal. Whatever his exact words – and Mao had probably uttered both versions at some point – the injunction to continue his work, and specifically the Cultural Revolution, was clear. Indeed, Hua had used the 'principles laid down' version himself on occasion.

But the spat over the wording became, in the words of two experts on the period, 'more a question of ownership and mutual antagonism than any profound ideological confrontation' and 'much ado about nothing'.[15] Hua's insistence on his version demonstrated his determination to be seen as the anointed successor, and to stamp his authority upon the Party. Yao tried to strike a bargain with Hua, pushing the use of both versions in different papers, but all this did was stir further suspicions when an article in *Guangming Daily*, authored by a study group controlled by the Gang, strongly put forward the 'principles laid down' line and went on to condemn 'revisionist chieftains'. Hua and the others saw this as a shot at themselves, and brought plans for the arrest of the Gang forward.

The original plan was to move against the leftists around ten days after National Day, leaving plenty of time to prepare. Ye started to hear rumours, however, that the Gang was claiming there would be 'great news' and a 'happy event' by 9 October. Jiang and Wang, in particular, were making factory and university visits, giving speeches, and attacking the eternal foe, the 'little Deng Xiaopings' and the greater beast behind them. They weren't attacking Hua and the others, but instead harping on about old enemies. Beating Deng for a second time had left them so satisfied that they kept focusing attacks on him and his supposed allies, rather than looking around to find genuine threats. When Jiang spoke of 'extraordinarily happy news', what she was probably referring to was the formal plenum of the Central Committee that would confirm her place in the post-Mao leadership.

Jiang's behaviour had a touch of hysteria about it. Losing her husband, and her political rock, had thrown her way off balance. She continued to launch into long rants in front of befuddled audiences, warned darkly of political enemies while continuing to ignore Hua, and ranted endlessly on about the role of women, which did nothing but hand her opponents ammunition. Her fixation on female leadership was easily turned against her; Wu Zetian, her model, had been a hate-figure for generations of patriarchal leaders, and the image of malevolent, usurping feminine power was easy for Hua and his group to exploit.

One of the last events Jiang and the others appeared at together as a group was a photo call, sometime around 3–4 October. The photographers were puzzled at the nature of the pictures they were asked for, which seemed to involve an unusual number of close-ups and a particular set of grimaces. Then they realised: they were poses for placard portraits of the type carried at parades. It was a pointlessly arrogant and presumptive gesture, sadly typical of many of the Gang's efforts since Mao's death.

Hua and the others saw strength and conspiracy in the Gang's various blunderings. Organised and determined themselves, it was hard for them to comprehend that their opponents could be so inept. Some of their fears were exaggerated or concocted afterwards, naturally, as part of the line that their own coup had been necessitated by the imminence of the Gang's, but they were also genuinely nervous. The article in *Guangming Daily* and the rumours about the plots pushed their plans forward by several days. Ye, Hua and Wang Dongxing agreed between themselves that they had to act now.

Still nervous about being watched, Hua took a circuitous route to Wang's home in Zhongnanhai, despite living extremely close by, and arrived just before midnight on 4 October. They sat up until 3:00, working themselves into a state of nervous exhaustion as they sketched out the details. Hua was worried about going home, where his late arrival might be noted by whatever watchers the Gang had set – as usual, they were attributing far more competence to the four than they possessed – and instead slept in temporary accommodation in Zhongnanhai, with a platoon of bodyguards personally picked by Wang placed outside his door.

The next morning they took separate cars to visit Ye, who was now, after moving from his old home to evade Wang Hongwen's spying, living in a mountainside villa inside the Summer Palace, another imperial resort. It was entirely appropriate that all this scheming took place inside the homes of the old emperors.

The plot for the arrest itself was beautifully simple. Wang Hongwen, Zhang and Yao were told to come to an 8:00 a.m. meeting on 5 October to discuss some revisions to chapter 5 of Mao Zedong's collected works. The legacy of the Chairman was serious business, and the three arrived at Huairen Hall in Zhongnanhai, a two-storey pagoda which was one of the regular meeting points for the leadership, ready for a heated ideological discussion. Zhang, foolishly, left his minders, his 'bears', behind.

Wang Hongwen was the first to arrive, coming through the door only to be seized by Unit 8341 guards, handpicked once again by Wang Dongxing, who was waiting with them in the reception hall. He tried to fight them off, shouting 'I'm here for a meeting!' and trying to pull out his gun, but was handcuffed and marched into the meeting room, where Ye and Hua were waiting. They read out charges against him, accusing him of 'crimes against the Party'. As he was marched away, he reportedly muttered 'I wasn't expecting it this soon . . .' Yao and Zhang went down more easily. Zhang, his glasses misted over, kept saying 'What's going on?' when he was grabbed, then said nothing as the charges were read out. Yao shouted out 'How dare you!' as the guards seized him, but is said to have fainted when told of the charges.

As these arrests were going on, a group of guards led by the commander of Unit 8341 knocked on the door of Zhongnanhai Building 201, to which Jiang Qing had recently moved. It was much easier than arresting her in her normal residence in Diaoyutai, where she had a considerable entourage; in Zhongnanhai she was more or less alone. The official accounts have her wearing silk pyjamas and watching a Hong Kong movie; neither of which is that implausible, but these decadent touches are a little suspicious. According to Mao's doctor, she looked at the commander as he announced the charges, and remarked 'You too! I have long anticipated this day!'[16] (Other accounts have her more confused, asking 'Why? Why?')

The Gang were placed in cells in the underground nuclear shelters, the same network in which Mao's body was being pickled. Across Beijing, Wang's men moved to pinch off the Gang's allies. Mao Yuanxin was seized – though without any formal charges, unlike the Gang – in his quarters at Zhongnanhai, while several supporters in the Ministry of Culture and other departments were quietly arrested, as were the Party secretary and vice-secretary of Tsinghua University, close followers of Jiang Qing. Most critically, they arrived at important media outlets, including *People's Daily* and *Liberation Daily*, and abruptly announced that they were under a new management. By 9:35 that morning, every prominent supporter of the Gang in Beijing was neutralised and Hua and Wang controlled the media. It was a precise surgical strike; now they just had to explain it to the rest of the leadership, and then the country.

The leadership wasn't a hard sell. Hua, Wang and Ye announced the arrests, presented as a forestalling of the Gang's own planned coup, to the Politburo that evening back at Ye's villa. Many of them already had a vague idea what had been planned, but the events themselves came as a surprise. It was clearly a done deal, and nobody present was willing to go down with the Gang, so there was almost no dissent. To make sure, none of them were allowed to return home that evening, instead sitting up for an all-night meeting.

Many of those present were jubilant at the news; Chen Xilian and his two roommates at Zhongnanhai, also both high-level officials, leapt about and excitedly hugged each other, despite all of them having been seen as allies of the leftists in the past. The celebrations were prompted by more than just personal dislike of the Gang; there was a feeling of deep relief that the uncertainty was over, and that a clear new order was emerging. That same evening, the Politburo officially voted Hua in as both Chairman and head of the Central Military Commission, the two most important posts in the country.

Announcing the news to the rest of the country, when the public had already shown their feelings about the 'Shanghai clique' and 'Jiang's little court' so vehemently, wasn't going to be that demanding. The information would be distributed to the regional leaders first, then down through the ranks, and finally be announced to a public already primed by rumour for the news.

The biggest problem was Shanghai, the Gang's power base and the second most important city in China. The Shanghai leadership had been worked up by Wang and Zhang into a fine state of justified paranoia. When Ma Tianshui and Zhou Chunlin, respectively head of the Shanghai Garrison Command and head of the Revolutionary Committee, were called to Beijing on 7 October for a meeting, it was a clear sign that something was up, since usually Wang or one of the others contacted the Shanghai leaders to let them know about important meetings beforehand. Anxious phone calls to the capital were in vain, and they had been unable to reach any of the Gang of Four or their allies.

The Shanghai bosses devised a code to let Ma and Zhou inform them about any threats, since their phone lines would invariably be tapped. 'My ulcer is acting up again' meant 'the rightists have gained the upper hand', 'good health' meant everything was OK, and 'a heart attack' indicated an actual coup. Ma and Zhou were kidnapped by Unit 8341 virtually as soon as they landed, and subjected to an intimidating series of meetings where they were told of the fall of the Gang of Four and bombarded with an impressive array of ideological reasons for the correctness of the new regime. Ma's secretary, meanwhile, managed to call the Shanghai Revolutionary Committee at noon on 8 October and inform them of the dire state of his ulcer, which prompted them to send another delegate to Beijing to investigate. He called back at midnight, with worse news; his mother had suffered, he said meaningfully, a 'heart attack'.

The Shanghai leaders panicked. They put the militia on high alert, and started distributing weapons, setting up command stations, and commandeering motorcycles, cars and a patrol boat. The next morning, they got a call from allies in Beijing that Hua had been officially appointed Chairman, but, more critically, they finally got through to Ma Tianshui. They asked him what was going on, and he assured them that everything was fine, and that 'I've seen [Zhang, Yao and Wang], they're all quite well, though rather busy and unable to talk to me one on one.'[17] The militia were stood down, and the Revolutionary Committee concluded that Hua must have the leftists' blessing, and that somebody else had been the victim of a brief internal struggle.

Ma, of course, was sitting in Beijing with a gun to his head – more or less literally. He was severely stressed by the sudden reversal of political fortunes, and later suffered a serious mental breakdown. Two other members of the Shanghai Revolutionary Committee went up to join him, and were promptly grabbed, told of the new reality, and given very little option but to conform. None of them had any stomach for a fight. In the meetings in Beijing, the coup had been presented to them as a *fait accompli*, and they had no desire to throw their lives away. They were no longer the young men who had bloodily seized power in 1967, but comfortable officials at the top of the totem pole, and they were keen to make their accommodation with the new order.

A couple of days later, news of the arrest of the Gang, though still not official, was now so widely rumoured that the Shanghai leaders became agitated again. In a last-ditch burst of rhetoric, one hardline supporter called, at a meeting on 12 October, for serious action:

Let's begin right now! Before six tomorrow morning, let's blow up all bridges, destroy all railways and highways, stop the armed troops of Jiangsu and Zhejiang provinces from entering Shanghai, and bring the industrial production of Shanghai to a halt. We should occupy the key departments. As soon as the action starts, we'll put up posters, create public opinion, and raise the slogan 'Release Jiang Qing! Release Chunqiao! Release Wenyuan! Release Hongwen!'

We'll also occupy the broadcasting station and issue a letter to the people of the entire country and the entire world! We'll be resolute to fight to the end. We'll fight like the Paris Commune members. If we can hold out for a week, we are bound to get the support of people of the entire country and the world. Even if we lose the battle, we shall have given a lesson in blood to later generations. But if we do not fight now, we'll leave only shame in the future.[18]

This was the kind of speech which, in 1966 or 1967, could have thrown a city into chaos. If the plan had been carried out, it would have been a huge political crisis for Beijing, and possibly provoked uprisings by hardcore supporters of the Gang elsewhere. But although people cheered, nobody showed any willingness to take to the barricades. Within a few days, the news of the Gang's fall was met with such widespread jubilation that any thoughts of a people's stand were abandoned.

The first ordinary Chinese came to know about the coup was on 15 October, when wall-posters started going up. The politically well-connected had known about it days before, of course – the UK *Daily Telegraph* reported it on 12 October, and anyone with connections knew about it in Beijing by the 10th. But although most people had heard that something had happened at the centre, just who had won out was still uncertain. People watched as the first characters were put on to the wall-posters. 'Down with . . .' – they strained their necks to see the next words. Down with whom? 'The Gang of Four!' This left most people scratching their heads; the 'Gang of Four' could be anyone. Mao's label for the leftists had been confined to the inner circles of the Party. Then the names went up.

The list of the Gang's crimes given to the public was extensive. They were accused of:

. . . keeping a nation of 800 million living in constant fear, ruthlessly attacking Party members, nearly destroying an economy, threatening civil war, committing national betrayal, hampering foreign trade, ruining the educational system, and preventing a single poem or play from being printed much less published without their approval.[19]

In a classic case of over-kill, some gossip was thrown in for good measure. This last was mostly about Mao's personal relations with Jiang, mixed in with some sexual scandal of the type often thrown at deposed and unpopular consorts.

For the public, the nature of the crimes showed clearly that this wasn't just the end of another set of leaders; it was, to one degree or another, the repudiation of the whole of the last ten years. That hadn't been Hua and Wang's intention: they were still determined to follow Mao's instructions to hew to the spirit of the Cultural Revolution, despite its mistakes. But people read the events nonetheless as the beginning of a new era.

The country heaved a sigh of relief. Foreign students in Beijing at the time remember a sudden openness on the part of their Chinese counterparts, a willingness to discuss things about which they'd been previously reticent or merely parroted a Party line. On 21 October, there was a mass parade in Tiananmen Square; in contrast to the lifeless anti-Deng parades in April, people flocked to join it, laughing and singing and setting off firecrackers. Many stores sold out of alcohol. People pinned up caricatures of the Gang, or defaced existing posters, with Jiang Qing being the most frequent target; one of the crudest and most common showed her with a speech bubble saying 'I suck dick.'

A certain amount of bandwagon jumping was going on, but the contrast between the jubilation with which the fall of the Gang was greeted and the hostile response to the campaign against Deng in April was enormous. Across China, local politicians scrambled to react. There were isolated clashes between die-hard leftists and the security forces, but they involved little beyond stone-throwing and shouting slogans. The vast majority of the Gang's supporters proved fair-weather followers, quite ready to adjust to the new order as long as it meant keeping their positions. After all, they could reassure themselves, the new leadership had promised to maintain the legacy of the Cultural Revolution. Surely their hard-won positions weren't in danger?

Cartoonists were allowed to unleash their most vicious satirical style, which they did with relish; the Gang were shown as fleeing demons, as rats and pigs, being trampled under children's feet in New Year's games, as three slaves led by a dominatrix-like Jiang Qing, having their photograph taken with Lin Biao, holding flags covered in swastikas, the Nationalist flag, and the rising sun of Japan, as gremlins sabotaging factories, as cackling goblins dancing round a bonfire of scientific textbooks and literary classics, and as tyrants forcing the great men of the past to kneel before them. Their infamy spread to every level; when one American, just arrived that winter from Detroit to work in Harbin, asked her young children what game they'd been playing that afternoon with their Chinese friends, they said 'Moooom! Smash the Gang of Four, *of course!*'

Among those who could afford it, a popular meal that autumn was crabs. Invitations were sent out. 'Please come and join us to celebrate the elimination of the "sideways-walkers".'[20] In Chinese stories, crabs were depicted as bullies, blocking the road for other creatures with their sideways scuttle. If possible, diners ordered one female crab and three males. The original four crabs themselves were now locked up in Qincheng Prison, a notorious institution near Beijing; it was the same jail that had once been used to hold many high-level political prisoners that the Gang had helped imprison.

As with the death of Mao, the fall of the Gang made little impact in Tangshan. 'We were pleased,' Chang Qing recalled, 'Of course, we were pleased. And I was very happy that Hua was now Chairman. He was a good man and I trusted him. But it wasn't a big concern.' They had nothing to spare for celebration, and much more immediate priorities.

National industry continued to override the needs of the Tangshan people. The limited electricity available was being used to fuel industry, not heat or light homes, and the still greatly reduced output of the coal mines went to factories elsewhere in Hebei.

Official media coverage of the disaster had dropped to almost nothing. Images of internal refugees and shanty towns didn't blend with socialist triumph. Propaganda about Tangshan's rebuilding reached delusional levels. The public was told that Tangshan citizens, thanks to the Party, were living better lives after the earthquake than they had ever done before. 'The number of restaurants and shops in the city has increased by 30 per cent,' proclaimed one report. After the initial fund-raising campaign, there were no channels for public donations. Word of the real extent of the devastation spread by mouth, prompting many to send private gifts to relatives or friends in the destroyed city, or to use their connections to arrange for their families to be moved to other provinces.

The winter cold was beginning to set in, and hundreds of thousands of people were still homeless. Even those who had shelter were reluctant to use it, terrified of the roofs over their heads. Families slept en masse, both because of a lack of bedding and to share body heat. The price of blankets, coats and fuel soared.

As people shivered in Tangshan, the Politburo made its final decisions about how to dispose of Mao. On 24 November, the first ground was broken on Mao's vast mausoleum, situated right in the centre of Tiananmen Square. Hua inscribed the calligraphy on the memorial stone, signing off on Mao's legacy for himself. Come the next May, the mausoleum would be opened, and Mao would be enshrined inside in a crystal coffin, ready for the crowds.

On 19 December 1976, in the back of a prison van on a frozen morning in the northern city of Changchun, a young man stared into the barrel of a gun. A couple of years earlier, in October 1974, Party organisations across the city had received leaflets denouncing Mao's personality cult. 'Even the leader of the Party is a common Party member! Oppose blind loyalty! Oppose individual worship! The CCP does not need a Party Emperor! The so-called Cultural Revolution is nothing but extreme leftist politics going out of control!'[21] A poster went up in the centre of town expressing the same sentiments.

The resulting investigation involved 300 detectives and 6,300 supporting staff. The leaflets had been reported to Beijing, where Wang Hongwen had expressed his serious concern, and signed off on the investigation with the rest of the Gang of Four. They were expecting to find a veteran cadre or other potentially juicy political opponent behind the affair, and were disappointed when it turned out to be Shi Yunfeng – an ordinary, if idealistic, worker at an optical instrument factory. Only twenty-six years old, his protests arose from nothing more than close reading of Marxist texts and his own sense of fairness.

Shi lingered in prison for months. As the day of his execution drew close, Shi's mother desperately petitioned the provincial Party headquarters. 'Why has the Gang been smashed, and he is still to be killed?' But the local Party boss, Wang Huaixiang, had been a keen supporter of the Gang,[22] and was now determined to protect his own shaky political position by demonstrating his loyalty to the Chairman's memory.

Shi was dragged out before a mass rally, wearing a billboard announcing his crimes, but he wouldn't play along. He kept shouting 'Unfair!' until his hands were bound, anaesthetic injected into his throat to stop him from speaking, and, for good measure, his mouth stuffed with cotton balls and his lips sewn up with surgical thread. He was bundled into a prison van, where his executioner drew a pistol and fired several shots into his forehead. Even months after the Chairman's death, criticising Mao could be fatal.

7 Aftershocks

Hua Guofeng emerged triumphant from the ruins of 1976. His picture went up next to Mao's on the Gate of Heavenly Peace, smiling down benevolently at the morning crowds at the daily flag-raising ceremony. The propaganda machinery began churning out posters of him in familiar Maoist poses, inspiring factory teams or being touched worshipfully by the simple folk of China's ethnic minorities.

A second series of posters revealed Hua's essential vulnerability. They showed him in a position Mao never assumed, performing routine chores, and drawn in a pencilled low-key style very different to the bold colours and square-jawed socialist supermen of early posters. Here was Hua cleaning a countertop at a pharmacy, or serving dinner in a communal hall. The attempts to project a leader with the common touch, immersed in everyday duties, showed up the cult-like nature of the other posters.

Hua's first problem was that, having been pitchforked to the higher levels of the Party only in the 1970s, he didn't have anything like the base of power or connections that Deng and his allies possessed. Besides, he didn't carry himself like a leader. His affability and skill as a social and political chameleon had been a big asset in his sudden ascent, but he lacked the kind of charisma, bite and insight needed to hang on at the peak of power. He never lost the look of a man who didn't quite know what he was doing in charge of 800 million people.

Hua's greatest failing was his inability to distinguish himself from the Cultural Revolution, and to embrace the deep-rooted desire for change. Nothing new was being offered here, only a watered-down version of the same old thing. Mao's blessing had carried him into power, but now, with the Chairman's heritage his chief source of legitimacy, he found himself trapped in a dead man's shadow.

The only new slogan Hua had to offer up was the 'Two Whatevers', one of the most feeble ideological efforts in Chinese political history – as well as sounding oddly like Valley Girl slang in its English translation. (It's narrowly rivalled only by Jiang Zemin's later 'Three Represents', a set of slogans of such extraordinarily deadening dullness and obscurity that even in Chinese they sound like they've been badly translated from a foreign language.) What bold words would carry China into its new era? 'We will resolutely uphold whatever policy decisions Chairman Mao made, and unswervingly follow whatever instructions Chairman Mao gave!'

The prospect of a continuation of Maoism had no appeal either for a public desperate for change or for a political elite who had spent the last decade under the Chairman's thumb. The Two Whatevers were dead in the water.

It wasn't entirely Hua's fault. The same allies who had helped him plot the coup against the Gang of Four, especially Wang Dongxing, pressed the policy upon him, demanding guarantees both of their own political–military power bases and of the ultimate legitimacy of the Cultural Revolution. They were derisively labelled the 'Whateverists', and the public were all too aware of the close ties many of them, like Chen Xilian and Wu De, had had with the disgraced Gang of Four.

Hua's attempts to invoke the talismanic power of Mao only served to remind people of his singular lack of leadership skills. His attempts to build up his own personality cult were not only another reminder of Mao's excesses, but came across as presumptuous and unearned. As Mao's clouded mental state during most of 1976 came to light, the blessing he gave to Hua started to carry less weight.

Meanwhile, Deng waited in the wings. The strange thing about his return was how inevitable it felt. For a man who had been the subject of a massive vilification campaign just a year before, and who had been stripped of all his positions, he returned to the top of Chinese politics with amazing speed. Deng was soon released from house arrest and given back his title of vice-chairman. The consensus was that the campaign against him had been an embarrassment best forgotten, a last spasm of the Gang of Four. From his new apartments in Zhongnanhai, he began to rally his allies and move against Hua.

It was a striking testament to his talent, to the ability of the Chinese public to shrug off propaganda, and to the propensity of many officials to shift with the Party line in order to keep their own privileges. Despite the big talk of guerrilla campaigns, very few of the one-time radicals were willing to risk their lives, or even their careers, in opposing Deng's rise. By the late seventies many local politicians who had once been fanatical leftists had calcified into political realists, and with the radical push from the centre gone, no new enthusiasm for revolutionary adventures was coming from the grassroots.

Deng didn't mince words when dealing with the 'Two Whatevers'. 'It will not do,' he said bluntly, 'In accordance with this doctrine, my rehabilitation is unjustifiable, and it is likewise unjustifiable to affirm that the activities of the broad masses of people at Tiananmen Square in 1976 were "reasonable".'[1] He pointed out that Mao, like other Communist luminaries from Marx to Stalin, had never claimed infallibility, and brought up the 70–30 doctrine that Mao liked to apply to his own efforts; '70 per cent correct' would soon become a standard verdict on Maoism, and especially on the Cultural Revolution itself.

Deng appreciated, more than anyone else at the top, the vast reservoir of public bitterness and anger the Cultural Revolution had left behind. True, the Whateverists had the millions of provincial cadres who had been promoted during the Cultural Revolution on their side. They were acutely aware that the political shift left them critically vulnerable, especially if the justification for their seizure of power was condemned from the centre. They figured, too, that the people they'd displaced, imprisoned and tortured during their rise to power would be only too keen to take revenge, or their families would. After all, it had happened after every other political hurricane of the last thirty years.

Deng knew that the beneficiaries of the Cultural Revolution were vastly outnumbered by those it had damaged. He began by starting a campaign to reinstate provincial cadres who had lost power over the previous decade – 400,000 in Hebei alone, for instance, and millions more across the country. This created a bureaucracy increasingly loyal to him. At the same time, he used the newly reinstated officials and his own political allies to purge the beneficiaries of the Cultural Revolution, putting his own men into place as each leftist official was pushed out.

At the centre, Deng concentrated on cracking Hua's fragile coalition of allies, spreading rumours and pressuring his own friends, such as the military leader Wei Guoqing, to withdraw their support of Hua. He concentrated on departments, such as the foreign ministry and the navy, which were full of old allies of Zhou Enlai. He was helped by Zhao Ziyang, the powerful Sichuan leader who had been attacked by the Gang of Four over the small earthquake there. Zhao, like Deng, saw Hua as a jumped-up no-account bureaucrat, and from the very start of his administration pointedly refused to back him.

Deng's third line of attack was intellectual and populist at the same time. He launched a new slogan in 1978, 'Seek truth from facts', a pointed contrast with the leftists' insistence on the primacy of ideology over reality. With his sponsorship, a 'Democracy Campaign' began in 1978. Hua was bullied into acquiescing in the campaign, which was both a genuine outpouring of popular feeling and another excuse to attack Hua's supporters.

In Beijing, a 'Democracy Wall' was established, on which people pinned big-character posters, long essays and slogans. The original postings were taken from a magazine, closed down on Wang Dongxing's orders, that had reproduced many of the poems of April 1976. Deng was particularly interested in promoting the idea of the rule of law, both in contrast to the anarchy of the last decade and in order to show that Hua's appointment as Premier had no clear legal backing. The idea of 'the rule of law', as opposed to 'the rule of man', came up over and over again.

'Scar literature', often semi-autobiographical, became popular. The protagonists were victims of Cultural Revolution persecution, such as in Liu Xinwu's groundbreaking story 'Class Teacher'. As indicated by the name, it concentrated upon the lingering mental and physical effects of the persecutions, not upon the political origins. The public ate up these tales of suffering and redemption through love, family or a renewed faith in Marxism. The government gave the genre tentative support, as long as it didn't veer too far from the official line.

One of the finest artistic responses came in the form of an exhibition in Guangdong, organised by the great cartoonist Liao Bingxiong, along with five other artists. It was hugely popular, attracting over 10,000 visitors a day. Liao had been active in the 1940s and 1950s, penning scathing depictions of Chinese corruption and colonial oppression, followed by propaganda work for the New China. He'd been caught up in the Anti-Rightist Campaign in 1956, and had sworn off cartooning, producing no new work for twenty-two years. Suddenly, following the fall of the Gang of Four, he began to work again.

Outside the exhibition, a standing tombstone was dedicated to 'Comrade Zhang Zhixin'. Zhang had been an ordinary middle-aged woman, and a critic of ultra-leftist policies in 1969. She had been arrested, imprisoned, raped, tortured and finally executed by decapitation, with her vocal cords slit first so that she couldn't cry out Marxist slogans at the end. Her two daughters, aged ten and eighteen, had been made to sign a document before her death.

Even though she gave birth to me and is my mother, she is a counter-revolutionary and is my enemy. She opposes the Party and Chairman Mao, and we must continue to struggle against her.[2]

A mirror had been placed above the tombstone, along with an invitation to all Party members to look in it, and measure themselves against Zhang's standards. It was a startling piece of confrontational memory, and the works inside the exhibition were no less powerful. One of the first showed Liao himself, freshly reborn from a broken burial urn, but his body still clenched in the shape of the urn. 'After the fall of the four demons,' the caption read, 'This is for me, and all the others like me.'

It was followed by a series of extraordinary works entitled 'Annals of a Nightmare', reminiscent of Goya's black paintings.[3] They mixed images of the Red Guards and the Gang of Four with the images of traditional Chinese culture, both heroes and demons. Here was Judge Bao, a renowned detective and magistrate, wearing a placard saying 'Big Black Gang' and arrested for political crimes by creatures of the underworld, the Red Guard usurping the role of judge of the dead and condemning scholars and philosophers, and gleefully elevating famous traitors to heroes.

The final cartoon showed a land awash with blood, with ruined walls labelled 'Cultural Revolution' and placards of Mao floating in the carnage. In a touch of hope, two large goldfish, a symbol of prosperity and happiness, are being hooked from the sea of red, but blood splatters fly from them as they are lifted up.

Most daringly, another of Liao's cartoons showed a fat cat in imperial robes. (Cat is *mao* in Chinese, though with a different tone to Mao's name.) It watches smugly as rats steal fish. The caption goes 'This cat, with his air of a god, sees the rats but doesn't catch them.' A final picture showed Liao's worries, as a clearly fanatical figure pores over the new liberal texts – noting down names for future use. This would be unfortunately prescient, although it would be pragmatists, not fanatics, who oversaw the next wave of persecution.

By the Party conference of December 1978, Deng had firm control. Hua was able to cling on as Premier for the moment, but his supporters were ousted, and Deng effectively ran the country. He began economic reforms, drawing on experiments by Zhao Ziyang in Sichuan, and set out to improve relations with Western powers. His biggest achievement was the official recognition of the PRC by the US government, building on Zhou Enlai's previous work. It was good for both sides, even if it did leave the Taiwanese convinced that Jimmy Carter, the then US president, was history's greatest monster.[4]

Apparently determined to demonstrate emphatically the shared values of the US and China, Deng went on to invade Vietnam in February 1979. The nominal excuse was border clashes, but the real reason was a long-running split over influence in the region and, in particular, China's discontent with Vietnam's ousting of Cambodian dictator Pol Pot, a Beijing protégé who had managed, proportionately, to excel even the Chinese standards for mass murder. In Chinese, with the usual over-protestation of innocence, it was called the 'Counterattack Against Vietnam in Self-Defence'.

The operation was a three-week, 100,000-man *chevauchée* that culminated in a brutal Chinese retreat, burning granaries and factories and murdering thousands of Vietnamese as they left. In turn, the Vietnamese persecuted ethnic Chinese, driving many of them out of the country. The campaign exposed the PLA's incompetence at fighting a real army, rather than a gaggle of civilians; losses may have run as high as a quarter of their men and half of their tanks.

The war finished the Democracy Movement, as protestors started to turn on Deng himself. Deng ordered a crackdown, going back to the usual language of 'counter-revolutionaries' and 'bad elements'. He evoked the spectre of the chaos of 1966 as he warned of 'ultra-democracy and anarchism'. With their usefulness over, Deng, like Mao, was quite willing to discard one-time allies. He would have very little truck with criticism of the Party's right to rule or with talk of democracy in the future.

Deng's anti-Hua campaign intensified. With his power base destroyed by Deng's manipulations, Hua was left stranded at the top. Many of his allies were pushed out at the 1979 Party conference, and Politburo meetings started to take on an increasingly bullying tone, as Hua was berated for his lack of abilities and the way he had assumed the Premiership. He soon capitulated, agreeing to resign his most important official titles. The final verdict was exceptionally humiliating, with Hua having to confess, before the rest of the Politburo, that he had never been capable of running the nation and had been promoted far beyond his abilities. By now his power was formal at best, and Deng and Hu Yaobang were effectively performing his job duties.

In his purge of China's top ranks, Deng was careful to signal that the days of exile and murder were over. Apart from the Gang of Four themselves, the ousted leaders were almost all put out to grass in comfortable sinecures, not imprisoned or executed. Deng would have hated the comparison, but the decision was very similar to Khrushchev's own actions against his fellow members of the Stalinist old guard in the 1950s, where once-powerful figures were stripped of their chief responsibilities and dispatched to minor positions – Stalin's foreign minister, Molotov, found himself appointed Soviet ambassador to Mongolia.

Hua and Wang Dongxing, for instance, were allowed to retain membership of top-level committees and to keep a variety of impressive official titles, while being kept away from any actual power or influence. Their children were permitted to rise to comfortable mid-level jobs in the army or state administration. The message was clear: the political game at the top levels would no longer be fought for fatal stakes.

The relative mercy shown at the top was echoed throughout the country. The focus was on rehabilitating the victims of the Cultural Revolution, not punishing the perpetrators. In one typical Hebei town, Raoyang, studied by the political scientist Edward Friedman, 1,241 people branded as 'bad elements' had their cases reviewed, and all but five of them were cleared. The investigations went back to the pre-Cultural Revolution era: out of 622 older cases, mostly dating from the Anti-Rightist Campaign, 564 were cleared. People were re-labelled as ordinary peasants, and no longer branded with the black mark of wealth. Out of 93 people in Raoyang who had been tortured, 77 were cleared.

The torturers themselves faced no great repercussions, though across the country tens of thousands of 'helicoptered' officials were demoted. Those who were found guilty of serious crimes lost their jobs, but rarely faced worse. Humiliation and degradation were usually as bad as it got, and even that was limited. 'Three kinds of people [were condemned]. Those who followed the Lin Biao and Jiang Qing cliques, those obsessed with factionalist ideas, and people who engage in smashing, beating and looting.'

The courts did try a few people involved in atrocities, but punishments were restricted, and rarely exceeded relatively short sentences. In Dao County, Hunan, for instance, the site of a massacre of over 4,000 people in 1967, 42 of the perpetrators were arrested in 1986 after a protracted investigation, and each sentenced to ten years in prison. The killings and rapes had been so bad that another 12 people, who had originally been arrested during the Cultural Revolution itself, were also condemned to serve short jail terms. Although 54 people had been punished, unofficial estimates showed that over 14,000 people must have been involved in the atrocities in Dao County.

The decision not to start a new round of persecutions was a clear sign that the days of fractured violence were over. The signals coming from the centre weren't the only reason for the lack of vengeance. The public was tired of politics and of killings. This hardly served justice, but it kept the peace. Many powerful local figures survived simply by switching to the Deng team as soon as it was obvious who was going to win. People had to keep working, living and serving on committees with the same people who had tortured them and killed their relatives, but the cycle of politicised revenge that had been repeated every few years in the countryside since 1945 was broken.

Even the Gang of Four faced imprisonment, not execution. Their show trial was held in 1980, when they were accused of having persecuted 727,240 people and being responsible for the deaths of 34,274 – a fraction of the real figures, with the victims' names carefully selected for maximum sympathy value and ideological correctness. Jiang Qing sneered at the court, smirking and yawning as the indictment was read, and insisting on conducting her own defence.

The prosecution combined the usual mixture of personal insult with legalistic denunciation, but tried to keep Mao's name as far from the listed crimes as possible. It was Jiang who kept bringing him back in, insisting – completely truthfully – that much of the time she'd been operating entirely in line with her husband's wishes. 'I was the one who stood by Chairman Mao Zedong! Arresting me and bringing me to trial is a defamation of Chairman Mao! . . . Do you think I was a monster with six arms and three heads, capable of doing all this by myself?'[5] Wang Hongwen, meanwhile, all but collapsed, admitting, with due expressions of shame, his role in starting riots and persecuting the innocent.

In the end Wang got life, Yao twenty years, and Jiang and Zhang got 'suspended' death sentences – an odd Chinese form of verdict, today most frequently handed out to corrupt officials and business executives, which in theory is designed to allow the criminal to 'reform', but in practice inevitably results in the sentence being commuted to 'life' (and, nowadays, a quiet release a few years later). Jiang hanged herself in 1991 after developing throat cancer, Wang died of cancer in prison the next year, while Yao and Zhang were released in old age and died in closely monitored obscurity.

As for Hua, the rest of his life was quiet. He occasionally complained to his children about mistakes he felt his successors were making, but he was never dominated by bitterness. His main interest became cultivating grapes. A famous photo taken at the 2007 Party Congress showed a crumpled Hua enjoying a nap as the delegates spoke. His death in August 2008 received extremely low-key coverage from the Chinese media, unwilling to remind people of a period of 'political errors'. For most people his time in power was a half-remembered curiosity.

Although he never took on either of what were, nominally, the country's two top jobs, Party Chairman or Premier, Deng was now undoubtedly the most powerful figure in China. Instead, he appointed two of his close allies, Hu Yaobang and Zhao Ziyang, to these positions. No new portraits went up next to Mao's as Hua's came down. Deng's own verdict on Hua's reign was brutal, but accurate. Hua's rule had been 'just a transition, not an epoch. His policies were a continuation of the late Mao's, and there was nothing original about him.'[6] Deng was determined that his own rule would be far more transformative.

And it was. Deng's new policies of 'reform and opening' let loose a gigantic flood of creative and economic energy, especially from the countryside. Farmers were released from the constraints of the collectivist system, and labour increasingly freed to move around the country. With the creation of Special Economic Zones in the south, huge factories sprang up, ready to put the flood of migrant workers to good use on the assembly line.

Individual entrepreneurs became multi-millionaires, taking to heart Deng's injunction that it was alright for some to 'get rich first'. Many of them wouldn't last, falling victim to accusations – mostly true – of mass corruption, political battles, or, in the case of Xinjianese businesswoman Rebiya Kadeer, who went from running a laundry to a gigantic cross-border trade empire, to charges of ethnic separatism. Millions of others moved from their marginal existence in the countryside to middle-class prosperity in cities and towns.

In the 1980s, the items everybody wanted shifted from radios, bicycles, sewing machines and watches to televisions, refrigerators, washing machines and tape decks. The four aspirational items of the 1970s put together cost an average worker two years' income; in the early 1980s, a mere seven months of savings sufficed. Private cars returned to the roads, though in very small numbers at first. Beijing began sprouting multi-storey apartment buildings and freshly built compounds, with walls and guards to keep the riff-raff out, as well as two new ring roads to cope with the influx of traffic.[7]

Tangshan came late to this new prosperity. For years after the earthquake, Tangshanese continued to live in what was in reality a gigantic refugee camp. It wasn't until 1979–80 that serious rebuilding of houses began, and as late as 1983 two-thirds of survivors still lacked permanent homes. In the meantime, they lived in lean-to shacks built of wood and tin, from where they travelled to work in factories with still-leaking roofs. Quake fears meant many people were reluctant to move into the new buildings, scared to have anything solid above their heads again. Some moved away, such as He Jianguo, who married and went to work as a teacher in the southern province of Anhui, but most stayed, whether out of *hukou* restrictions, work commitments or civic pride.

The city was essentially rebuilt by 1986 – to exhaustive anti-earthquake standards. It benefitted from the industrial boom of the 1980s, its coal now fuelling factories turning out cheap toys and plastic goods for the export market. Older Tangshanese are still very proud of the new buildings of the era, clean, well-built and safe compared to the past, and a symbol of the city's resilience. They're proud, too, of their mines, which maintain safety standards far higher than the infamous private operations which surfaced in the 1980s in other provinces. Chang Qing, the photographer – now so universally respected that I never heard anyone refer to him as other than 'Teacher Chang' – took pictures of the city each year, showing the gradual rise of a new, modern town from the ashes of the old. The phoenix became the city's symbol.

Along with China's fiery consumerism came a great surge of culture from the outside world. Mainland Chinese thrilled for the first time to the Hong Kong movies that Mao, Wang Hongwen, Jiang Qing and a very few others had enjoyed in the seventies. Smuggled tapes introduced eager teenagers to rock 'n' roll, though the first foreign music to become popular was Indian pop, echoing a brief post-war period when Hindi films had been hits. Many middle-aged Chinese have a disconcerting familiarity with classic Bollywood songs.

Many of the preoccupations of the 1980s were a deliberate rejection of Cultural Revolution values. Anything from the outside had been scorned, so people embraced imports; intellectuals and technicians had been degraded and humiliated, so people became obsessed with technology and learning from Western experts. The only aspect the two eras shared was a disdain for China's history, but for very different reasons. In the 1980s, as one veteran of the era put it to me, 'Everybody loved money because money had no history, and all that history meant was pain.'

Money wasn't the only value. There was a new delight in words too. Poetry readings attracted crowds of hundreds, new books sold out one week and were banned the next. Underground artists, writers and musicians mingled, dodging the police who were determined to crack down on 'spiritual pollution', and pushing the envelope in any way they could.

Imported Western values were – and still are – blamed for the breakdown in traditional culture, the materialism and selfishness of young Chinese, and the complete lack of social trust. But the ten years of denunciation and betrayal, the destruction of every non-state institution that tied people together, and the denigration of all alternative value systems, from religion to conservatism to family, seemed a more plausible cause.

The leadership was keen to embrace modernism in some fields, but deeply unnerved by the new 'bourgeois' habits of the public. Numerous campaigns of petty harassment were launched, failing to have much impact on the giddy embrace of the new by ordinary people. Women started to wear make-up and daringly low-cut dresses; fortune tellers and Daoist soothsayers returned to the streets; young men gathered to smoke, sneer and play billiards.

Deng had to walk an uneasy line between old revolutionaries, especially in the military, unhappy with the speed of change, reformists such as Hu Yaobang and Zhao Ziyang pushing for faster change and real political reform, and a newly empowered public both giddy with possibilities and angry at the loss of security. The dismantling of large portions of the state-run economy meant an end to the 'iron rice bowl' of a guaranteed job and a guaranteed income that some had enjoyed; workers who had assumed they had a post for life found themselves floundering in a terrifying new world as their factories were closed down or sold off to private owners keen to bring in cheaper labour. In 1987, Hu was forced out of power, undone by an old guard tired of his fierce contempt for Maoism and his open enthusiasm for radical change.

Political liberty was high on the agenda for many young Chinese. Grassroots meetings saw fierce discussion of where China should be going next, what was happening, what radical reforms were needed. Speakers defiantly exclaimed, 'I'm not a member of the Party!' and were cheered for it. Officials were slammed for their laziness and corruption, and the Party for its slowness to change. In 1986–8, student protests became common, sparked both by high-minded concerns of political liberty and discontent over rising tuition fees, terrible canteen food and crumbling dormitories. Tiananmen was a frequent site of protests, such as the thousand who marched there in 1988 to protest the killing of a fellow student in a brawl, or the tens of thousands who protested Hu Yaobang's sacking in the winter of 1986–7. Big-character posters became popular again, complaining about everything from crime to intellectual persecution to the 'second Japanese invasion' of consumer goods.

1989 was when Deng's new order temporarily came unstuck. Hu Yaobang died that April, and, like Zhou Enlai's, his passing away triggered mourning that rapidly turned into protest. Hundreds of thousands of protestors filled Tiananmen Square for weeks, student intellectuals backed up by workers angry over job losses and stagnating wages. Like the Qing Ming protests of

1976, the protests had a wild atmosphere at first, full of music and ideas and sudden bonding between strangers.

It was all too much for a frightened leadership. The shadow of the Cultural Revolution hung over them. They were scared – scared of an angry crowd that reminded at least some of them of the spectre of the Red Guards, scared of a new wave of civil war, scared that what was happening in the USSR and Eastern Europe might happen to China. After initial attempts at negotiation and soft force failed, they felt something had to be done. Beijing army units weren't thought politically reliable enough. The prospect that they might side with the protestors was exceptionally terrifying, bringing up images of Russia's revolution in 1917 and Hungary's in 1956, so soldiers were brought in from outside the city, pumped full of propaganda about counter-revolutionaries, and unleashed on the public.

In contrast to the popular image of the massacre, almost none of the killings actually took place in the square itself. But the murders started early, in the outskirts of Beijing, as crowds of ordinary Beijingers tried to block the advance of the army into the square and soldiers opened up with live ammunition. As the tanks rolled in, most of the protestors scattered. As in 1976, the authorities were looking to crush protest, not commit mass murder, but they were also largely uncaring about the consequences of unleashing the army against the people.

Throughout the city, and especially in the alleys and backstreets near the square, fearful young soldiers shot randomly at anybody who seemed to be a threat. It echoed the panicked killings carried out by the people's militia in the aftermath of the Tangshan earthquake. You could be shot for as little as poking your head out of a window to see what was going on. Hundreds of people were murdered by an army that had long lost any claim to be liberators.

Some of the protestors fought back, improvising Molotov cocktails or beating individual soldiers caught in back alleys. Beijing stood with them; crowds of ordinary citizens swarmed to block the army's way, throwing stones and jeering at the troops for betraying the people. Xi Chuan, a prominent poet and intellectual, saw a cluster of protestors grab a submachine gun from a ruined tank, wrapping it in cloth and blowing on the metal, overheated from firing, to ready it for use against the soldiers. The grand battle that Hua and the others had feared would overtake the capital in 1976 had finally happened.

In the end, inevitably, the army won. Tiananmen, and the wave of political persecution that followed, killed the freewheeling atmosphere of the 1980s for good. The brightest and fiercest minds went into exile or prison, or simply lay low to avoid trouble. Xi Chuan, who had lost two friends over the course of the protests, later commented, 'For me, that day was like the big bang. I witnessed deaths, losses and departures. The moral and aesthetic values within me collapsed. Like a useless man, I started to accept evil with my mouth shut.'[8]

Three bleak years in which the political hardliners seemed close to rolling back many of Deng's reforms came after Tiananmen. Zhao Ziyang, who had made his sympathies with the protestors very clear, walking and talking with them in the square, was placed under house arrest until his death; he passed the time writing a memoir that called for liberal democracy and an end to the one-party state, but that was now further off than ever.

Deng had been complicit in the decision to unleash the troops, but he was also the one who helped break the freeze. In yet another masterful political stroke, and despite having nominally resigned his political positions, he exploited his old power base in 1992 on what would become a famous 'southern tour', visiting the areas that had boomed most under his economic reforms in Guangzhou, Shenzhen and other parts of South China. The tour was a wild success and a new course had been firmly set for Deng's successors.

Deng died in 1997, at ninety-three. He'd seen almost the whole of the Chinese century, from the warlord era to the Japanese invasion to Maoist insanities, ending in his own triumph. Although he never built his own personality cult, many Chinese feel the same respect for him as they do for Zhou Enlai. Despite everything, in the end he was on their side. I have a small plastic statue from Guangdong which seems to sum up much of the Chinese feeling for Deng; he's sitting in pyjamas on a large armchair that almost dwarfs him, enjoying a smoke, while wearing two slippers in the shape of cats, one black and one white. It's impossible to imagine a statue of Mao showing the same kind of joking affection.

After his death, the economy continued to grow, fuelled by a seemingly insatiable American consumer market and the flow of cheap credit. In 1998, the old system of Foreign Exchange Certificates was abolished, where foreigners had been given special currency which allowed them to buy import items – a perk discreetly shared by officials and the rich. At this point, the lifestyle of the average upper-middle-class urban family, with their own phone, two-bedroom apartment, car, big TV, CD player and VCR, was better than that of most of the leadership in Zhongnanhai in the 1970s.

Personal liberties increased at the same time. For instance, in 1999, the government stopped assigning graduates jobs after university, instead throwing them into an open labour market. In 2003, it became possible to get married or divorced without permission from your work unit. Other policies were allowed quietly to lapse into disuse, such as the once-common police habit of arresting unmarried couples at hotels.

The new order came with an implicit bargain: stay out of politics and you won't get hurt. This was all very well if you were part of the up-and-coming middle class in the cities, getting rich off exports to the West. For a worker whose state-owned factory had just been closed, or a young farmer whose sister had been raped by the local cadre, or a woman forced to have an abortion because it was her second child, or a family whose home was bulldozed without compensation in order to make way for a shopping mall or a new ring road it was a little less appealing.

The economic benefits, too, were increasingly confined to a coastal urban majority. The incomes of unskilled workers stagnated when measured against inflation, while the country's new wealth was devoted to holding on to US government bonds instead of being spent on improving the lives of ordinary people. (In the words of one US economic analyst to me, 'For Christ's sake, I'm a Texas Republican and this country's lack of welfare is enough to convert me to socialism.')

Private charities stepped in to fill what gaps they could as rural education and healthcare crumbled; between 2000 and 2005, for instance, the absolute number of illiterate people in China *increased* by 30 million, reversing one of the regime's few successes since 1949.

Today, failures in the tax system mean that local governments increasingly rely on selling off land to raise funds, leaving farmers dispossessed and pushing up housing prices to unaffordable levels. Officially, rural residents aren't supposed to pay tax; in practice, local officials extort money from them on a regular basis as 'fees' and 'fines', money that goes into their pockets rather than to the state. As a result of the One Child Policy, tens of millions of Chinese don't even have an official existence, leaving them completely unable to get public benefits without using fake ID numbers. (Graffiti advertising where you can get these is common as you come into second-tier cities.)

Yet the political bargain still clings on, just about. Politics classes are compulsory for both students and officials, but are also stunningly – perhaps even deliberately – boring, a mere repetition of outdated slogans and Marxist theories the teachers themselves rarely grasp. There's no attempt to bring a political lens to bear on modern issues, and the classes are essentially opportunities for students to enjoy some hard-earned rest. Only inside Party colleges does real debate take place over political theory, and how to keep control. One professor, back from teaching cadres, commented slyly, 'You have to be willing to kill a couple of hundred people if you want to advance in local politics.'

The fiercest and most effective indoctrination is the one provided by nationalism; the Taiwan reunification drum is beaten at every opportunity, and history and politics distorted to produce an ever-victimised China. After the 1989 Tiananmen incident, students were required to undergo two weeks of military training after matriculation, along with an inoculating dose of nationalist rhetoric. There's hot competition among single PLA officers to teach these classes, not because of any desire to mould the young, but because they're stationed in remote army bases most of the time and this is their only chance to meet girls.

At the higher levels, the struggle for succession has been replaced with a careful rotation of leadership, with each new generation selected and cultivated as possible contenders long before they reach the top levels. Technocracy is the order of the day, with engineering degrees and overseas study common attributes of the new mandarins. There are factions within the Party, but they're largely based on the networks that brought leaders to power. For instance, the seventy-year-old Hu Jintao is considered to head the 'Youth League' faction.

There are no personality cults among senior leaders any more; indeed, Hu seems to have gone so far as to eliminate his personality altogether. The current Chinese premier, Wen Jiabao, seems to be following in Zhou Enlai's footsteps, deliberately building up an image of himself as concerned, kind and connected to the public. But Wen's attempts to pitch himself as the nation's favourite grandfather are deliberately non-ideological, and his calls for reform carefully circumscribed.

Yet the government has also surrendered a tremendous amount of rhetorical ground, on terms that started with Deng's own changes in 1978. When you are publicly calling for the rule of law, it becomes harder and more embarrassing to lock people up on spurious national security grounds. When talking about the need to protect private property, driving farmers off their land to build shopping malls doesn't look good. When claiming that democracy is the future of China, even if the Chinese aren't 'ready' for it yet, the very idea of the one-party state is weakened. Activists, intellectuals and reformers inside the government increasingly press for change within ideological frameworks accidentally constructed by the state itself.

The legacy of radical protest has continued far beyond Tiananmen, and remains inspired by memories of past struggles. A limited study by Chinese sociologist Feng Chen at two factories found that 'almost all instances of factory-based resistance were led by people who strongly believed in Maoist socialism, and most of the leaders were former Cultural Revolution activists whose thinking and actions showed a strong imprint of that time'.[9] The tools they used, like 'leaflet distribution, group meetings, mass rallies, placards, slogans, red armbands and factory takeovers', were all methods they'd learnt in the early years of the Cultural Revolution.

The appeal of Maoism in a materialist and often brutally authoritarian society isn't limited to factory protestors. The Utopia bookstore in Beijing – the name, alas, is not ironic – was founded in 2003, and stocks a full case of Mao's works alongside Noam Chomsky, Naomi Klein and other anti-globalisation writers. Its walls are covered with Cultural Revolution posters showing miners, factory workers and schoolchildren swooning over Mao. The website, Land of Utopia, saw its hits per day rise from 10,000 to 300,000 between 2006 and 2010, as the global financial crisis struck and the appeal of neo-liberalism dimmed even further.

According to the 33-year-old owner, Fang Jingqing, 'Mao is a symbol of equality and justice. In his time workers and farmers lived with dignity and their rights were guaranteed.' The bookshop is frequented both by young neo-leftists, enthusiasts of European post-modernist thinkers, and old-school Maoists given to walking out or throwing temper tantrums when irritating realities like starvation deaths and political murders are mentioned.

Today's Maoist activists, even those who were alive at the time, dream of a Maoist era when, 'Cadres did their jobs in accordance with Chairman Mao's instructions. They were not corrupt and did not have many privileges.' And when 'Workers and peasants were the masters . . . People lived a happy life without worry and anxiety and got paid for their work. Everybody worked hard for the country without trouble back home, as the state provided housing and medical insurance.'[10]

This is clearly as much of a fantasy as, say, William Morris's dreams of medieval England as a land of contented families and rosy-cheeked guild workers turning out everyday art, or neo-Confederate fantasies of benevolent plantation owners guiding happy slaves. But it appeals, too, to something older and stronger than just politics, to the old millennial dreams of a world turned upside down. Living in a country where the gap between rich and poor grows daily, the lifetime income of a factory worker won't buy a one-bedroom apartment in a provincial city, and real wages for most workers have been flat since the 1990s, you can hardly blame people for dreaming.

Fantasies of the past are not limited to the political fringe, though. In many Chinese cities, the revolution has become a dinner party.[11] Cultural Revolution theme restaurants are masterpieces of kitsch featuring musical extravaganzas of singing workers and dancing soldiers, where staff address customers as 'Comrade'. When I went to one, the young people there seemed to find it camp and funny (helped, no doubt, by the word for 'comrade' having shifted meaning among the young to 'homosexual'[12]). For the middle-aged, it was more stirring. 'It reminded me of the friends I was with in the countryside,' one 54-year-old business-man told me. 'We really believed in something at that time, you know? It wasn't as bad as they say.' He handed me his business card and got into his Audi.

The most disturbing form of Cultural Revolution nostalgia is not in China. Maoism retains a powerful appeal in India, in the countryside, where a rebel movement, the Naxalites, controls entire regions, and thrives among dissatisfied youth in the cities. At the same time, the Indian police use accusations of Naxalite connections to stitch up political activists and crack heads among the poor. Among Indian students, often bitter and radicalised, the violence of the Cultural Revolution is the very point of its appeal. A Tsinghua professor visiting India in 2007 was dismayed by the number of young Indians who, after his talk, would come up to praise the Cultural Revolution for its courage in destroying the old order, attacking traitors to the nation, and tearing down corrupt officials and stagnant university authorities. He returned in the same kind of profound shock that would grip a modern German who'd just been told 'The Third Reich, eh? Sounds like a good idea to me.'

In China, violence, once a political mainstay, has taken on different forms. Countryside thugs now beat people up for getting in the way of forced demolition programmes, or for trying to block the local village leader's attempts (literally) to stuff the ballot box in a village election. The most politicised form of aggression is the regular beating and illegal imprisonment of people attempting to petition higher authorities.

In 2010, the most famous example of this was the attack on Chen Yulian, a 58-year-old woman petitioning the higher authorities over the death of her daughter through medical malfeasance six years earlier. Six policemen found her outside the Hubei provincial Party headquarters and proceeded to beat and kick her for sixteen minutes, which was caught on a cameraphone by passers-by. The video of the beating might not have been enough to have a public impact – but, unfortunately for the policemen, Chen was not a usual village mother, but the wife of an Hubei provincial official. When this was discovered, the police chief visited her in hospital and offered an apology, explaining – in so many words – that they would never have attacked her if they knew she was the wife of someone important.

Both the central government and local authorities have massive budgets for 'maintaining stability', but this kind of violence is never publicly defended, only overlooked and tacitly encouraged, especially around sensitive political events. When it comes to the public, you get defenders of many forms of authoritarianism in China – one-party systems, technocracy, censorship, even the imprisonment of dissenters – but nobody speaks out in favour of thuggery, which is seen as an endemic problem, like corruption and organised crime.[13] But there's one form of violence that wins favour among the Chinese public, at least online, and that's against officials.

This was beautifully demonstrated in April 2010, when Chinese diplomat Yu Boren, attached to the consulate in Houston, Texas, accused the local police of roughing him up after he refused to stop when signalled to pull over. I expected it to become another excuse for nationalist posturing, of the kind common online, but instead it disappeared from the Chinese news cycle within a day. Why? Because the overwhelming reaction online was to praise the Texas police for beating up an official, and regret that the Chinese police didn't do the same.

No evidence existed to show that Yu was in any way corrupt, but the automatic reaction of most Chinese 'netizens' to any story involving an official is that he *must* be dirty, and deserves whatever he gets. The slightest whiff of a story around an official can trigger a 'human flesh search' that pores over any evidence available to prove his corruption.

As Chinese political scientist Yu Jianrong put it,

You're wearing a really nice watch. Everyone's cell phone nowadays can take pictures, so they take a picture of you and post it on the web saying that you are one of the nation's civil servants and are named Leader XXX. They ask, how then can this person, on the basis of their salary, afford to wear a several hundred thousand RMB watch? They start to search online and are able to search out your ancestors going back eighteen generations. They find out what your wife is doing, what your son is doing; finally they come up with this conclusion – you are a corrupt official.[14]

The widespread anger against officials, the feeling that anybody in office must be corrupt – all of this was as familiar in 1966 as in 2010.

What about Mao's legacy? Unlike other former 'princelings', his children haven't become prominent figures. His surviving daughters were neatly sidelined by Deng and rarely exposed to public view. In 2009, his only direct adult male descendent, Mao Xinyu, the son of the mad Mao Anqing, was given the rare honour of becoming China's youngest major general, only nine years after he joined the army.

This was a purely symbolic gesture; his duties largely involve the maintenance of his grandfather's archives. He wanted to study English literature, but got bullied by his mother into becoming an expert on his grandfather's works instead. Young Chinese find him a laughable figure, since he looks like a giant cartoon baby in a soldier's costume.

Mao's picture still hangs over Tiananmen Square, but all the other big pictures came down in the early 1980s 'for cleaning' – very, very long cleaning. Statues of him stand in every university and many town squares, often with his hand out in a way that suggests he's directing traffic.

The Maoist cult enjoyed a resurgence in the early 1990s, with the religious aspects even more heightened. Mountains that looked vaguely like his outline became tourist attractions, while his image became a brand in itself. You can still buy Mao yo-yos, Mao electronic toys, Mao teacups, glow-in-the-dark Mao clocks, Mao watches – it's a festival of cheap tat that the Chairman himself would have loathed as a sign of consumerist decadence. Visitors to Hunan, Mao's home province, can visit the birthplaces of Mao Zedong and Liu Shaoqi in the same day; it's a rare pilgrimage that lets you venerate a murderer *and* his victim on the same tour.

Chinese banknotes, which used to include pictures of Sun Yat-Sen and other important revolutionary figures, now purely feature a rather smug-looking Mao. (At the time of writing, there was a rumour that a supposed new 500 yuan note would feature Deng. Appropriately enough, it would have five times the face value of any previous note.)

Children read Mao's poems in school and learn his sayings, while his name is ritually invoked at political events. It looks like he's dodged Stalin's fate for good; permanently established as a kind of George Washington figure, associated with the struggle against the Japanese and the foundation of the nation rather than anything that came after.

The actual Maoist content in Chinese media and popular culture is tiny. Individual Chinese often come to their own harsh conclusions about him, just as others still worship him, but for the majority of the public he's simply part of history. He's respected as a national figure, not a Communist one. It's highly unlikely that he'll ever stop being held up as a hero, but it's equally unlikely that, outside of an idealistic or angry fringe, his bloody ideology will ever have the same sway.

It's almost impossible to estimate accurately how many people died from political violence or artificial starvation under Maoism. The figures for deaths during the Great Leap Forward, for instance, began at 17 million when knowledge of the extent of the famine first became common outside China in the 1980s; and now, based on extensive archival research by scholars like Frank Dikotter and Yang Jisheng, the figure has been convincingly pushed up to over 40 million – a figure higher, for instance, than civilian deaths worldwide in World War II.

Estimates for deaths during the Cultural Revolution alone start at around 400,000 and go up to over 10 million. Lowballing the statistics, 2 or 3 million deaths is a reasonable figure. By the standards of Chinese political violence, this would be relatively low, about the same number as died in the 'Land Reform' process and the persecution of Nationalists and 'rich peasants' in 1949–51 – though this figure, again, could plausibly be as high as 8 million.

Six or seven million deaths in the Cultural Revolution is possible; the rather eccentric 'democide' scholar R. J. Rummel, in his idiosyncratic survey *China's Bloody Century*, estimates

7,731,000. Any of these numbers exclude, of course, the millions crippled physically or mentally, not to mention the art, historical sites and religious artefacts destroyed.

The numbers for Tangshan are in a slightly more limited range. Government household surveys after the earthquake recorded the names of 242,000 deceased. This is the lowest figure possible. The survey teams were largely confined to the environs of Tangshan itself, and didn't venture far into the massive region hit by the quake. The figure also took no account of the many outsiders to the area killed during the disaster, from migrant workers to the victims in the train station. A survey conducted in the early 1980s, using casualty estimation techniques based on projecting proportional household casualty figures to the entire region, placed the number of deaths as somewhere around 650,000, which seems a reasonable estimate.

Every 28 July, Tangshan remembers its dead. Like families returning to sweep tombs on Qing Ming, Tangshanese from all over the country return to honour the lost. Late into the night, survivors and relatives sit round fires, burning paper images of grave goods – traditionally money, today including cars, DVD players and designer clothes – for the dead, chanting prayers and telling stories. People cry in the street, letting out thirty years of grief. It's a strange place to be as an outsider, whether Chinese or foreign; when I talked to newcomers to Tangshan, they mentioned that they avoided going out that day, unwilling to intrude on a pain they couldn't fully know.

Except on the anniversary, very little sign of the quake is visible in Tangshan, save for the prevalence of 'Anti-Earthquake' squares and roads. A couple of collapsed buildings, such as the fallen dormitory in which Zhu Yinlai was once buried, are preserved as memorial sites. The most visible signs of the earthquake's impact remain the bodies of survivors. Every so often in Tangshan, you'll see a man with a missing arm, or a woman walking on an artificial foot. Over 6,000 survivors of the earthquake have been permanently crippled, and I went to visit some in a hospital dedicated to their care.

The home felt like a slow death. It wasn't an unattractive building, with a set of shared dorm rooms around a grassy quad, but it was still and lifeless, a sharp contrast to the usual lively outdoor life of any Chinese community. The patients had nothing to do beyond trundle about in their wheelchairs, read old magazines and play cards or mah-jongg with each other. There were no computers, and only an ancient VCR attached to the TV. I was the only visitor whenever I went.

The patients were visibly nervous of the staff, and worried about being caught talking to me. The entire pension they received from the government, they said, went directly to the hospital, leaving them no money of their own other than whatever cash relatives provided. When I offered to bring one patient some books and English materials, she called me from a public phone a few days later and asked me not to, worried that it would make other patients jealous and resentful. There were no organised trips outside the hospital, and it was virtually impossible for them to leave the place on their own. Their wheelchairs were enormous, motor-driven affairs that gave their users a robotic quality, and nothing in China is built to be wheelchair accessible.

Other crippled victims found better lives. I met Little Ma in a park in northern Tangshan, where she was telling horoscopes, sitting in her wheelchair covered in a blanket and smiling at passers-by. I've never met anyone who made me feel so immediately and utterly happy; joy bubbled out of her like a spring. After being told by doctors that she would never walk again, she wanted to commit suicide, convinced that she would only be a burden to her family. Her parents and siblings encouraged her to live as close an approximation of a normal life as she could, coming with her to events to help lift her wheelchair upstairs. A few years after the earthquake, she married a man who loved her deeply and they had a son.

Feeling frustrated at home, she decided to take up Daoist fortune-telling, buying some books on palmistry and the *I Ching* and taking up a regular spot in the park alongside other sooth-sayers. 'Seventy per cent of it is psychology', she told me, 'I spend most of my day listening to people. If it's a young woman, I tell her she'll get married and have a son, if it's a middle-aged man I tell him he'll be promoted at work. I just like to make people happy.'

Not being able to marry was the greatest pain for many crippled survivors. The Chinese have a pronounced fear of physical deformity or incapability, which makes finding a husband or a wife even more difficult than it is in the West for a disabled person, and there is a near-complete lack of understanding from many medical authorities about the possibility of sex. 'I was told it was impossible, and that I should put it out of my mind entirely,' said one survivor. Through support groups, some found their own solution. Two wheelchair-bound survivors would marry each other in a 'sexless marriage' – though not all of them matched the name, thankfully – providing companionship and support. Where possible, they adopted children, especially earthquake orphans.

For the thousands of children who lost their parents in the earthquake, both the government and the public stepped up. Many were taken in by immediate relatives, others adopted, often by army families. Orphanages were set up for the rest. Chinese orphanages run the gamut from the truly horrifying, like the institution a friend of mine visited as a child in Changsha where she was told not to give presents to the children because they were being punished for their sins in past lives, to the excellent, with kindly, dedicated staff and a determination to make sure the children have the same chances as anyone else.

Fortunately, the experiences of Tangshan orphans were mainly at the better end of the spectrum. Other cities set up specialised institutions to help the children, especially the Hebei provincial capital of Shijiazhuang. Not only did most earthquake orphanages have dedicated and caring staff, who became adept at dealing with the traumas of their young charges, the government supplied funds to help the orphans into adulthood.

As usual, orphans in the countryside got the shorter end of the stick, being shoved into regular homes rather than ones that specialised in earthquake survivors. Zhang Youlu and his sister spent the rest of their childhood in one such institution. 'It was OK,' he shrugged, 'At least there was food every day, which was a change.' He went on to pass the gruelling national entrance exam and go to university, eventually becoming the owner of a fine independent bookstore in Tangshan.

At first, little attention was paid to the psychological impact of the quake. Chinese mental health care is relatively primitive, and concepts of post-traumatic stress disorder highly underdeveloped in a country where anybody born before 1970 or so would be a reasonable candidate for PTSD. The government considered 'that its attitude, policy, actions and publicity made survivors feel better. Besides, it was concluded, survivors would talk to each other and learn self-help.'[15]

Informal groups of survivors did comfort and aid each other, and by the mid-eighties local psychologists had made a speciality of treating quake cases. But the mental scars ran deep. After his four-day ordeal under the rubble, it took years before Zhu Yinlai could go to the toilet comfortably. Other small spaces were uncomfortable, but it was toilets, for some reason, that triggered the worst memories. His class was transferred to Beijing, and he went on to become a successful engineer, but every time the cubicle door swung closed he found himself wanting to scream and scratch in terror.

Yu Xuebing married, worked in a factory, and became, after her husband was laid off from his job in the early twenty-first century, a taxi driver to help support her family. When she turned on her TV on 12 May 2008, her immediate thought was 'My god, it's happened again.' The pictures of the devastating earthquake in Sichuan that afternoon triggered flashbacks for many Tangshanese as they watched scenes of howling mothers, wrecked houses and bodies being carted from the ruins.

Sichuan's tragedies were all too familiar to Tangshanese, even if the casualty figures, at 80,000 dead, were lower. A far more extensive and capable media ensured that individual stories got the attention they never had after Tangshan, such as the young mother whose body was found bent over her still-living three-month-old baby, shielding him. She had typed a message on her mobile phone while dying. 'My dear baby, if you survive, remember your mother loves you.'

The PLA's efforts were impressive, too, rapidly flying in the kind of special equipment and heavy vehicles that had been missing in Tangshan. With the images all over the Chinese media, volunteers jumped in cars or trucks and drove straight to the disaster-struck region, bringing food, blankets, water and medicine. This time China had no hesitation in accepting foreign aid, with millions pouring in from abroad. Both companies and celebrities faced massive social pressure to donate, with those seen as stingy being panned in the media. False promises led to later scandals, such as actress Zhang Ziyi's failure to deliver on the $1 million in funds she claimed to have raised.

Yet, as in Tangshan, the aid pooled in certain areas, leaving vast swathes untouched. Sichuan's landscape is more mountainous and tougher than Hebei's, so it had even more remote communities that never, in the words of one middle-aged Sichuan woman, 'saw a *mao* of help for us. We just picked things up ourselves and carried on.' Help was there for those who travelled to find it, but disaster relief efforts and reconstruction money were largely confined, yet, again, to the big towns.

According to Australian journalist John Garnault, even in the immediate aftermath of the quake the disaster relief efforts were often more about show than substance. He reported how he 'watched People's Liberation Army soldiers loitering aimlessly and helping themselves to goods looted from shattered shops, while the cries of trapped citizens rang out from buildings nearby'.

Of the tens of thousands of soldiers in Beichuan in the days after the quake, the only ones we saw raise a sweat were a dozen who jostled in front of Premier Wen as they rushed to an imaginary rescue for the benefit of the China Central Television camera.[16]

And earthquake funds often went straight to official banquets and the purchase of new Land Rovers, rather than to the people they were supposed to help, prompting public calls for increased government financial transparency, a perpetual sore spot. Officials exaggerated the death toll in their districts in order to secure more funds, or simply filed paperwork twice with different departments.

Locals had been rightly cynical straight from the start, 'The government will have to give me money to rebuild my house, but I have no confidence in the local officials. They'll put the money in their own pockets,' said one fifty-year-old factory worker a few days after the quake, looking at his ruined house.[17] UNESCO made sterling efforts to reach remote areas and provide new housing programmes, just as it did later after a smaller, even more remote earthquake in the Tibetan county of Yushu in 2010, and so did other international agencies. There were definitely benefits to bringing in outsiders.

The reaction in Tangshan to the Sichuan earthquake was both generous and bitter. The Tangshan government sent numerous rescue teams, while donations from the city were among the highest in China. Yet, talking with Tangshan survivors about the Wenchuan earthquake, they showed an odd tone of jealousy. Wenchuan was getting all the attention, they felt, while their experiences were forgotten. 'Tangshan was worse than Sichuan,' I was told over and over again, 'Ours might have been a 7.8 and theirs an 8.0, but we were right at the centre.'

The most disgraceful part of the Sichuan quakes was the '*dofu*-paste schools', public buildings where money meant for construction had been siphoned off by local authorities in collusion with the builders. Real estate is a very corrupt industry in China, where lack of effective and adequate local taxation means that many local governments have become dependent on the sale of land, and officials expect hefty bribes from any bidder for a contract.

The cost for bribing officials to get a tender is often then taken in turn from the funds for building, which in Sichuan resulted in a greater percentage of schools and other public institutions collapsing in the quake than private buildings. The quake hit at 2:48 in the afternoon, when classes were packed, and at least 5,000 students were killed. It was even more devastating for the parents than for those who lost children at Tangshan, since the One Child Policy meant that a high percentage of the dead were the only child in their family. The assurances by the authorities that the One Child Policy had a provision allowing a second child in the event of the first's death was little consolation.

The government went on to throw away much of the credit it had gathered in the initial response to the Sichuan earthquake by harassing, beating and attacking parents and activists. Tan Zuoren, a noted dissident and environmentalist, tried to set up a database to record how many children had died and where, only to find himself arrested and his materials seized. In March 2009, he was tried for 'subverting state power' and sentenced to five years in prison. Yet even this disgraceful abuse of state authority took place in a very different atmosphere to the past. The sentence was publicly condemned by prominent Chinese intellectuals, and Tan's lawyer mounted a vigorous defence on the grounds that it was no crime to use democratic methods in a people's democracy.

The Sichuan earthquake sparked wild stories everywhere. Within a few days of the quake, I had heard that the government had predicted the quake, that the year was cursed, and that a new earthquake was about to hit Beijing, which the government knew but was keeping secret to avoid panic, even as officials secretly fled. That last part was particularly widespread; Beijing and other major cities were noticeably empty the weekend after the quake.

One reporter was able to trace the origins of a rumour in the city of Chengdu, which had suffered slightly from the quake. 'At 11:30 a.m. on 15 May, the businessman Wu Fengjun . . . received a call from a stranger who said that there would be a magnitude 7 earthquake in Chengdu.' Wu called the paper, who traced it from him to a middle school teacher called Li, who had meant to call his mother, but dialled the wrong number. He'd got the wrong information from the school head, who'd got it from a chemistry teacher – who'd merely passed on news he'd heard from his daughter that there might be strong aftershocks, which she'd got from a friend of a friend who worked in the Earthquake Bureau. It had gone from aftershock to immediate threat in less than an hour, and the rumour was still being recorded on internet bulletin boards days later.

Many towns and counties had some variant of the rumour that a quake was about to hit, prompting official announcements from local disaster relief boards that no earthquake was imminent. Seventeen people were arrested for 'spreading malicious rumours', but there was no malice in most cases, only fear and a shared disbelief in the honesty of the authorities.

The immediate reaction of many Chinese to the Sendai earth-quake of March 2011 was to marvel at the calm discipline of the Japanese public, the open media coverage, and the sturdiness of Japan's buildings. Zhang Lei, a writer for the Chinese edition of the *Financial Times*, implicitly contrasted the situation with that in China:

I wondered: Was Japan's government not afraid that it would cause instability for them to report the quake on the TV without fear like this? But in the TV reports on the quake, you rarely saw pictures of high-level Japanese leaders 'dealing with the disaster', and there seemed to be no images of the Japanese Prime Minister directing the relief effort, spilling his tears over the disaster-stricken area.

Online commentators noted the lack of looting, the Japanese public's trust that the government would provide food and shelter, and the open media coverage of issues around the quake. 'In China,' one wrote, 'I bet [people] would have immediately broken into and looted the surrounding supermarkets,'[18] while another noted that the difference is that 'over there they have something called trust'.

In 2010, two different films captured different parts of the Chinese collective memory of the Tangshan disaster. The first, *The Great Tangshan Earthquake* – in English, actually rather more appropriately titled *Aftershock* – had a huge budget for a Chinese movie, coming in at 150 million yuan (around $22 million), and was accompanied by a giant marketing blitz. It broke box office records for a domestic movie (though still trailing a long way behind the *Avatar* juggernaut, which the Chinese audience read as a parable of forced demolition and resistance to real estate companies), though it seemed to have relatively little staying power; few people were going to see it twice, or talking of it as a favourite movie. It was simply something you were expected to see.

It was a competently done movie, and occasionally very moving, though the earthquake itself was over by the first twenty minutes.[19] It put forward, unsurprisingly, a completely conventional narrative of China's progress since the earthquake, following a brother and sister, torn apart when their mother was forced to choose which of them to save. The sister ends up being adopted by heroic PLA officers, while the son, one-armed, remains with the mother and becomes a successful businessman, until the siblings are reunited by chance when they go to aid victims of the Sichuan earthquake. China's material progress is much emphasised throughout the film, as the characters' homes fill up with electronic goods, revolutionary posters shift to pictures of sports stars and movie icons, and transport changes from bicycles to BMWs.

It was much criticised for product placement ('What company should we use for insurance for the trip?' 'Use China Life, they're very reliable'), but the political placement was shoehorned in almost as crudely. Scenes of Mao's death appear out of nowhere, taking up two minutes of the film with mourning music and white flags for no particularly good reason. The PLA come in for abundant praise. The real political message is more subtle. As one commentator approvingly put it, 'The message of the film is that China has moved on from the historical pain of the past.' The son's lack of an arm doesn't prevent him achieving business success, while the daughter cannot be truly happy until she puts aside the bitterness she feels towards her mother for abandoning her.

All this was a change from the original message of the story on which the movie was based, in which there are no clear emotional consolations and the wounds of the past are implied never fully to heal. The movie only hinted at a subplot made somewhat more explicit in the original text: the adoptive father of the rescued girl develops a sexual attraction to his new daughter. That the nurturing PLA family, which acts in the movie as a symbol of national conscience and government care for the survivors, might also be a source of emotional trauma was not something mainstream audiences were quite ready for.

The second film, *Buried,* was made for almost no money at all by independent director Wang Libo.[20] It's a simple documentary, consisting mostly of talking heads and the occasional archival record, which repeats the claims of covered-up predictions around the Tangshan earthquake. Made in the aftermath of the Sichuan quake, and based largely on the work of reporter Zhang Qingzhou, it linked the two, and suggested that the Chinese government had deliberately concealed the success of the Qinglong county government and the extent of pre-earthquake warnings.

Buried won praise at the 2009 Beijing Film Festival, and was a sleeper hit online, despite being repeatedly taken down from Chinese sites. Yet the fundamental premise, as I outlined earlier in this book, was wrong. The earthquake forecasts were vague, covered huge areas, and nowhere near the level of specificity or urgency that would have prompted immediate action, let alone evacuation, under any system. As with the validity of any prediction, it looks stronger in hindsight because we don't have access to the full volume of predictions made, in different times and regions, that *didn't* prove true. They were similar to the 'predictions' of 9/11 within the US intelligence agencies – general forecasts that any system throws up on a regular basis. Qinglong's prediction was a remarkable work of intuition and guesswork, but it was so far distant from the epicentre that the number of lives saved was very small. Although Hebei officials cautioned Qinglong staff to keep quiet, there was no systematic long-term cover-up of the prediction – knowledge of it was already common currency in Tangshan soon after the earthquake, and articles on Qinglong were appearing in Chinese papers by the early 1980s.

There was also a certain amount of personal bitterness involved. The scientists interviewed in *Buried* are all keen proponents of the validity of earthquake prediction and continue to tout the Haicheng story as a success. In the meantime, the State Seismological Bureau has moved back towards a more mainstream scientific understanding of the limitations of prediction, putting them distinctly at odds with their former colleagues.

Yet the film went beyond the earthquake. It expressed much deeper doubts about the official historiography of the period, the feeling that the truth of what had happened was still being covered up and smoothed over. The slogan of the film was simple: 'The truth cannot be buried.' A similar work, the 2006 satirical essay 'Did the Tangshan Earthquake Really Happen?' by blogger Han Song, was full of the same kind of doubts, using the official reports of the quake to highlight political hypocrisies and fictions.[21] What is being talked about here is not just the earthquake, but the cover-ups, fictions and false histories surrounding the whole of the Cultural Revolution.

The Cultural Revolution actually gets one of the better treatments in terms of recent Chinese historiography and censorship. This isn't saying much. Honest history is hard to do in China, given the determination of Beijing to put forward a historical narrative that presents an essentially benevolent Communist Party guiding China from weakness to strength and occasionally going astray through no fault of its own.

Still, the crimes of 1966–76 are acknowledged even in the official media, even as their scope and origins are minimised. Details are kept very much out of the mainstream; scar literature is never going to be televised on Chinese Central Television. All the blame, naturally, is heaped upon the Gang of Four, and criticism of Mao's role is very largely absent. But it can be talked about and the period's horrors recognised while, for instance, the atrocities committed during the land reform process simply can't be discussed, nor the oppression of the Anti-Rightist Campaign, or, most glaringly, the political causes of the Great Leap Forward.

Apart from the gaping absence of Mao, the greatest flaw in the official line on the Cultural Revolution is how it treats the period as if it was conjured out of nowhere, sprung full-grown from Jiang Qing's thigh. Apart from the startling role of the very young, there was no form of political violence or oppression in the Cultural Revolution that was new to the Maoist regime. Attacks on intellectuals, mass murder of class enemies, the denigration of past traditions, campaigns against religion, paranoia about counter-revolutionaries, factional conflict, 'struggle sessions' – all of these well pre-dated 1966. The Cultural Revolution, like the Gang of Four, has become a general scapegoat; all of the Party's past atrocities can be dumped on it.

The Tangshan earthquake has contributed something unique and powerful to Chinese historical memory. Both *Aftershock* and *Buried* end on the image of the new Tangshan memorial wall, finished in 2010. The wall is, as far as I know, unique; it's the only memorial of a major disaster in China which lists the names of every known victim. Most of China's disasters aren't memorialised at all, and those that are, such as the 1937 Nanjing Massacre, focus on general images of martyrdom. Tangshan's is the first to recognise individual loss, rather than collective sacrifice.

The memorial wall itself had a sketchy start. It was set up at first as a private operation, which demanded that anybody who wanted a relative's name inscribed pay around 800 yuan (about $100 at the time) to get a name on the back of the wall, or 1,000 yuan if they wanted it on the front. Local anger over this coincided with the appointment of a new reformist mayor, who had the city government take over the project and execute it on a far grander scale.

I visited the wall while it was being built. The construction workers had set up camp in a quake-ruined factory nearby, the flames of their cooking fire flickering on the looming black walls on either side, which rose like the remains of a medieval cathedral. It had no ceiling, but provided at least some shelter from the harsh wind. They were all Sichuanese or Hunanese, part of the vast wave of migrants from the south looking for work, and felt little personal connection to the memorial site.

The memorial itself was bleakly moving, even half-finished. Eventually it would have over twenty-five blocks, and be more than 300 metres long. The names were ordered by stroke count, which must have been a nightmare to compile. Each block looked like a tombstone, the names engraved in gold. Like everything in China, it was big, far more overwhelming and much less intimate than its original model, the Vietnam Wall in Washington – also designed, as it happens, by a Chinese architect. Each block was nearly ten metres tall; to read the names at the top you had to stand back and stretch your neck. Before it was a small lake, the grey waters broken by jagged rocks. A few wreaths had already been laid at the base of the wall; on the anniversary of the quake it would be covered with flowers.

I wandered along the wall, writing down blocks of names:

Liu Xue Chun	Liu Lianzhong	An Xiaoyi	Xu Xiaolian
Liu Xuen Sun	Ma Dianyi	Dai Xiurong	Xu Fengxia
Wang Li	Liu Cunjin	Yang Guilan	Xu Gengdong
Lia Xilin	Liu Junling	Li Lianmao	Xu Genzhu

Lia Xiujun	Tan Aiguo	Xu Gengju	Xu Xiaopei
Liu Ai	Dai Liying	Xu Genglin	Zheng Shuhua
Dou Guangrong	Dai Lina	Liu Faping	Liu Xudong
Liu Xuemin	Dai Ruexing	Xu Huanqing	Yu Langui

After the memorial was completed, the Tangshan government built a new earthquake museum, which I visited shortly after its opening in late 2009. It was a step up from the old city museum, which had focused mostly on statistics, with long lists of the various donations from different provinces, technical diagrams crammed with seismological details, and long corridors full of Tangshan's industrial advances. The new museum was largely below ground, and was heavy on dioramas, models, flashing lights and dramatic films. There was a model of the red ambulance that had borne the four messengers to Beijing, scenes of soldiers feeding grateful survivors and individual accounts of heroism and survival. It was a fine effort, and I was moved, as were the other visitors that day, all Chinese and mostly locals.

Before leaving the museum, visitors had to pass down a long corridor, with five heavy inscriptions on the left-hand side. They repeated the same themes found on the Tangshan Earthquake Monument in the centre of the city. 'The great Chinese Communist Party is wise, the socialist system is incomparably superior, and the People's Liberation Army is loyal and reliable.' Each one had several paragraphs of political bombast, detailing how the earthquake relief efforts had shown the perfection of socialism and the continued wisdom of the Party as the sole leaders of China.

I was the only one reading them. Everyone else in the crowd walked straight past, heading up the stairs to the sunlight outside.

Acknowledgements

I could not have written this book without the help of Peter Yang, my tireless fixer and translator in Tangshan and Qinglong, who found interviewees, conducted his own archival and photographic research, and organised bus tickets and hotel rooms. His diligence, intelligence, and curiosity were invaluable. His parents welcomed me into their home and gave their own accounts of the disaster.

The toll of spending fourteen hours a day translating told on him when, one Spring Festival, after being plied with drink by his girlfriend's relatives, he woke up and began translating the conversation into English as if I were present, with explanatory cultural notes, and continued undeterred by my absence, for a good half hour before falling asleep again.

The people of Tangshan were warm, welcoming, and generous with their time. I owe particular thanks to Chang Qing, Yang Zhikai, Yuan Wuyi, Zhang Wenzhong, Zhang Youlu, Zhu Yinlai, He Jianguo and Yu Xuebing. The Tangshan Publicity Bureau was both open and helpful.

I owe a huge debt to the pioneering 1980s work of Qian Gang, and, in my understanding of Cultural Revolution politics, to the books of Roderick MacFarquhar, Michael Schoenhals, Frederick Teiwes and Warren Sun.

Neil Belton's detailed and thoughtful editing was invaluable, as was the careful work of Donald Sommerville. Many thanks also to Kate Murray-Browne at Faber, Lara Heimert at Basic Books and my agent, Gillon Aitken. Much gratitude to Shastri Ramachandaran, who read and gave detailed comments on the entire manuscript.

My mother, Sandra Palmer, gave me the same support and love she always has. My father, Martin Palmer, and his wife,

Acknowledgements

Victoria Finlay, read and commented on the initial drafts of the book, as well as providing a countryside refuge in the UK. Many thanks also to my aunts Yan Chi and Sheila, as well as my uncle Nigel. In London, Colin Thubron gave both encouragement and hospitality, as did Alice Cairns and her family.

My Australian relatives, particularly my beloved grandmother Janet and my aunts Lindi and Sue, embraced my fiancée as one of the family during her studies in Australia, while I was working on the book in China, as did Rebecca and Rachel Jee. My cousin Jane Gleeson-White also arranged a highly entertaining visit to the Sydney Literary Festival. From Hungary, I received the encouragement of my grandfather Rudi, his wife Dagmar and my aunts Roxi and Ralou.

My colleagues at the late *Bilingual Time,* especially Tina, Nicole and Cynthia, were exceptionally helpful and tolerant of occasional absences. My co-workers at *Global Times* make working for the Party surprisingly pleasant; particular thanks to the indefatigable Jingxian and Chen Ping.

Online, a big shout-out to all my colleagues Backstage, and to the *schlachtbummlers* at Blood and Treasure.

Many thanks too to Jeremiah Jenne, Nick Cyr, Liz Licata, Nick Vogt, John Jamie Kenny, Bill Joseph, Isaac Stone-Fish, John Garnault, Tom McGrenery, Jeff Becker, Graham Earnshaw, Justin Mitchell, Nancy Pellegrini, Isabel Hilton, Robert Foyle Hunwick, Logan Wright, James Tiscione, Frank Dikotter, Paul French, Richard Burger, John Pretty, John Churcher, and most especially to my brother in cheese and Cultural Revolution trivia, Michele Scrimenti.

I have forgotten the names of some people who should be here; in particular the Brazilian seismologist who pointed me to the British mining surveys, and whose name, shamefully, completely eludes my best efforts at searching both my memory and my inbox.

My friend Ian Sherman died in 2009. He was much loved, though he would have derided it as un-English for any of us to tell him so.

Notes

Chapter 1 Who will protect us now? *(pages 5–42)*

1 *Brother* and *sister* in Chinese refer to any relative of the same generation, both siblings and cousins, as well as frequently being used about best friends, classmates, etc. It seemed uncouth for me to ask for biological details when talking to people, and so the terms are used in that sense in this book.

2 The standard unit of currency in China at the time was the RMB (*renminbi yuan*, people's currency). Ten *mao* made up one *yuan*, ten *fen* made up one *mao*. The average salary in 1976 was around 10 RMB or less a month.

3 Gao Wenqian, *Zhou Enlai: The Last Perfect Revolutionary* (New York, 1997), p. 181.

4 Ibid, p. 289.

5 This was not at all a new development; the first Ming emperor, formerly a wandering monk, banned the use of any written characters that resembled *monk* or *bald*, and executed scholars for what he read as coded references to his past.

6 Roderick MacFarquhar and Michael Schoenhals, *Mao's Last Revolution* (Cambridge, Mass., 2006), p. 112.

7 Lu Xing, *Rhetoric of the Chinese Cultural Revolution* (Columbia, 2004) p. 23.

8 Wang Youqin, 'Student Attacks against Teachers: the Revolution of 1966', *Issues and Studies* 37 (March–April 2001).

9 Yang Su, 'Mass Killings in the Cultural Revolution', in *The Chinese Cultural Revolution as History*, ed. Joseph W. Esherick, Paul Pickowicz and Andrew Walder (Stanford, 2006), p. 99.

10 MacFarquhar and Schoenhals, pp. 204–5.

11 Ralph Thaxton, *Catastrophe and Contention in Rural China* (Cambridge, Mass., 2008), p. 148.

12 Thaxton, p. 196, quoting Jia Yanmin, *Dayuejin Shiqi Xiangcun Zhengzhide Dianxing*, pp. 221–7, 230–1.

13 Frank Dikotter, *Mao's Great Famine* (London, 2010), p. 100.

14 R. J. Rummel, *China's Bloody Century*, (New Brunswick, 1991), pp. 241–2.

15 Richard Aldrich, ed., *The Faraway War: Personal Diaries of the Second World War in Asia and the Pacific* (London, 2006), p. 663.

16 Gao Yuan, *Born Red: A Chronicle of the Chinese Cultural Revolution* (Stanford, 1997), p. 25.

17 China's school grades correspond to those used in the USA. 'Second grade' is therefore roughly equivalent to the British Year 3.

18 Lin Jing, *The Red Guards' Path to Violence: Political, Education, and Psychological Factors* (New York, 1991), pp. 88–91.

19 Sang Ye, *Beijing's Red August,* available at http://www.danwei.org/scholarship_and_education/beijings_bloody_august_by_gere.php.

20 MacFarquhar and Schoenhals, p. 334.

21 Yan Jiaqi and Gao Gao, trans. Daniel Kwok, *Turbulent Decade: A History of the Chinese Cultural Revolution* (Honolulu, 1996), p. 431.

22 Yan and Gao, p. 437.

23 Dikotter, p. 134.

24 So-called because they (probably) originally migrated from central or northern China to the south-west. It has never been clear whether Deng actually had any Hakka ancestry or not, but he certainly didn't speak Hakka or consider himself a member of the minority.

25 This seems to have been coined by government officials in rural areas struggling to keep people alive during the Great Leap Forward.

26 Yan and Gao, p. 483.

27 Like most of these titles, it sounds snappier in Chinese.

Chapter 2 Living in coal country *(pages 43–70)*

1 Matthew Connolly, *Fatal Misconception: The Struggle to Control World Population* (Cambridge, Mass., 2008), p. 179.

2 Ironically, North Korea in the 1960s and 1970s had far higher living standards than China, and North Koreans would frequently congratulate themselves on not having fallen into the chaos and backwardness of their giant neighbour. It was only in the early nineties, with the end of Russian and Chinese subsidies, that the North Korean economy collapsed.

3 Anita Chan, Richard Madsen and Jonathan Unger, *Chen Village: Revolution to Globalization* (Berkeley, 2009), p. 253.

4 Chan, Madsen and Unger, p. 254.

5 Big character posters (*dazhibao*) were handwritten posters using over-sized Chinese characters, normally intended as messages of political protest or to display support for one faction or another. They have a long history in Chinese political protest, but became particularly common in the twentieth century, and especially during the Cultural Revolution.

6 Feng Jicai, *Ten Years of Madness: Oral Histories of China's Cultural Revolution* (San Francisco, 1996), p. 2.

7 Paul Fussell, *Wartime: Understanding and Behavior in the Second World War* (Oxford, 1990), p. 80.

8 For a point of comparison, the Aberfan mining disaster killed 144 people in Wales in 1966, and I, born in 1978, had at least a vague idea of what had happened by the time I was a teenager.

9 James Tong, *Collective Violence in the Ming Dynasty* (Stanford, 1991), p. 83.

Notes

10   Qian Gang, trans. Nicola Ellis and Cathy Silber, *The Great Chinese Earthquake* (Beijing, 1989), p. 285.

11   Central Party Document 69, issued 29 June 1974.

12   Qian, p. 160.

Chapter 3 Tomb-Sweeping Day *(pages 71–113)*

1   I watched the funeral on youku, a Chinese video-sharing website, where the scenes of weeping crowds were slightly undercut by the large bouncing breasts on the right advertising a plastic surgery hospital.

2   Famously achieved in part through 'ping-pong diplomacy', where the Chinese team reached out to their US counterparts at an international tournament. They had to do so, however, without the guidance of China's former table tennis world champion, Rong Guotuan, who had been accused of being a foreign agent, attacked by the Red Guards, and hanged himself in 1968 with a note in his pocket saying 'I am not a spy.' Two other members of the national team were also driven to suicide around the same time.

3   He was heartbroken when, after the conservatories reopened in 1978, he was told that at thirteen, he had come to the instrument too late. But while he was there, they said, why not see if he could sing? He went on to become one of China's great operatic performers. Like the rest of the material on music and ballet during the Cultural Revolution, I owe this story to Nancy Pellegrini, who, when she gets around to it, will write a fantastic book on the topic.

4   The modified version used in the immediate aftermath of the Cultural Revolution is hilarious in its political correctness. It begins 'March on! People of all heroic nationalities!' (a sop to the idea of China's '56 peoples') and reminds everyone that 'The Great Communist Party leads us in continuing the Long March'. The chorus tells us that the Chinese people will 'for generations, raise Mao Zedong's banner'. It was abandoned in 1982.

5   Frederick Teiwes and Warren Sun, *The End of the Maoist Era* (Armonk, 2007), p. 439.

6   MacFarquhar and Schoenhals, p. 417.

7   Benjamin Yang, *Deng: A Political Biography* (Armonk, 1998), p. 193.

8   Chang Jung and Jon Halliday, *Mao: The Unknown Story* (London, 2005), p. 318.

9   Ye Yonglie, *The Rise and Fall of the Gang of Four* (Beijing, 2009), p. 1157.

10   My father-in-law, also from Hunan, looked like Hua when he was young too, but as far as I know is no relation to Mao Zedong.

11   Teiwes and Sun, p. 519.

12   Genny and Kam Louie, 'The Role of Nanjing University in the Nanjing Incident', *The China Quarterly* (No. 86, June 1981), p. 335.

13   *People's Daily*, 10 April 1976.

14   Edward Friedman, Paul Pickowicz, and Mark Selden, *Revolution, Resistance, and Reform in Village China* (New Haven, 2007), p. 2.

15 Several people told me, too, that their parents or grandparents retained strong memories of the ideas of American liberty they'd learnt from foreign media or teachers in the 1930s or 1940s, and passed them on to their children.

16 'The Fengster', as he is affectionately known, was a young soldier who spent his spare time studying Mao's works and helping old ladies across roads, kittens down from trees, and such, before dying in 1962, aged twenty-two, after a telephone pole fell on top of him when he accidentally directed a truck into it. Rather oddly, this made him a martyr of the revolution. His diary was found (and probably suitably embellished) and he was promoted as a national hero and role model for children.

17 Zhu Di Xiao, *Thirty Years in a Red House: A Memoir of Childhood and Youth in Communist China* (Boston, 1999), p. 166.

18 Sebastian Heilmann, *Turning Away From the Cultural Revolution: Political Grassroots Activism in the Mid-Seventies* (Stockholm, 1996), p. 33.

19 Ye Yonglie, p. 1190.

20 Roger Garside, *Coming Alive: China after Mao* (London, 1981), p. 256.

21 Yan and Gao, p. 493.

22 MacFarquhar and Schoenhals, p. 423.

23 Teiwes and Sun, p. 473.

24 Yan and Gao, p. 494.

25 Heilmann, *Turning Away*, p. 29.

26 Heilmann, *Turning Away*, p. 33.

27 MacFarquhar and Schoenhals, p. 526.

28 Ye Qing, *Deng Xiaoping zai 1976* (3 vols, Beijing, 1993), Vol. 1, p. 197.

29 Li Zhisui, *The Private Life of Chairman Mao* (London, 1996), p. 612.

30 MacFarquhar and Schoenhals, p. 430.

31 Teiwes and Sun, p. 493.

32 Sebastian Heilmann, *Sozialer Protest in der VR China. Die Bewegung vom 5 April 1976 und die Gegen-Kulturrevolution der siebziger Jahre* ['Social protest in the PRC: The April 5th Movement and the Counter-Cultural Revolution Movement of the 1970s'] (Hamburg, 1994), p. 47.

33 Zheng Yi, *Scarlet Memorial: Tales of Cannibalism in Modern China* (Boulder, 1998), p. 167.

Chapter 4 Four hundred Hiroshimas *(pages 114–143)*

1 Qian, p. 301.

2 Ibid, p. 313.

3 *Buried* (2009), dir. Wang Libo, viewable at http://dgeneratefilms.com/critical-essays/controversial-earthquake-documentary-now-on-youtube/.

4 Zhang Qingzhou, 'A Record of Warning from Tangshan (Tangshan Jingshilu)', *Reportage* (Baogao Wenxue), Vol. 65, 2005, p. 70.

5 Ibid, p. 75.

6 Li Zhisui, p. 620.

Notes

7 Qian, p. 31.
8 Today it's a local government headquarters, carefully and tenderly maintained by a staff aware of its historical importance. The only damage it suffered, as buildings collapsed all around it, was shaken tiles.
9 This wasn't a spontaneous quotation; we were in a church and I had to call a friend to Google the lines when neither of us could remember how it went, then we found it in her Bible.
10 Qian, p. 52.
11 Qian, p. 44.
12 A practice that continues today to punish families who have more than one child, or who go against village bullies.
13 Qian, p. 54.
14 Li Zhisui, p. 622.
15 After US shock comic Gilbert Gottfried made similar jokes about the Sendai earthquake in March 2011, he lost a lucrative advertising deal.
16 Qian, p. 57.
17 Qian, p. 61.

Chapter 5 Everybody saved me *(pages 144–172)*

1 Mencius, II.A.6.
2 I am pathetically unable to tell the age of rural Chinese over 35 or so, because even by 45 they're often so weathered, toothless and worn as to look decades older than their real age by Western standards. I was convinced that a beloved auntie in one compound I lived in was at least 60 until I discovered she was 47, and I once met a Daoist hermit who looked about 102 and turned out to be barely 50. Meanwhile the sprightliness of my 83-year-old grandmother when she visited me in Beijing slightly amazed my colleagues. But I was pleased to discover that this inability to judge accurately the rural aged is shared by many young urban Chinese, which in its own way is an indicator of better times.
3 The officer responsible, Amakesu Masahiko, was sentenced to ten years, served three, and was then put in charge of police repression and propaganda in Manchuria, where he helped create the culture of brutality that led to a vast swell in support for the Communists. There would have been survivors of interrogation by his secret police force among the Tangshan victims. If you drew a diagram of East Asian horrors in the twentieth century and how they connect to each other, Amakesu and others like him would be thick threads in a very tangled web.
4 Qian, pp. 206–7.
5 Most Chinese institutions had swimming pools, thanks in part to Mao's own enthusiasm for a dip.
6 Chinese are far more likely to know their own blood type than Westerners, and believe it to be linked to personality, which originates from a piece of quackery conducted by the Japanese military in testing soldiers for its puppet armies in China.
7 Qian, p. 91.

8 And still are. I once saw a children's playground with a wall mural showing, in English and Chinese, such perennial favourites as 'Truck', 'Car', 'Bicycle', 'Tank', 'Attack Helicopter' and 'Armoured Personnel Carrier'. All of the vehicles had smiley faces.

9 Qian, p. 232.

10 Qian, pp. 127–8. If it was possible, I would quote the whole of the marvellous testimony she gives, full of life and vigour and courage. Qian Gang interviewed her in 1985; I tried to find her again twenty-four years later but, alas, she seems to have died some time in the 1990s.

11 Feng, p. 3.

12 Qian, p. 214.

13 Feng, p. 97.

14 Qian, p. 143.

Chapter 6 You die, I live *(pages 173–210)*

1 Ross Terrill, *Madam Mao: The White-Boned Demon* (Stanford, 2000), p. 321.

2 Li, p. 7.

3 Ye Qing, Vol. 2, p. 5.

4 Li, p. 13.

5 Zhu, p. 170.

6 Jerrold Schecter, 'Last Respects for Chairman Mao', *Time*, 27 September 1976.

7 Teiwes and Sun, p. 595.

8 Terrill, p. 393.

9 Yan and Gao, p. 517.

10 MacFarquhar and Schoenhals, p. 419.

11 Albert Speer, *Inside the Third Reich: Memoirs* (New York, 1970), p. 291.

12 Yan and Gao, p. 514.

13 Liu Huixian, ed., *The Great Tangshan Earthquake of 1976* (Pasadena, 2002), Vol 3.6, p. 754.

14 *People's Daily*, 17 December 1976.

15 Teiwes and Sun, p. 565.

16 Li, p. 635.

17 MacFarquhar and Schoenhals, p. 448.

18 Yan and Gao, p. 527.

19 Andres Onate, 'Hua Guofeng and the Fall of the Gang of Four', *The China Quarterly* (No. 75, September 1978), pp. 540–1.

20 Zhu, p. 170.

21 Zheng, p. 155.

22 So keen a supporter that he was ousted in the early 1980s, which is why we have such a clear record of this case. Many others like it were hushed up.

Notes

Chapter 7 Aftershocks *(pages 211–249)*

1 *Beijing Review*, 24 May 1977.
2 http://www.southcn.com/news/community/shzt/party/first/200206271778.htm.
3 A collection of the cartoons is in Ralph Crozier, 'The Crimes of the Gang of Four: A Chinese Artist's Version', *Pacific Affairs*, Vol. 54, No. 2 (Summer, 1981), pp. 311–22. Some of Liao's cartoons can also be found at 'The Life and Times of Liao Bingxiong', http://www.zonaeuropa.com/culture/c20061003_1.htm.
4 Guard-dogs in Taiwan frequently used to be named Hitler, Stalin and Carter.
5 Terrill, p. 343.
6 Hua Guofeng obituary, *Guardian*, 21 Aug 2008.
7 Now up to six. Rather confusingly, they started with the Second Ring Road; there is no First. Equally, Beijing's subway lines go 1, 2, 4, 5, 8, 10, 13.
8 Xi's comments were made during an interview with *Global Times* – http://special.globaltimes.cn/2010-09/571106.html – but the sections dealing with Tiananmen were censored in the final print version.
9 Feng Chen, 'Worker Leaders and Framing Factory Based Resistance', in *Popular Protest in China*, ed. Kevin O'Brien (Cambridge, Mass., 2008), p. 89.
10 Ye Yonglie, pp. 1146–53.
11 I stole this line from the title of a paper by Jennifer Hubbert in *China Review*, Vol. 5, No. 2 (2002).
12 The same linguistic shift happened in the former USSR.
13 Naturally, it's tightly linked to both of these. Petitioners are often attacked or imprisoned when attempting to expose local government corruption, and some towns are controlled by 'black gangs' that collude with the authorities to eliminate those who oppose them. I once asked an engineering student from Shandong why he was moving to Australia. 'Because after my family bid against them for a road construction project, the mafia in my home town murdered my uncle by chopping off both his legs and leaving him to bleed to death on top of a building, then they had my father arrested for six months on false charges. So I decided I wanted to live in a country where you didn't have to be a criminal to succeed.'
14 http://chinadigitaltimes.net/2010/03/yu-jianrong-%E4%BA%8E%E5%BB%BA%E5%B5%98-maintaining-a-baseline-of-social-stability-part-6/. This talk to the Beijing Lawyers' Association is essential reading for anyone interested in protest, corruption and the Party's attempts to maintain 'stability' in China.
15 Louise T. Higgins, Xiang Gao and Song Zhu, 'The development of psychological intervention after disaster in China', *Asia Pacific Journal of Counselling and Psychotherapy*, 1:1, pp. 77–86.
16 John Garnault, 'Journey Through An Earthquake', *The Age*, 9 May 2009. Garnault told me in personal communications that he and his fixer attempted to alert PLA soldiers to trapped civilians, and were ignored.

17 William Foreman and Anna Cara, 'China earthquake brings suspicion, relief corruption', *USA Today*, 29 May 2008.

18 http://www.chinasmack.com/2011/pictures/chinese-netizens-admire-japanese-post-earthquake-behavior.html.

19 For a generally very well-acted film, it also has a jarringly awful moment when a 'white guy' actor shows up as the heroine's new Canadian husband and gives the single most wooden performance I've ever seen, which prompted my fiancée to lean across and whisper, 'She's escaped the Tangshan earthquake only to marry a serial killer!'

20 The film is available in its entirety on YouTube: see http://dgeneratefilms.com/critical-essays/controversial-earthquake-documentary-now-on-youtube/#more-3370.

21 http://hansong.blshe.com/post/57/51231.

Bibliography

Journals and Periodicals

The Age (Melbourne)
Beijing Review
China Youth Daily (Beijing)
Global Times (Beijing)
Liberation Daily (Beijing)
Newsweek (US)
People's Daily (Beijing)
Red Flag (Beijing)
Shanghai Daily
The Telegraph (UK)
Time (New York)
The Times (UK)

Published Sources

Aldrich, Richard, ed., *The Faraway War: Personal Diaries of the Second World War in Asia and the Pacific* (London, 2006)

Baum, Richard, *Burying Mao* (Princeton, 1992)

Becker, Jasper, *Hungry Ghosts* (London, 1996)

Bonavia, David, *Verdict in Peking* (London, 1984)

Chan, Anita, Madsen, Richard, and Unger, Jonathan, *Chen Village: Revolution to Globalization* (Berkeley, 2009)

Chen Yong et al., *The Great Tangshan Earthquake: An Anatomy of Disaster* (New York, 1988)

Cheng Guimin, *Tangshanren zai Wenchuan* ['Tangshan People in Wenchuan'] (Beijing, 2009)

Clark, Paul, *The Chinese Cultural Revolution: A History* (Cambridge, 2008)

Col, Jeanne-Marie, 'Managing Disaster: The Role of Local Government', *Public Administration Review* (December 2007)

Connolly, Matthew, *Fatal Misconception: The Struggle to Control World Population* (Cambridge, Mass., 2008)

Crozier, Ralph, 'The Crimes of the Gang of Four: A Chinese Artist's Version', *Pacific Affairs*, Vol. 54, No. 2 (Summer, 1981)

Dai Qing, trans. Yi Ming, *The River Dragon Has Come!: The Three Gorges Dam and the Fate of China's Yangtze River and its People* (Armonk, 1998)

Deng Rong, *Deng Xiaoping and the Cultural Revolution*, trans. Shapiro, Sidney (Beijing, 2002)

Dikotter, Frank, *Mao's Great Famine* (London, 2010)

Evans, Humphrey, *The Adventures of Li Chi: A Modern Chinese Legend* (New York, 1967)

Fenby, Jonathan, *The Penguin History of Modern China: The Rise and Fall of a Great Power* (London, 2008)

Feng Jicai, *Ten Years of Madness: Oral Histories of China's Cultural Revolution* (San Francisco, 1996)

Friedman, Edward, Pickowicz, Paul and Selden, Mark, *Revolution, Resistance, and Reform in Village China* (New Haven, 2007)

Fussell, Paul, *Wartime: Understanding and Behavior in the Second World War* (Oxford, 1990)

Gao Wenqian, *Zhou Enlai: The Last Perfect Revolutionary* (New York, 1997)

Gao Yuan, *Born Red: A Chronicle of the Chinese Cultural Revolution* (Stanford, 1997)

Garside, Roger, *Coming Alive: China after Mao* (London, 1981)

Guo Jian, Yongyi Song, and Yuan Zhou, *A to Z of the Chinese Cultural Revolution* (Lanham, 2006)

Heilmann, Sebastian, *Sozialer Protest in der VR China. Die Bewegung vom 5 April 1976 und die Gegen-Kulturrevolution der siebziger Jahre* ['Social protest in the PRC: The April 5th Movement and the Counter-Cultural Revolution Movement of the 1970s'] (Hamburg, 1994)

Heilmann, Sebastian, *Turning Away From the Cultural Revolution: Political Grassroots Activism in the Mid-Seventies* (Stockholm, 1996)

Huang Yasheng, *Capitalism With Chinese Characteristics* (Cambridge, 2008)

Jung Chang and Halliday, Jon, *Mao, the Unknown Story* (London, 2005)

Li Zhisui, *The Private Life of Chairman Mao* (London, 1996)

Li Zinfang, 'Social Responses to the Tangshan Earthquake' (preliminary paper, Delaware University, 1991)

Lin Jing, *The Red Guards' Path to Violence: Political, Education, and Psychological Factors* (New York, 1991)

Liu Huixian, ed., *The Great Tangshan Earthquake of 1976* (Pasadena, 2002)

Louie, Genny, and Louie, Kam, 'The Role of Nanjing University in the Nanjing Incident', *The China Quarterly* (No. 86, June 1981)

Lu Xing, *Rhetoric of the Chinese Cultural Revolution* (Columbia, 2004)

MacFarquhar, Roderick, and Schoenhals, Michael, *Mao's Last Revolution* (Cambridge, Mass., 2006)

Mitter, Rana, *A Bitter Revolution: China's Struggle with the Modern World* (Oxford, 2004)

O'Brien, Kevin, ed., *Popular Protest in China* (Cambridge, Mass., 2008)

O'Brien, Kevin J., and Li Lianjiang, *Rightful Resistance in Rural China* (Cambridge, 2006)

Onate, Andres, 'Hua Guofeng and the Fall of the Gang of Four', *The China Quarterly* (No. 75, September 1978)

Qian Gang, trans. Ellis, Nicola, and Silber, Cathy, *The Great Chinese Earthquake* (Beijing, 1989)

Quan Yanchi, *Mao Zedong: Man, Not God* (Beijing, 1992)

Rummel, R. J., *China's Bloody Century* (New Brunswick, 1991)

Bibliography

Sandschneider, Edward, 'Political Succession in the People's Republic of China: Rule by Purge', *Asian Survey* (Vol. 26, No. 6, June 1985)

Sang Ye, *China Candid: The People on the People's Republic* (Berkeley, 2006)

Schoenhals, Michael, *China's Cultural Revolution* (Armonk, 1996)

Shambaugh, David, 'Deng Xiaoping: the Politician', *The China Quarterly* (No. 135, September 1993)

Shapiro, Judith, *Mao's War Against Nature* (Cambridge, 2001)

Shapley, Deborah, 'The Maoist Approach to Seismology', *Science* (Vol. 193, No. 4254, August 1976)

Short, Philip, *Mao: A Life* (London, 1999)

Solnit, Rebecca, *A Paradise Built in Hell: The Extraordinary Communities that Arise in Disaster* (New York, 2009)

Speer, Albert, *Inside the Third Reich: Memoirs* (New York, 1970)

Spence, Jonathan, *The Gate of Heavenly Peace* (Harmondsworth, 1981)

Spence, Jonathan, *Mao* (London, 1999)

Teiwes, Frederick, *Politics at Mao's Court* (Armonk, 1999)

Teiwes, Frederick, and Sun, Warren, *The End of the Maoist Era* (Armonk, 2007)

Terrill, Ross, *Madam Mao: The White-Boned Demon* (Stanford, 2000)

Thaxton, Ralph, *Catastrophe and Contention in Rural China* (Cambridge, Mass., 2008)

Tong, James, *Collective Violence in the Ming Dynasty* (Stanford, 1991)

Wakeman, Edward, 'Historiography in China After Smashing the Gang of Four', *The China Quarterly* (No. 76, December 1978)

Walder, Andrew, *Fractured Rebellion: The Beijing Red Guard Movement* (Cambridge, Mass., 2009)

Wang Youqin, 'Student Attacks against Teachers: the Revolution of 1966', *Issues and Studies* 37 (March–April 2001)

Whiting, Allen, 'China After Mao', *Asian Survey* (Vol. 11, No. 17, November 1977)

Winchester, Simon, *A Crack in the Edge of the World: America and the Great California Earthquake of 1906* (London, 2005)

Witke, Roxanne, *Comrade Chiang Ch'ing* (New York, 1977)

Wright, Tim, *Coal Mining in China's Economy and Society, 1895–1937* (Cambridge, 1984)

Yan Jiaqi and Gao Gao, trans. Kwok, Daniel, *Turbulent Decade: A History of the Chinese Cultural Revolution* (Honolulu, 1996)

Yang, Benjamin, *Deng: A Political Biography* (Armonk, 1998)

Yang Su, 'Mass Killings in the Cultural Revolution', in *The Chinese Cultural Revolution as History*, ed. Esherick, Joseph W., Pickowicz, Paul and Walder, Andrew

Yang Zifa, *The Great Tangshan Earthquake: A 30 Year Perspective* (Newark, NJ, 2006)

Ye Qing, *Deng Xiaoping zai 1976* (Beijing, 1993)

Ye Yonglie, *The Rise and Fall of the Gang of Four* (Beijing, 2009)

Zhang Liang, Nathan, Andrew, and Link, Perry, *The Tiananmen Papers* (New York, 2001)

Zhang Qingzhou, 'A Record of Warning from Tangshan (Tangshan Jingshilu)', *Reportage* (Baogao Wenxue), Vol. 65, 2005

Zhang Yu and Lu Xin-An, 'Shunkouliu as China's Evidential Social Communication', *Studies in Popular Culture*, 2003

Zheng Yi, *Scarlet Memorial: Tales of Cannibalism in Modern China* (Boulder, 1998)

Zhu Di Xiao, *Thirty Years in a Red House: A Memoir of Childhood and Youth in Communist China* (Boston, 1999)

Online Sources

Integration of Public Administration and Earthquake Science, the Best Practice Case of Qinglong County: http://www.globalwatch.org/ungp/qinglong.htm

Chinese Posters, hosted by the International Institute of Social History: http://chineseposters.net/

Marxists Internet Archive: www.marxists.org

Index

ff

The Bloody White Baron

This is the shocking, epic and largely unknown story of one of the strangest and most violent men in twentieth-century Russian history.

Roman Ungern von Sternberg was a Baltic aristocrat, a violent, headstrong youth posted to the wilds of Siberia and Mongolia before the First World War. After the Bolshevik Revolution, the Baron – now in command of a lethally effective rabble of cavalrymen – conquered Mongolia, the last time in history a country was seized by an army mounted on horses. Driven by a cocktail of esoteric beliefs, anti-Semitism and violent obsessions, he invented ever more cruel ways to slaughter and torture his enemies. James Palmer's book is a fascinating recreation of this barely believable man who also foreshadowed the Nazis in his terrible combination of mysticism and genocide.

'A wonderfully lucid and intelligent resurrection of a forgotten history and its terrible protagonist. James Palmer here establishes himself both as scholar and writer.' Colin Thubron

'Palmer has written as serious a history as is possible for such an unbelievable subject, without stinting on the gore or dodging the big, awkward questions Ungern raises about the capacity of humans to revere monsters.' Giles Whittell, *The Times*

'With deftness and grace, Palmer makes an extraordinary man legible.' Robert Hudson, *Financial Times*

ff

Faber and Faber is one of the great independent publishing houses. We were established in 1929 by Geoffrey Faber with T. S. Eliot as one of our first editors. We are proud to publish award-winning fiction and non-fiction, as well as an unrivalled list of poets and playwrights. Among our list of writers we have five Booker Prize winners and twelve Nobel Laureates, and we continue to seek out the most exciting and innovative writers at work today.

Find out more about our authors and books
faber.co.uk

Read our blog for insight and opinion on books and the arts
thethoughtfox.co.uk

Follow news and conversation
twitter.com/faberbooks

Watch readings and interviews
youtube.com/faberandfaber

Connect with other readers
facebook.com/faberandfaber

Explore our archive
flickr.com/faberandfaber